Eleanor de Montfort

Eleanor de Montfort

A Rebel Countess in Medieval England

Louise J. Wilkinson

continuum

Continuum International Publishing Group
The Tower Building   80 Maiden Lane
11 York Road   Suite 704
London SE1 7NX   New York, NY 10038

www.continuumbooks.com

First published 2012

British Library Cataloguing-in-Publication Data
A catalogue record for this book is available from the British Library.

ISBN: HB: 978-1-8472-5194-7

Library of Congress Cataloging-in-Publication Data
A catalog record for this book is available from the Library of Congress.

Typeset by Fakenham Prepress Solutions, Fakenham, Norfolk NR21 8NN
Printed and bound in India

Contents

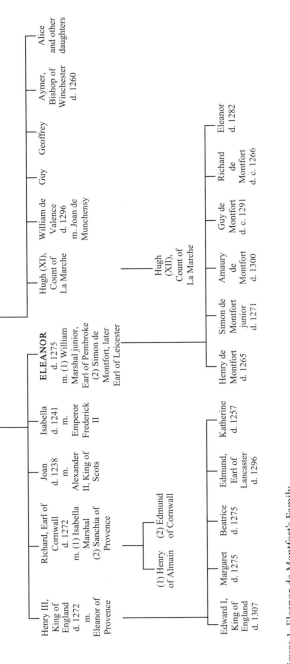

Figure 1 Eleanor de Montfort's Family

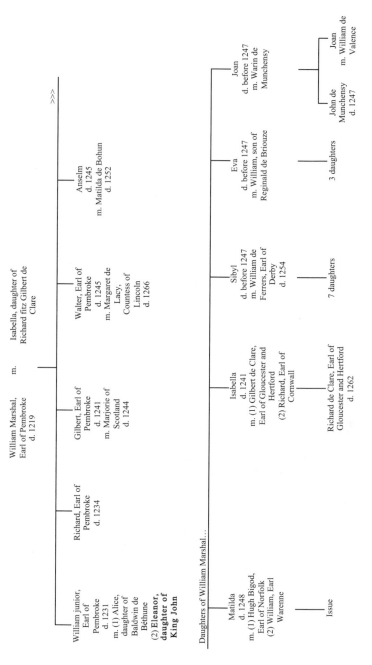

Figure 2 The Children of William Marshal, Earl of Pembroke (d. 1219)

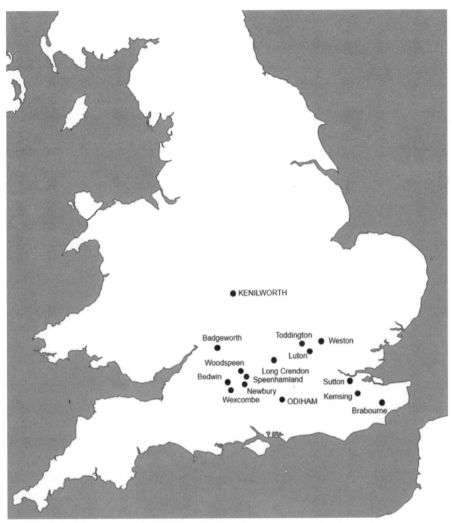

Figure 3 Eleanor's Principal Marshal Manors in England. The castles of Kenilworth and Odiham which Eleanor received as gifts from Henry III are also shown.

Preface

In his magisterial study *King Henry III and the Lord Edward* (1947), F. M. Powicke celebrated Eleanor de Montfort as 'the most vigorous and passionate of the daughters of King John and Isabella of Angoulême, a greater force in affairs than her sisters the queen of Scots and the [Holy Roman] empress.'[1] Yet the life of this remarkable woman has long been overshadowed by the controversial career of her second husband, Simon de Montfort, Earl of Leicester, and his death and mutilation at the battle of Evesham in August 1265. Earl Simon was one of the leading figures in a baronial movement to reform the government of the realm that emerged during the latter part of King Henry III's reign and reduced the king to a mere cipher at the hands of his opponents. As one of the key architects of what is now regarded by many historians as England's first political revolution and the man who effectively held the king captive for fifteen months after Henry's defeat at the battle of Lewes in May 1264, Earl Simon's life has, quite understandably, attracted the interest of a whole host of modern scholars. The most recent biography, that by John Maddicott (1994), offers a fascinating insight into Earl Simon's political career in England and France, the financial insecurities that he faced in supporting his growing family throughout the 1240s and 1250s, and the strength of his religious beliefs. Yet, there has been no new, detailed biography of Eleanor, his wife, since that which M. A. E. Green published in her six-volume work, *Lives of the Princesses of England from the Norman Conquest* in the mid-nineteenth century.[2]

Admittedly, a surviving account roll from Eleanor's household for 1265, the year of Evesham, has awakened the interest of a number of scholars. A printed edition of this roll in the original Latin was published by T. H. Turner in *Manners and Household Expenses of England in the Thirteenth and Fifteenth Centuries* (1841), and I am now preparing a separate English translation of Eleanor's roll for publication by the Pipe Roll Society with a view to making this remarkable source accessible to as wide an audience as possible. William H. Blaauw devoted a chapter of his seminal work *The Barons' War including the Battles of Lewes and Evesham* (first published 1844, second edition with additions by Charles H. Pearson 1871) to 'Eleanor de Montfort and her sons'. Blaauw used the roll to discuss the provisioning of Eleanor's household during this critical period in the Montfort family's fortunes, the countess's itinerary, the garrisoning of the castles at which she stayed, the visitors to whom she offered hospitality and the Montfortian allies with whom she corresponded. It was, however, Margaret Labarge, who, having examined Earl Simon and Countess Eleanor's 'personal quarrels' with Henry III for a University of Oxford B.Litt thesis in 1939, made the most extensive study of the roll to date. Her analysis of Eleanor's household roll formed the basis for a study of thirteenth-century baronial lifestyles, first published in 1965 as *A Baronial Household of the Thirteenth Century* and reprinted in 2003 as *Mistress, Maids and Men: Baronial Life in the Thirteenth Century*. Although Labarge readily acknowledged the impact of the civil war on the household, observing that 'Even the sober items of ... [Eleanor's] account show how much political initiative ... [this noblewoman] displayed',[3] her work was primarily concerned with the practicalities of running a great household, focusing on the domestic concerns of the countess as its lady and the internal organization of her establishment. It therefore included chapters on 'The Castle as a Home', 'The Lady of the House', 'The Daily Fare', 'The Spice Account', 'Wine and Beer', 'Cooking and Serving of Meals', 'Cloths and Clothes', 'Travel and Transport' and 'The Amusements of a Baronial Household'. By comparison, relatively little was said about Eleanor's political career and her personal role in the Barons' War of 1263–5. A valuable step towards remedying this omission was made in 2010, when, in a piece that readily acknowledged its debt to Labarge, the Japanese scholar Keizo Asaji devoted a chapter of *The Angevin Empire and the Community of the Realm in England* to a fresh appraisal of Eleanor's account roll, with a view to examining 'the importance of the baronial household against the background of thirteenth-century English political society'.[4] Somewhat intriguingly, Asaji compared Eleanor's role in gathering and disseminating information for her husband and sons to that of a modern 'relay station'.[5] More recently, in an article published in the *Journal of Medieval History* in 2011, Lars Kjær analysed the use made of food, drink and hospitality in the countess's account, creating a persuasive case for treating them as 'ritualised' forms of 'communication' that were intended to bolster Eleanor's and the Montfortians' standing in the localities in which she resided in 1265.[6] This biography also makes use of Eleanor's household roll in a way that is grounded, first and foremost, in examining Eleanor's political activities and in considering the extensive networks of family and friends that she nurtured and maintained at this critical period in English history.

This present work is, then, the first detailed account of Countess Eleanor's life for more than 150 years. It fills an important gap within the existing literature and serves as a timely companion volume to other biographical works on medieval women, such as Margaret Howell's splendid study, *Eleanor of Provence: Queenship in Thirteenth-Century England* (1998). This book draws on the wealth of information from chronicles, letters, charters, public records, household accounts and the remains of the Montfort family archives to reconstruct the narrative of Eleanor's life. In doing so, it provides an intimate portrait not only of Eleanor as a wife, mother and politician, but also of her changing relationships with her eldest brother, King Henry III, and with her nephew the Lord Edward, the future King Edward I, before, during and after the period of baronial reform and rebellion in England (1258–67). This biography also sheds significant new light on the countess's experiences as a young bride during her marriage to her first husband, William Marshal junior, Earl of Pembroke, and as a widow after his untimely death in 1231. In particular, it challenges the motives traditionally ascribed by historians to her decision to take a vow of perpetual chastity during her first period of widowhood, arguing that Eleanor's actions need to be considered against the political background of the settlement of England in the aftermath of the rebellion by her brother-in-law, Richard Marshal, Earl of Pembroke, in 1233–4.

If Eleanor's close kinship with the English king and her subsequent remarriage to a court favourite, and later reformer and rebel, Simon de Montfort, make her an exceptional woman in many respects, then her career still raises wider questions about the nature of, and potential for, women's political agency in this period. As the sister of King Henry III, an aunt of the Lord Edward and the wife of Earl Simon, Eleanor straddled the bloody conflict between Henry III and the barons who wished to reform his government in the 1250s and 1260s. Yet she remained resolutely wedded to the cause of her second husband, sharing his political ambitions, energy and fiery nature. She stood firm in her opposition to the English crown during the mid 1260s and defended Dover Castle for the Montfortian cause during the summer of 1265 as her family's enemies closed in around her.

I first encountered Eleanor as a doctoral student in the late 1990s, when I researched the life and political allegiances of another prominent thirteenth-century lady, Margaret de Lacy, Countess of Lincoln and Pembroke (d. 1266), who corresponded with Eleanor in 1265. It was not until 2006, when heavily pregnant with my first daughter, that I began to undertake more extensive research into Eleanor herself, and the idea for a biography gradually began to evolve from two papers that I wrote on Eleanor's political involvement in the Barons' War for the International Medieval Congress at the University of Leeds in 2006 and for a conference at The National Archives (UK) at Kew in 2007. In developing, researching and writing this study, I have, therefore, incurred a number of long-standing personal debts. Dr Adrian Jobson, Dr Liz Oakley-Brown, Dr Michael Ray and Dr Jennifer Ward have all kindly given me the benefit of their particular areas of expertise and have all read parts of this work. Any errors that remain are my own. I have also benefitted from the encouragement and friendship of Professor David Carpenter, Professor Michael Clanchy, Dr David Crook and Dr Paul Dryburgh at various stages of this project. Chapters 7 and 8 of this book are based upon earlier papers that I gave at Leeds, Kew, Oxford and Canterbury between 2006 and 2008; the people who attended these events made numerous valuable suggestions that I have tried to incorporate. The record copying department at the Bibliothèque nationale de France has been extremely helpful in providing me with images of MS Clairambault 1188 (the remains of the Montfort family's archive) and MS Clairambault 1021 (the Montfort confraternity letters from St Albans Abbey in Hertfordshire), while the staff at the British Library furnished me with a copy of Eleanor de Montfort's household roll (BL, MS Add. 8877). My thanks go to the staff of the reading rooms at the British Library, the Hampshire Record Office and The National Archives, who have provided valuable assistance during the course of my research. My colleagues and students at Canterbury Christ Church University have offered friendship and encouragement throughout the whole process. I am also particularly grateful to Michael Greenwood and all the staff at Continuum for their enduring patience and guidance. My greatest debt, though, is to my husband, Lee, for his love and support, and to our daughters, Emma and Katie, who were both born during the years when this book was first conceived.

A NOTE ON MONEY

In the thirteenth century, £1 was equivalent to 20 shillings, and 1 shilling was made up of 12 pence. A mark was a unit of account worth 13s. 4d.

Abbreviations

Ann. mon.	*Annales monastici*, ed. H. R. Luard (1864–9). London: Longman, Rolls Series, 5 vols.
BL	British Library.
BnFr	Bibliothèque nationale de France.
Cal. Docs. Ireland	*Calendar of Documents relating to Ireland, 1171–1307*, ed. H. S. Sweetman (1875–86). London: Longman, 5 vols.
CChR	*Calendar of the Charter Rolls* (1916–). London: HMSO.
CClR	*Calendar of the Close Rolls* (1892–). London: HMSO.
CFR	*Calendar of the Fine Rolls of the Reign of Henry III* (2007–2011), available online at http://www.frh3.org.uk/home.html.
Chronica majora	*Matthaei Parisiensis, monachi Sancti Albani, chronica majora*, ed. H. R. Luard (1872–83). London: Longman, Rolls Series, 7 vols.
CIM	*Calendar of Inquisitions Miscellaneous, Volume I, 1219–1307* (1916). London: HMSO.
CLR	*Calendar of the Liberate Rolls* (1916–). London: HMSO.
CPR	*Calendar of the Patent Rolls* (1906–). London: HMSO.
CR	*Close Rolls of the Reign of Henry III* (1902–75). London: HMSO, 13 vols.
CRR	*Curia Regis Rolls of the Reigns of Richard I, John and Henry III* (1922–). London: HMSO.
DBM	*Documents of the Baronial Movement of Reform and Rebellion, 1258–1267*, ed. R. F. Treharne and I. J. Sanders (1973). Oxford: Clarendon Press.

Diplomatic Documents   *Diplomatic Documents, Volume I, 1101–1272*, ed. P. Chaplais (1964). London: HMSO.

EHR   *The English Historical Review.*

Flores historiarum   *Flores historiarum*, ed. H. R. Luard (1890). London: Longman, Rolls Series, 3 vols.

Foedera   *Foedera, conventiones, litterae et cujuscunque generis acta publica*, ed. T. Rymer (searchable text edition, 2006). Burlington, Ontario: TannerRitchie.

GEC   G. E. Cokayne, *The Complete Peerage*, ed. V. Gibbs et al. (1910–59). n.p.

Historia anglorum   *Matthae Parisiensis, monachi Sancti Albani, historia anglorum*, ed. F. Madden (1872–83). London: Longman, Rolls Series, 3 vols.

HRO   Hampshire Record Office.

Manners   *Manners and Household Expenses of England in the Thirteenth and Fifteenth Centuries*, ed. T. H. Turner (1841). London: Roxburghe Club.

Monasticon anglicanum   W. Dugdale, *Monasticon anglicanum*, eds R. Dodsworth, J. Stevens, J. Caley, H. Ellis, B. Bandinel and R. C. Taylor (1817–30). London: Longman, Hurst, Rees, Orme and Brown, 6 vols in 8.

ODNB   *Oxford Dictionary of National Biography*. Oxford: Oxford University Press, 2004–11, available online at http://www.oxforddnb.com.

Pipe Roll 16 John   *The Great Roll of the Pipe for the Sixteenth Year of the Reign of King John*, ed. P. M. Barnes (1962). London: The Pipe Roll Society, new series, vol. 35.

PR   *Patent Rolls of the Reign of Henry III* (1901–3). London: HMSO, 2 vols.

PRO   Public Record Office.

RLCl   *Rotuli litterarum clausarum in Turri Londoniensi asservati*, ed. T. D. Hardy (1833–4). London: Record Commission.

RLP   *Rotuli litterarum patentium in Turri Londoniensi asservati*, ed. T. D. Hardy (1835). London: Record Commission.

Royal Letters   *Royal and Other Historical Letters illustrative of the Reign of Henry III*, ed. W. W. Shirley (1862–6). London: Longman, Rolls Series, 2 vols.

SCLA   Shakespeare Centre Library and Archive.
TNA   The National Archives.
Treaty Rolls   *Treaty Rolls, Volume I, 1234–1325* (1955). London: HMSO.
Wendover   *The Flowers of History by Roger of Wendover*, ed. H. G. Hewlett (1886–9). London: Longman, Rolls Series, 3 vols.

Childhood

'descended from a race of kings'[1]

In 1917, a French scholar, Max Prinet, published a detailed description of a tomb housed within the church of the Abbey Royal of St-Antoine-des-Champs, a medieval nunnery on the outskirts of Paris. The tomb, which depicted a woman wearing a religious habit, was heavily decorated with armorial bearings typical of those employed in the thirteenth century. It bore no inscription that immediately identified its owner, but an analysis of its heraldic devices suggested that this was none other than the funerary monument constructed to house the heart of Eleanor (d. 1275), Countess of Leicester, the daughter of King John of England and the widow of William Marshal (d. 1231), Earl of Pembroke, and Simon de Montfort (d. 1265), Earl of Leicester. The arms depicted on the tomb included two emperors, those of the Holy Roman and Latin Empires, four kings, those of England, France, Sicily, and Castile-León, and those of the Montfort family, which an earlier French heraldist, Claude-François Ménestrier, had identified with Eleanor's sons by her second marriage. This evidence, coupled with that from an ancient inventory of the abbey's goods referring to a cloth placed 'on the heart of the countess of Leicester' on feast days and at Lent, confirmed that Eleanor's heart was probably housed within this tomb or that, at the very least, there had later emerged a strong local tradition that this was so.[2]

Whether or not this monument contained the heart of the youngest daughter of King John of England, Eleanor was certainly a remarkable woman who could claim close kinship with the most powerful ruling dynasties of Western Europe and the Latin East in the thirteenth century. This point was not lost on her contemporaries. Eleanor's impeccable connections, and those of her sisters – Joan Queen of Scots and Isabella, the Holy Roman Empress – were detailed in an elaborate genealogy compiled to celebrate the latter's marriage in 1235 to Emperor Frederick II of Hohenstaufen. On their father's side, these women claimed descent from the kings of England, dukes of Aquitaine and Normandy, and counts of Anjou, Maine and Touraine. Through the marriages of their aunts in the paternal line, they were associated with the kings of Castile and Sicily, the dukes of Saxony and the counts of Toulouse.[3] As members of the European political elite, Eleanor's and her sisters' lives were, therefore, played out on an international stage. This was, after all, an era in which the language, life and culture of the English royal family and high aristocracy were closely integrated with Europe and especially with France.

These continental connections were especially important for Eleanor, the only English royal sister not to acquire a crown through marriage. Like her grandmother and namesake, the formidably talented Eleanor (d. 1204), Duchess of Aquitaine, who had been the wife of King Louis VII of France and King Henry II of England in turn, the key events in the younger Eleanor's life took place on both sides of the English Channel. The political capital invested by the younger Eleanor, her two husbands and, ultimately, her children in *her* lineage and *her* natal family ties offers a window onto female agency and the opportunities that existed for medieval noblewomen, primarily through the mediums of marriage, motherhood and lordship, to foster their own interests and those of their closest kin. It was, after all, precisely these ties that located the younger Eleanor at the very heart of the conflict for control of English government that emerged between her brother, King Henry III, and his barons. The years 1258 to 1267 – a period of baronial reform and rebellion – were of tremendous significance in English history. They saw the king reduced to a cipher and a baronial council, led by Eleanor's second husband, Simon de Montfort, pushing through legal and administrative reforms far more radical and wide ranging than those envisaged in Magna Carta in 1215. This book, therefore, considers the life and career of Eleanor, the youngest daughter of King John, against the turbulent background of thirteenth-century English politics and Anglo-French relations, and considers her transformation from the king's beloved youngest sister into his bitter political enemy.

BEGINNINGS

The earliest years of Eleanor's life, in common with those of other medieval English princesses, remain clouded in obscurity, with few hints of what was to come.[4] No English chronicler saw fit to record the birth of Eleanor to King John and his wife, Isabella of Angoulême, in or around 1215.[5] The arrival of the couple's fifth surviving child and third surviving daughter went unremarked by contemporary chroniclers in an age of high rates of infant mortality and at a time when the Angevin dynasty faced a grave political crisis – civil war in

England between Eleanor's father and his barons.[6] King John, the youngest son of Henry II and Eleanor of Aquitaine, had seized the English throne in 1199 on the death of his elder brother, Richard. The loss of Normandy to the French king, Philip Augustus, in 1204 seriously dented the prestige of the English crown, so much so that John devoted the remainder of his reign to raising money to help secure its recovery. John's plans, though, came to nought, thanks, in large part, to the disastrous defeat of his allies at the battle of Bouvines on 27 July 1214. Defeat at Bouvines left the English crown financially embarrassed and critically exposed to its enemies at home, to the barons, knights and free men who bore financial and other grievances against John, and who resented the intrusive and rapacious system of government over which John and his predecessors had presided.[7] The outpouring of these grievances culminated in civil war, in the issue of Magna Carta in June 1215, in its failure as a peace treaty and in the renewal of hostilities between the warring parties in August 1215. Thoroughly disenchanted with John, the rebel barons invited Philip Augustus's eldest son, Louis (the future King Louis VIII of France), to take the English throne; Louis's arrival in England in May 1216 posed a serious threat not only to John but also to his wife, his sons and his daughters.[8]

John's wife and the younger Eleanor's mother, Isabella of Angoulême, was none other than the daughter and heiress of Adomar, Count of Angoulême, the lord of a strategically important territory in south-western France, situated between Poitou and Gascony.[9] Eleanor's maternal grandmother, Alice de Courtenay, was the daughter of the French lord of Montargis and Châteaurenard, and a cousin of Philip Augustus. Through her Courtenay connections, Isabella also enjoyed kinship with the kings of Jerusalem, and was a half-sister to Peter, Count of Joigny, the child of one of her mother's earlier marriages.[10] Isabella's marriage to John in August 1200 accorded well with Angevin interests south of the River Loire, promising increased stability across the border regions of Poitou and Gascony. In marrying Isabella, John also decisively stepped in to prevent her union with another powerful Poitevin neighbour, Hugh (IX) de Lusignan, Lord of Lusignan and Count of La Marche, a union that threatened John's dominance within Aquitaine.[11] It was unfortunate, to say the least, for John that the offence he caused Hugh (IX) led to this count's rebellion and an appeal to Philip Augustus's court. These events, in their turn, resulted in the French king declaring John's continental territories forfeit, thereby helping to trigger the ultimately successful Capetian invasion of Normandy, Maine, Anjou and Touraine, along with a significant slice of Poitou.[12]

Isabella of Angoulême did not enjoy anything like the level of personal wealth or political influence enjoyed by some of her twelfth-century predecessors as queens of England.[13] In short, John deliberately denied his queen consort access to material resources that might have allowed her sufficient independence to act as a patron and thereby make a significant mark on court politics, possibly by forging her own faction.[14] Isabella was unable to avail herself of the full revenues from her inheritance or her dower (those lands set aside to provide for her in the event of her husband's death) during John's lifetime. It is also probable that she did not receive, as Eleanor of Aquitaine had done, any income from Queen's Gold, a surcharge on voluntary offerings, Jewish amercements and sums owed by moneyers that was traditionally levied by the crown.[15] In this way, John ensured that his queen remained dependent upon his continued generosity and goodwill for her day-to-day maintenance. Furthermore, the presence of royal mistresses and, until her marriage to the Earl of Essex in 1214, of Isabella of Gloucester, John's former wife, at royal residences in the south and south west of England (Winchester, Sherborne and Bristol) potentially posed a more direct threat to Isabella of Angoulême's personal relationship with her husband.[16] In spite of this, though, John and Isabella of Angoulême remained on sufficiently intimate terms for this Isabella to give birth to five surviving children between 1207 and 1215, and for the king and one of his most trusted aides, Peter des Roches, Bishop of Winchester, to bestow occasional gifts upon the queen as her household moved from one royal residence to another.[17] Fourteen years after their marriage, John still spent time in his wife's company, especially when it was politic to do so. In 1214, John used Isabella's position as countess of Angoulême to his advantage in his dealings with the Poitevin nobles, when she accompanied him overseas.[18] During this trip the couple's eldest daughter, Joan, was betrothed to Hugh, the eldest son and namesake of the lord of Lusignan and count of La Marche to whom Isabella had previously been betrothed before her marriage to John.[19] Later that year, after the king and queen's return to England and a brief sojourn together at Exeter, John placed Isabella under the armed protection of one of his most trusted servants, Terric the Teuton. This was probably for the queen's personal safety as the political situation in England deteriorated, rather than for more sinister reasons.[20] In November 1214, Terric, the constable of the royal castle at Berkhamsted in Hertfordshire, escorted the queen when she visited Berkhamsted, a castle earmarked as part of Isabella's future dower.[21] When, during the following month, the king visited the great fortress at Corfe in Dorset, he instructed Terric to convey the 'lady queen' to Gloucester Castle. Once at Gloucester, Isabella was installed in the chamber where, John recalled with a surprising eye for fatherly detail, their eldest daughter, Joan, had been nursed.[22] During the early months of 1215, under Terric's watchful supervision, the queen and her household visited Berkhamsted again and later Winchester in Hampshire, where she enjoyed the company of her eldest son, Henry.[23] Mother and son then travelled on together to Marlborough Castle in Wiltshire in May 1215.[24] With the resumption of civil war between the king and his rebel barons later that summer, when the king refused to be bound by the terms of Magna Carta, Isabella and Henry moved, yet again, on John's orders so that they might enjoy the greater protection offered by Corfe.[25]

It was against this immediate political backdrop that Isabella of Angoulême gave birth to Eleanor, her third daughter to survive infancy. The chroniclers' failure to note Eleanor's entry into the world was also, in part, a reflection of the patriarchal values to which the noble landholding elite of thirteenth-century England subscribed. These values were firmly underpinned by church teachings on gender roles and scientific beliefs about gender difference inherited from the ancient world. Women were regarded as weak and irrational creatures, who were inferior to men, and who therefore ought to be subject to male authority.[26] The male-dominated military society into which Eleanor was born favoured patrilineal primogeniture, the descent of lands through the eldest male child.[27] Sons were typically preferred to daughters as a means of securing the succession, stabilizing the future of the bloodline and exercising effective lordship.[28] Thirteenth-century chroniclers noted the births in 1207 and 1209 of Henry, the heir to the throne, and of Richard, King John's younger son, as well as that in 1210 of the royal couple's eldest daughter, Joan, but not apparently those of the younger Isabella or Eleanor.[29] In order to establish the dates of birth of John's youngest daughters, we are reduced to conjecture. If the statement of the St Albans chronicler, Roger of Wendover, is accurate and Isabella was twenty-one at the time of her marriage to the Holy Roman Emperor, Frederick II of Hohenstaufen, in 1235, then she was probably born in 1214.[30] Other, circumstantial evidence indicates that 1214 was, indeed, the year of Isabella's birth. Isabella was not a name that had previously been used within the Angevin ruling dynasty. In naming his second daughter Isabella, John therefore introduced a new woman's name into his lineage. If, as seems likely, the younger Isabella was born when her parents were in Poitou, then this might explain their decision to name her after the queen, who was, after all, heiress to the county of Angoulême. It might be seen, in part, as a move that was designed to curry favour with her mother's vassals by acknowledging the older Isabella's presence on the Poitevin expedition and thereby reminding them of her position as their liege lady.

If the younger Isabella was born in 1214, presumably Eleanor as her younger sister was born in 1215 or perhaps 1216.[31] The practice among the nobility of handing over babies to wet nurses soon after birth allowed noblewomen to recover their fertility relatively swiftly, paving the way for multiple pregnancies in quick succession.[32] Perhaps it was when the queen was in residence at Winchester, the location of Henry III's birth, during the early months of 1215 that she had her lying-in and delivery. An alternative location for Eleanor's birth is Marlborough. Isabella of Angoulême's need for larger clothes, or for new robes for the celebration of her churching after the birth, possibly lay behind a gift of cloth and furs that John bestowed upon his wife there in August that year.[33] In the later Middle Ages, when more detailed records for lying-in survive, it was customary for an English queen consort to withdraw into her birthing chambers one month before the baby was due. She remained within them for a further six weeks after the birth until she attended church for her purification. It is not inconceivable that the English royal ordinances of the fifteenth century had their roots in much longer established ceremonies and practices, some of which were observed in Isabella's day.[34] The ceremony that attended the churching at Westminster Abbey in early August 1239 of Isabella's daughter-in-law and successor as queen consort in England, Eleanor of Provence, took place around six weeks after the birth of her eldest son, Edward, and was noted by the chronicler Matthew Paris.[35]

Isabella of Angoulême's residence in the south and west of England throughout 1215 and 1216 made perfect political as well as practical sense. Winchester was not only home to a royal castle, but was also the episcopal seat of des Roches, her husband's ally and the man in whose charge Henry, Isabella and John's eldest son, was placed in 1211–12.[36] Furthermore, Winchester possessed strong associations with queenship that might have stood the crown in good stead at this difficult time; it had formed part of the traditional dower lands assigned to widowed queens consort since Anglo-Saxon times.[37] It might well have been hoped that the birth of a royal daughter there would strengthen the resolve of the king's subjects to remain loyal to the crown. Yet such associations were not enough to prevent this city from falling, during the summer of 1216, to the forces of Louis, the son of the king of France who had been invited to take the English throne by the rebels.[38] For his part, John also enjoyed strong personal connections with the west and south west through his earlier marriage to Isabella of Gloucester. In fact, the king contrived to ensure that he retained possession of Bristol, with its strong trading links to Ireland and the Continent, after his first wife's remarriage in 1214.[39] By the summer of 1216, Terric, the queen and possibly the infant Eleanor were in residence at Bristol, apparently ready, should the need arise, to flee abroad.[40]

King John's death at Newark during the night of 18 to 19 October 1216 deprived Isabella of Angoulême of a husband and her children of their father.[41]

It was followed, in 1217, by Isabella's own departure to Angoulême, ostensibly to escort her eldest daughter, Joan, to her bridegroom, Hugh (X) de Lusignan.[42] Although one of the first acts of Henry III's minority government on 1 November 1216 had been to award Isabella seisin of her dower in Devon, Essex, Hampshire, Hertfordshire, Rutland and Wiltshire,[43] the new queen dowager rapidly found herself excluded from the regency council and from effective political influence within her son's kingdom. Henry III's coronation at Gloucester on 28 October 1216 was celebrated under the direction of the papal legate, Guala, a legacy of John's submission to Innocent III at the end of the Interdict, and under the watchful eyes of William Marshal, Earl of Pembroke, into whose care John had entrusted his son.[44] John's will had not anticipated that Isabella might play a role in English government and in securing their children's inheritances after his death, hence her exclusion from the list of his thirteen executors.[45]

Marginalized from English political life in marriage and in widowhood, it is perhaps unsurprising that Isabella decided to return to her inheritance in the south of France and preside over her own comital court at Angoulême. Viewed through the eyes of modern scholars, however, she has been criticized for taking 'the earliest possible opportunity to abandon four of the five children [including the baby Eleanor] that she had borne to John'.[46] It is, however, possible to place more of the blame, if indeed that is what it should be called, at the door of the regency council. It was only with the Treaty of Lambeth in September 1217 that the civil war was concluded in England and Louis agreed to leave the realm.[47] To put it simply, the regency council under William Marshal might well have feared the consequences of Isabella's influence over her young children. Isabella's effective exclusion from court politics during John's reign meant that she was an untried, untested and therefore a potentially damaging force on the English political stage at a time when her son's supporters were fighting for the very survival of his crown. She was also possibly regarded as a divisive figure due to popular perceptions of her relationship with her late husband; the St Albans chronicler, Roger of Wendover, for example, blamed the loss of Normandy, at least in part, upon John's infatuation with Isabella.[48] While Isabella's possession of her dower meant that those lands remained in loyalist hands during the final stages of the war, it also meant that significant resources were now in the hands of the queen dowager, resources which might at last allow her to forge her own, possibly destabilizing, faction at the Henrician court. Although Isabella had apparently danced to John's tune during their marriage, within that marriage John had allowed and expected Isabella to play at least a supervisory role in their children's upbringings in accordance with the social conventions of their day.[49] Isabella certainly spent time in the company of her older children, especially during their early childhoods and the civil war that preceded John's death. Richard, for example, accompanied his mother and elder sister to Poitou in 1214.[50] The queen continued to take an interest in Henry's and Richard's affairs after they were placed in the separate charges of des Roches and Peter de Maulay in 1211–12 and in 1215 respectively.[51]

There was, admittedly, nothing unusual in placing children from high-status families in other households for part of their upbringing. This practice accorded well with contemporary English and European expectations that, by the age of seven or sometimes earlier, the boys of the high nobility be removed from their nurseries in order to enter another lord's household for their education in courtly manners and knightly skills.[52] In the troubled political climate of 1216–17, however, the personal influence that the queen potentially wielded over Eleanor's brothers might well have been regarded with alarm by the men to whom her late husband had assigned the task of safeguarding the throne for his dynasty.[53] The regency council's suspicions about Isabella and Isabella's own sense of political isolation in England were apparently confirmed in 1220 by the queen dowager's subsequent decision to remain in Poitou, and take the place of her daughter, Joan, as Hugh (X) de Lusignan's bride.[54]

UPBRINGING

The queen dowager's return to Angoulême in 1217 and her continued absence from England meant that she was not a significant physical presence in the upbringings of Eleanor and her older sister, Isabella. These two daughters, like their older brothers, were placed, instead, in the guardianship of the crown's most loyal servant, Peter des Roches, or in that of men closely allied to him.[55] By June 1220, if not earlier, Isabella was in the custody of Philip Mark, who escorted her to York during the negotiations for the marriage of her sister, Joan, to Alexander II, King of Scots.[56] As the youngest child, Eleanor was placed under the overall supervision of Henry III's protector, des Roches, while Richard remained in de Maulay's care at Corfe.[57] It is curious, bearing in mind their closeness in age, that Isabella and Eleanor were not raised in one another's company. One possible explanation for this arrangement is that it reflected contemporary concerns about the royal children's safety: if they were all placed in the hands of the same guardian, they might have been more vulnerable to attack from external foes, or more vulnerable to the political machinations of des Roches. There might well have been an underlying fear that a single guardian might marry off all the children to further his own political agenda.[58] Similar concerns were certainly evident by June 1221, when Peter de Maulay fell from grace, following rumours of his alleged involvement in a plot to deliver Eleanor of Brittany, the king's cousin and captive then in de Maulay's care, to the French king.[59] Much later in Henry III's reign, in February 1234, the English episcopate expressed their fears about des Roches's control of the king's sister (which sister is not specified), fears that might have taken root much earlier.[60]

In common with her older siblings, Eleanor possessed her own separate household from early infancy, staffed by attendants who looked after her everyday needs. Such arrangements were not unique to John's children, but arose partially from the exalted status of the ruling dynasty and partially from necessity – the disruptive, itinerant lifestyle of the royal court was not necessarily one suited to the emotional and physical wellbeing of young children, especially in an age when children were particularly vulnerable to disease.[61] Payments to meet all manner of expenses for the maintenance of Eleanor and her household staff feature regularly in the records of the bishopric of Winchester for the years 1217–21 and reveal tantalizing details about Eleanor's early upbringing and its material comforts. The bishop's officials accounted for the expenses – in cash and goods – of Eleanor, who was styled initially as the 'king's daughter' and later as the 'king's sister', her nurses and other members of her domestic establishment.[62] Accounts (the Winchester pipe roll) for 1217–18, for example, record expenses incurred on Eleanor's behalf by those who cared for her for items that included candles, cloth, oil, robes and soap for washing.[63] When, during the following year, Eleanor and her household resided on the bishop's manor of Taunton in Wiltshire for twenty-six weeks and three days, the bishop's officials accounted for purchases of cloth for clothing, grain, oil and writs, and for oblations.[64]

As Eleanor's brothers, Henry III and Richard, grew older, they were placed in the care of knights such as Philip d'Aubigny, the keeper of the Channel Islands under John, who looked after the young king and instructed him in riding, hunting and the use of weapons.[65] They were also assigned tutors like Roger of Acaster, who was appointed to serve the younger Richard between 1217 and 1223, and who presumably educated them in letters and manners.[66] The king and his brother probably received instruction in the seven liberal arts, the cornerstones of a learned – or Latin – education in the Middle Ages. These were grammar, rhetoric and dialectic, known as the *trivium* or the three arts of language, along with geometry, music, astronomy and arithmetic, the *quadrivium* or the four arts of number. Knowledge of Latin on the part of Henry and Richard is indicated by the metrical grammar commissioned from Master

Henry of Avranches for them.[67] After all, their father, like their paternal grand-father before him, had been extremely well educated, and possessed an extensive personal library of French and Latin texts.[68] As an adult, Henry III owned texts in Latin (mainly liturgical works), as well as romance tales in French.[69] His wife, Eleanor of Provence, purchased romances based upon Arthurian legends and classical figures, and probably possessed a range of religious texts to assist in her daily devotions; a vernacular history of the Anglo-Saxon king, Edward the Confessor, was dedicated to her.[70]

The education that Henry and Richard received reflected their status, the public roles they were expected to assume in adulthood and their gender. The education of girls, like Eleanor and her sisters, in royal and aristocratic circles differed markedly from that of their brothers, reflecting medieval Christian and scientific teaching on feminine intellectual, physical and psychological inferiority.[71] Their upbringings prepared them for marriage or for admission to the cloister. It usually fell to royal mothers, albeit in a supervisory capacity, to induct their daughters into the rituals, ceremonies, gift-giving and conspicuous consumption associated with queenship and diplomacy, as well as seeing to it that they acquired courtly manners and practical skills in household management.[72] It was also under maternal supervision that they received religious instruction, presumably from household chaplains. The *Life* that Agnes of Harcourt, abbess of Longchamp, wrote of Eleanor's cousin and contemporary, Isabella (1225–70), the sister of King Louis IX of France, recalled the parental concern of Isabella's mother, Queen Blanche, and her close involvement in her daughter's affairs.[73] Although Isabella was destined to become the founder of Longchamp, near Paris, and lived out her life in a residence within its grounds, the close cultural and royal familial ties between England and France at this time mean that the descriptions within her *Life* of her qualities, upbringing and education resonate with the occasional glimpses of Eleanor and her sisters within English sources. Isabella of France was commended for her grace, beauty, lineage and the nobility of her morals. As a woman who dedicated her adult life to spiritual works, the French princess was also praised in her childhood for her innocence, patience, piety, chastity and mercy.[74] When Queen Blanche saw to it that her daughter was dressed in richly ornamented clothes appropriate to her position, Isabella expressed her personal preference for more humble, religious attire.[75] While other girls of her rank attended entertainments at the French court, Isabella studied divine scripture in her chamber, learning her letters and how to work in silk in order to make vestments for the church.[76] Much of Isabella's day was spent in prayer or studying holy works, such as the Bible and saints' lives. According to her biographer, she also 'understood Latin very well', so well, in fact, that 'when her chaplains had written her letters for her … in Latin, and … would bring them to her, she would amend them when there were any wrong words'.[77] Isabella was evidently schooled in writing as well as reading Latin, two skills which were not necessarily taught together in the Middle Ages.[78]

Even if we make allowance for the hagiographical nature of Agnes's work, with its heightened emphasis on Isabella's religiosity, contemporary English chroniclers made similar claims about the characters and attributes of Henry III's sisters. Although their comments are indicative of the shared social conventions of the French and English courts, they are also revealing of the manner in which the behaviour and outward countenances of the English king's sisters conformed to contemporary expectations. During the viewing of the bride that preceded Isabella of England's marriage to the Holy Roman Emperor, Frederick II, this young English bride left the imperial ambassadors impressed by her 'virgin modesty' and her 'royal dress and manners'.[79] In a similar vein, Eleanor's 'beauty' and royal descent were said, by the St Albans chronicler, Matthew Paris, to have played an important role in attracting her second husband, Simon de Montfort, in 1238.[80] Religious instruction – and instruction in the arts of literacy – also loomed large in both Isabella's and Eleanor's upbringings. In the queen mother's absence overseas, the English royal sisters received their educations at the hands of the *magistrae* or 'governesses' who resided in their households. The younger Isabella's governess was Margaret Biset, a noblewoman whose family possessed a long history of service to the English crown.[81] Margaret, who subsequently entered the household of Henry III's queen, Eleanor of Provence, was pious and literate in Latin as well as the French of Henry III's court. She successfully foiled an assassination attempt on the king one night in 1238 when the court was in residence at Woodstock, having stayed awake to read her Psalter.[82] Another similarly experienced woman, Cecily of Sandford, whom the St Albans chronicler, Matthew Paris, described as 'of noble blood, but with nobler manners', served as Eleanor's governess.[83] Cecily was the wife and later widow of William de Gorham, a knight who held lands near St Albans in Hertfordshire.[84] Cecily was also, in Paris's eyes at least, clearly a woman of exceptional qualities – 'exceedingly learned, and courteous, and eloquent' – and after leaving Eleanor's service, she was governess to Joan, the wife of Henry III's half-brother, William de Valence.[85] The reputation for learning and the noble background and character of Cecily of Sandford indicate that a great deal of thought, as well as practical considerations, lay behind her initial appointment as Eleanor's mistress. This was probably just as well. Eleanor's education at Cecily's hands made a significant impact upon her subsequent life and piety. The influence Cecily exerted over the younger woman's spirituality was seen a few years after the death of Eleanor's first husband, William Marshal junior (d. 1231), when Cecily and her charge took a vow of chastity and perpetual widowhood in the presence of Edmund of Abingdon, Archbishop of Canterbury.[86]

It was under Cecily of Sandford's guidance and that of others like her, as well as household chaplains and priests, that Eleanor presumably received instruction in the Bible and other religious works. Eleanor's formative years also coincided with the arrival of a new religious movement in England – the Mendicant Orders of friars. The arrival in 1221 of the Dominicans or Black Friars, the followers of St Dominic of Castile, was followed in 1224 by that of the Franciscans or Grey Friars, the followers of St Francis of Assisi. Both groups quickly attracted royal, noble and local patronage, and established houses in Oxford and numerous other English towns.[87] As an adult, the Oxford Franciscan friar Adam Marsh, an intimate of Henry III's court, directed Eleanor's attention to biblical passages which he clearly expected her to know.[88] The texts of eight letters that Marsh wrote to Eleanor between the late 1240s and early 1250s have been preserved down to the present day.[89] Two letters in particular are littered with allusions or references to biblical passages from the book of Genesis (2:18), the gospel of St John (6:37), the Wisdom books (Job 5:2 and Wisd. 11:24, 27), St Paul's Epistles to the Philippians (4:7), the Corinthians (2 Cor. 1:3) and Timothy (1 Tim. 2:9–10), and the writings of St Peter (1 Pet. 3:1–4).[90] Both letters, significantly, addressed Eleanor's conduct and exhorted her to follow long-established Christian models of acceptable feminine behaviour, models with which Eleanor would have been familiar since childhood. Although seven years younger than her second husband, Eleanor was of a sufficiently forthright, passionate and strong disposition to incur Marsh's criticism for her failure to act as an obedient, passive and submissive wife in line with biblical teaching. The first letter, for example, counselled Eleanor on her relationship with her husband and offered advice on how to modify her character and temperament in accordance with the church's ideals of wifely obedience, humility, passivity, restraint and subjection. Marsh criticized her, in a highly provocative way, for departing from her Christian duty towards her second husband and, by impli-cation, for failing to show due care and attention to his commands and wishes. The friar rebuked Eleanor in no uncertain terms for her tendency to resort too quickly to anger ('Anger killeth the foolish') and cautioned her on the damaging effect that this might have upon those nearest and dearest to her.[91] Yet it was not just Eleanor's temper that earned Marsh's disapproval. In addition to criti-cizing Eleanor's personal failings, the friar also extended to her the universal ecclesiastical censure of dress and vanities. Marsh rebuked the king's youngest sister, at length, for the excessive extravagance of her clothing. Women, he counselled, ought to adopt modest and sober apparel, rather than elaborate hairstyles, costly jewels and luxurious robes ('women also [should be] in decent apparel, adorning themselves with modesty and sobriety, not with plaited hair, or gold, or pearls, or costly attire; but as it becometh women, professing godliness with good works').[92] Eleanor ought to abandon outward displays of vanity, extravagance and 'wanton style'.[93] Marsh's comments are indicative of an enjoyment of finery on Eleanor's part as an adult and, more importantly, perhaps, of an awareness of how the outward trappings of wealth might serve as visual reminders of her regal status to those around her. In the second letter, Marsh warned Eleanor of 'an increasing number of unpleasant and vexatious reports of improprieties that are soiling your reputation not a little'.[94] He went on to urge and even 'admonish' her to mend her ways,

> to multiply your good deeds for the future and both to make a zealous effort to make your conscience clear before the Most High [God], and to repair your reputation with men, showing yourself in every way, in matters that affect your husband and children, your household and in general those closest to you, ever watchful, reasonable, and peaceable, following the example of praiseworthy matrons.[95]

Eleanor's correspondence with Marsh, who acknowledged and thanked her for her missives, in the late 1240s and early 1250s raises the question of the level of Eleanor's literacy.[96] The existence of Marsh's letters, which were written in Latin rather than in the French vernacular, certainly suggests that Eleanor possessed at least a competent reading knowledge – or level of comprehension – of this language. It is also possible, although difficult to prove, that, like Isabella of France, Eleanor did not leave the composition of her letters to Marsh solely in the hands of her clerks, but checked their contents in person. On one occasion at least, Marsh thanked the countess 'for remembering to tell me in your letter to my poor self, so carefully written' some heartening news concerning her family.[97] When Eleanor became a mother later in life, she was certainly aware of her maternal responsibility to oversee the religious and literary instruction of her only surviving daughter and namesake, Eleanor.[98] The fragment of the adult Eleanor's household roll that survives for the year 1265 records the purchase in February that year of twenty dozen sheets of parchment in London by Brother G. Boyon in order to make a portable breviary for the countess's daughter.[99] The parchment was then carried to Oxford, where the breviary was written and the text completed by the spring.[100] The breviary, which usually took the form of a small, thick volume or series of volumes, was a type of devotional work popular with priests, monks, nuns and the laity alike in the Middle Ages, due to its size.

Breviaries usually contained material including hymns, Psalms, prayers for the religious offices from Matins to Compline, and, indeed, often the Psalter in its entirety.[101] In commissioning such a work for her daughter and in appointing a male religious to oversee its execution, Countess Eleanor took a guiding hand in her daughter's spiritual guidance and counsel, and perhaps recognized the opportunity to instil her own religious values and views on morality into her offspring.

The role played by figures like Cecily of Sandford in Countess Eleanor's upbringing might well have provided an element of stability and emotional support that was perhaps lacking elsewhere in her daily life. Indeed, established in their respective households and, for the most part, in the custody of different guardians, Henry III, his brother and his sisters emerge as remarkably isolated figures in their childhoods. It is, for example, difficult to gauge how often they maintained contact with one another, remembered significant family anniversaries and celebrated the great feasts of the religious calendar. Obvious occasions when they might have been permitted to come together and socially interact with one another were the Christmas courts of Henry III's minority, which were usually held at Winchester until 1221, under the watchful eyes of Peter des Roches.[102] If anything, the shared experiences of their parents' absence after 1217 might well have heightened the value placed upon sibling relationships, especially among Eleanor's older siblings. The relationship that Eleanor's eldest sister, Joan, enjoyed with her brothers is strongly suggestive that this was, in fact, the case. The text of a letter survives that was addressed to Henry III and written in Joan's name in or around 1220, when she was nine or ten years old and in the household of Hugh (X) de Lusignan. Its purpose was ostensibly to reassure her brother, the king, of Hugh's continued loyalty, against the immediate political background of Isabella of Angoulême's impending marriage to him. Having set the king's mind at rest with regard to her own safety, Joan asked for news of Henry and their brother Richard. Even if allowance is made for the possibility that this letter was written under Hugh's or Isabella's guidance, with their interests firmly at heart, its tone was that of a caring younger sister and encouraged Henry to respond as an affectionate older brother.[103] After Joan's marriage to Alexander II, King of Scots, in 1221, she became a regular visitor to the English royal court, especially when it visited York. She also corresponded with Henry, imparting Scottish intelligence about the activities of Hugh de Lacy and his fellow rebels in Ireland in or around 1224.[104] In fact, as Jessica Nelson observes, Joan's preference for the English royal court, and by implication for her natal family, over her husband's court, company and kin, attracted contemporary comment. Matthew Paris noted, with a critical eye, her refusal to return to Scotland in spite of her husband's repeated requests for her to do so.[105] When Joan died on 4 March 1238, it was in England, at Havering in Essex, and her deathbed was attended by her brothers. According to the Melrose chronicler, she passed away in their arms, in a moving family deathbed scene.[106] She was subsequently buried 'with great grief and with equal magnificence' at the abbey of Tarrant Keynes in Dorset, a house in the patronage of Henry III's wife.[107]

The circumstances of Eleanor's early upbringing and the physical remoteness from her siblings during infancy might help to explain her later 'independence' of character, observed by John Maddicott in his biography of Simon de Montfort.[108] The chastising tone that Eleanor's correspondent, Adam Marsh, was prepared to adopt towards her when the need arose indicates Eleanor was prepared to receive and, perhaps, listen to his advice. Indeed, a striking feature of Marsh's letters is their candid language. From the pen of Marsh, the adult Eleanor emerges as his friend and valued patroness, as well as the determined, forceful, wilful and, at times, quarrelsome wife to Earl Simon, a woman who manipulated and subverted gender expectations, themes that will be explored in this book.

2

The Marshal Marriage

'we have no greater treasure than our own marriage and [the marriages] of our sisters'[1]

Royal marriage in the thirteenth century was a highly valued and, indeed, valuable tool in the diplomatic armoury of the English king and his kingdom. It offered a potential means of recruiting powerful political allies to cement the king's position as well as a way of engineering peace between neighbouring rulers through the creation of a personal, dynastic bond. Inheritance customs and the property settlements that accompanied royal unions also meant that prudently arranged alliances might bring with them movable wealth and new territories to augment the prosperity of the ruling house. The high level of personal importance that King Henry III attached to marriage was made clear in a memorandum dispatched to the English proctors at the papal curia in 1224. This document furnished Henry's agents with the reasons for the marriage of his youngest sister, Eleanor, then just nine years old, to a man twenty-five years her senior, William Marshal junior (d. 1231), Earl of Pembroke. The political background to Eleanor's first marriage and the relationship that she subsequently forged with her new husband are the subjects explored within this chapter. In particular, we shall consider precisely why it was that the young king felt compelled in 1224 to justify and defend his choice of bridegroom for this sister to his agents in Rome.

WILLIAM MARSHAL JUNIOR AND THE CROWN

The father of Eleanor's bridegroom, William Marshal senior, was a younger son of John Marshal, a minor baron who held the hereditary post of royal master-marshal, by his second wife, Sibyl, the sister of Earl Patrick of Salisbury.[2] Through service in the households of Henry the Young King (d. 1183), Henry II (d. 1189), Richard I (d. 1199) and John (d. 1216), William senior had reaped the rewards of royal patronage. Most notably, he secured the hand in marriage of Isabella de Clare (d. 1220), the daughter and sole heiress of Richard fitz Gilbert de Clare,

Lord of Striguil and of Leinster, and a claimant to the earldom of Pembroke, thereby acquiring her extensive estates in England, south Wales, Ireland and Normandy.[3] It was a measure of William Marshal's importance within the Angevin dominions that, unlike the queen, he was appointed as one of King John's executors and was personally charged with safeguarding Henry III and the English throne.[4] With the agreement of the remaining loyalist barons, the older Marshal was appointed regent just a short time after the young king's first coronation at the end of October 1216, and helped to secure a decisive royalist victory against the supporters of the French prince Louis at the battle of Lincoln in May 1217.[5] Ill-health and old age brought William senior's regency to an end in early April 1219; he died a month later and was buried at the New Temple in London.[6] William junior, William senior's eldest surviving son and heir, stood next in line to inherit the earldom of Pembroke (bestowed by King John upon his father in 1199) and, on his mother's death in 1220, the bulk of the couple's English, Irish and Welsh lands.[7] The deaths of his parents left William junior one of the wealthiest and most eligible magnates in the kingdom.

William Marshal junior had already made his own mark on English politics by 1220. Whereas his father had been an unswerving loyalist during the civil war of 1215–17, William junior had sided initially with the rebels and was one of the twenty-five barons appointed to oversee the enforcement of Magna Carta in 1215.[8] In the event, William junior's rebellion was not long lived: the young Marshal successfully retook Marlborough Castle from the rebels and fought for the royalists at the battle of Lincoln in May 1217.[9] William's change of heart was rewarded when he received a grant of the lands confiscated from the rebel, David, Earl of Huntingdon, which included Fotheringhay Castle.[10] Although Earl David's lands were restored to him in 1218, William junior hung on tenaciously to Fotheringhay in the face of growing pressure for him to relinquish this stronghold until the summer of 1220, when events in Wales conspired against him.[11] The unexpected invasion of Pembrokeshire by Llywelyn the Great, Prince of North Wales, devastated the Marshal lands there and forced William junior's supporters to agree peace on unfavourable terms.[12] When the new Earl of Pembroke sought the aid of the justiciar, Hubert de Burgh, against the Welsh settlement, he was met with a demand for Fotheringhay's return to the crown.[13]

In the letter in which William junior announced his intention to answer for Fotheringhay, he claimed that he was prepared to do so because 'I endeavour to obtain the preferment of the lord king and his sister by all means.'[14] The royal sister in question was Joan, Eleanor's oldest sister. The negotiations for Joan's marriage to Alexander II, King of Scots and Earl David's overlord, subsequently concluded in June 1221, were, by this time, already well underway.[15] As part of the Anglo-Scottish talks held at York in August 1220, Alexander pushed for, and was promised, Fotheringhay's restoration.[16] On 11 September 1220, a curt letter addressed by Henry III to William junior ordered the latter to yield this castle forthwith, 'lest the whole business of the marriage remains incompleted to our great damage and shame'.[17]

The match agreed at York in August 1220 reworked the terms of an earlier treaty that had provided for a double marriage between Alexander II and Joan, and Alexander's eldest sister, Margaret, and the English king. It was now agreed that Alexander's sister would marry a subject of the English king instead.[18] For the time being, the identity of the new English bridegroom remained unclear. Yet the royal memorandum of 1224 that announced William's later marriage to Eleanor indicates that the young Marshal, as one of the greatest lords of Henry's realm, was regarded as a serious, and potentially threatening, alternative candidate for the hand of the Scottish princess to that championed by the English crown.[19] In the event, Margaret married the justiciar, Hubert de Burgh, during the autumn of 1221 in a union possibly arranged at Joan's wedding to Alexander earlier that year.[20]

In the meantime, the young Marshal was tempted by the prospect of an alternative match between himself and a daughter of Count Robert of Dreux, his erstwhile competitor for Marlborough.[21] As the royal memorandum of 1224 also explained, this potential match was similarly fraught with danger for the English crown: Robert was an alien (a foreigner) and such an alliance might introduce more aliens into England.[22] This was an especially pertinent consideration in view of the events of 1215–17 and the fact that William's younger brother, Richard, held all his lands in Normandy and owed homage to the French crown, a point that the king readily acknowledged.[23]

Another candidate for the Marshal's hand who emerged at this time, and was named in the English memorandum, was none other than a daughter of Henry (I) de Louvain, Duke of Brabant (r. 1183–1235). Although Henry de Louvain supported his son-in-law, the Holy Roman Emperor Otto IV, as an English ally at the battle of Bouvines in 1214, the duke had subsequently allied with the victor, the Capetian king Philip Augustus.[24] This change of alliance was not altogether surprising: Henry (I)'s second wife was Philip's daughter, Marie of France, the widow of the Marquis of Namur.[25] By 1221, Henry was the father of four daughters by his first wife, all of whom had already made highly advantageous marriages.[26] Perhaps the recent death of Arnoul (III), Count of Loos and Graf of Rieneck, the husband of one of Henry's younger daughters, Adelaide, prompted the Earl of Pembroke to consider applying for her hand.[27] A marriage alliance between William junior and the Brabantine house, with its Capetian sympathies, clearly presented yet another threat to the future security of the English crown and to any long-term ambitions for the recovery of Henry III's lost continental possessions.

It is, of course, possible that the royal memorandum of 1224 was written as much as an apology, as well as a justification, for the decision taken by the boy king and his counsellors to marry his youngest sister, Eleanor, to a nobleman, rather than a foreign potentate. In view of the sheer extent of the Marshal's estates within the English king's dominions, it is easy to appreciate the appeal of allying these considerable resources to a cash-strapped crown.[28] The proposed marriage between William junior and Eleanor was a match with a clear political purpose, a union that not only promised safety against internal foes, but also increased protection against external foes by countering the potential threat of a Francophile Marshal marriage.[29]

The situation in England in or around 1221 made arrangements for a Marshal/Plantagenet alliance all the more urgent. From the safer vantage point of 1224, Henry III later recalled that William junior's loyalty to the crown had come under suspicion: 'magnates in England ... were struggling to turn the heart of [Pembroke] from us by malicious confederations'.[30] Faced with a possible rebellion, Hubert de Burgh, the main architect of this new union, now sought to placate Pembroke, his former rival for the hand of Margaret of Scots.[31] The prospect of a marriage between the younger Marshal and Eleanor also served the immediate purpose of providing a bargaining counter with which finally to recover control of the royal castles of Marlborough and Ludgershall (whose custody was often linked to the former) from Pembroke.[32] As the memorandum of 1224 explained, the crown hoped that this would encourage other custodians to resign possession of further royal castles. This was all part of a wider programme for the recovery by the crown of its castles and estates from the nobility of the realm.[33] 'After Easter [1221]', the Dunstable annalist recorded, 'William Marshal the younger was being urged by the royal council to surrender the castle of Marlborough' into the hands of Pandulf, the papal legate. If other lords failed to follow suit, the annalist continued, then Pembroke would receive Marlborough back again, presumably as a conciliatory gesture.[34] In actual fact, under the terms of the marriage settlement, Marlborough's return was promised if the king failed to deliver the bride to her groom within a specified timeframe.[35] If concerns about the direction of William junior's loyalties were conducive to a royal marriage, then the prospect of Marlborough's return sealed the deal for the minority government.

There was, however, no escape from the fact that the marriage of the king's sister, even that of his youngest sister, was a matter of tremendous political importance. According to the papal mandate of June 1222, it was with the counsel of numerous bishops, earls and barons that the Earl of Pembroke agreed to marry one of the king's sisters, and swore an oath to this effect. Hubert de Burgh, for his part, then took an oath on behalf of the king to deliver one of Henry's sisters to him as his bride.[36] It was not enough for the papal legate and the justiciar, Hubert de Burgh, to agree the match with Pembroke in line with their own political agenda; the marriage was made conditional upon the consent of the English magnates. The initial absence of leading figures like Ranulf (III), Earl of Chester, slowed down proceedings, as did the veracity of the debate generated by the more widely perceived advantages and disadvantages of a union such as this.[37] David Carpenter has argued that Chester, one of the greatest barons in the realm whose estates easily rivalled those of Pembroke, might well have been one of the magnates who initially opposed the proposed alliance with Eleanor. This just might explain why the memorandum of 1224 singled out Chester by naming him as one whose consent had expressly been secured.[38] As a result of a lack of consensus, and to Pembroke's deep frustration, the marriage was delayed.

THE QUESTION OF DISPARAGEMENT?

One of the issues seized upon with great vigour by critics of the match, so the memorandum of 1224 recalled, was the fact that in marrying the younger Marshal, Eleanor was not entering into a union that obviously facilitated 'a great alliance in foreign parts'.[39] In the aftermath of Joan's marriage to the King of Scots, Hubert de Burgh and Pandulf found themselves open to accusations that they were disparaging Eleanor by marrying her to one of Henry's subjects, rather than finding her a husband of equal status. The disparagement of minors was such an important and highly topical political issue that it had merited inclusion in Magna Carta in 1215: cap. 6 had specifically laid down that heirs ought to be married without disparagement, that is, not to someone of lesser social status.[40] This was also an accusation to which de Burgh was vulnerable on a far more personal level. From obscure beginnings as the son of a minor Norfolk landholder, Hubert's meteoric rise in royal service to justiciar had facilitated his own marriage to Margaret, the sister of the king of Scots, on 3 October 1221.[41] The obscurity of de Burgh's birth was not lost on other members of the nobility. When, for example, false reports reached the English royal court in 1225 of the

Earl of Salisbury's death overseas, the justiciar's nephew solicited the Countess of Salisbury's hand in marriage. According to Roger of Wendover, the countess sternly rebuked him 'because the nobility of her family', as well as the fact, as she first pointed out, that her husband was alive, prevented such a union.[42]

In comparison with that of de Burgh, Pembroke's noble status and lineage was, on his mother's side at least, far better established. Yet, in the memorandum of 1224, the matter of Eleanor's possible disparagement was considered of sufficient weight to be tackled head on. The memorandum noted how the younger Marshal was a 'great potentate' in England and Ireland, and recalled how he had recaptured for the English crown 'our castles which Llywelyn, prince of North Wales, held'.[43] This was a clear reference to Pembroke's successful Welsh campaign of 1223, as a result of which Cardigan and Carmarthen had been captured for the crown from the Welsh and William junior regained control of Cilgerran for himself. Pembroke had subsequently been placed, alongside the Earl of Salisbury, in charge of a cavalry force that recovered the castle and lordship of Kidwelly.[44] These events all conspired to bring Llywelyn to terms in the autumn, whereupon Pembroke was appointed custodian of Carmarthen and Cardigan in November that year.[45] Having thus established Pembroke's credentials, the memorandum of 1224 pointed to the example of the former king of France, Philip Augustus (d. 1223), whom, it was claimed, had married 'his daughters, sisters and nieces' to 'the Count of Namur, and the Count of Ponthieu, and his other men', that is to other great subjects.[46] In a similar fashion, the memorandum went on, the 'niece' of the present king of France, Louis VIII, 'namely the daughter of Guichard of Beaujeu', had lately been given in matrimony to the Count of Champagne.[47] Taking this all into consideration, Henry III and his counsellors finally agreed that it would be 'to our profit and honour to marry our sister' to Pembroke.[48]

A point often overlooked by modern scholars is that William junior might also have made attempts of his own to counter claims of disparagement when his marriage to Eleanor was in negotiation. Between 1224 and February 1225, William junior took the remarkable step of commissioning an account of his father's life, the *History of William Marshal*, in Middle French verse. The work of a poet called John, it drew on the memories of those closest to William Marshal senior, including John of Earley, one of the regent's executors, and ran to 19,214 lines in length.[49] Probably completed by the autumn of 1226, the biography celebrated the older Marshal's career as a warrior, courtier and great statesman, and included vignettes that demonstrated his heroism, loyalty and nobility of conduct.[50] Indeed, it might be argued that the elder Marshal was portrayed in such a way so as to make it clear that these values more than amply compensated for the relative obscurity of his birth as the younger son of a Berkshire baron. In the textual introduction to the modern edition of this work, A. J. Holden expresses his belief that 'The poem was commissioned as an act of filial piety by the hero's eldest son and successor.'[51] In the historical introduction to the same work, David Crouch argues that the author's 'most pressing task was to repudiate the criticisms being made of his hero in the 1220s', including those relating to the family's retention of their French estates after the loss of Normandy in 1204.[52] Crouch also, significantly, draws attention to passages in the text concerning the older Marshal's claims over Caerleon, which resonate with William Marshal junior's ultimately successful attempts to recover this Welsh lordship in August 1226.[53] While this might, indeed, have been the case, the text served the additional purpose of enhancing William junior's reputation through his association with his father precisely at a time when William junior's own background and personal attributes were under particular scrutiny, as evidenced by Henry III's memorandum to the papal curia. Crouch suggests 'that the commissioning of the *History* was one aspect of the earl's need to put his affairs in order before he departed to Ireland [in 1224] for an indeterminate period'.[54] It might have done this and rather more. William junior's appointment as justiciar of Ireland was intimately connected to his marriage to Eleanor, as we shall see below.[55] By praising the older Marshal's character and achievements, perhaps with an eye also to celebrating the connections of his eldest son, William junior might well have hoped that the *History* would help to counter criticism of his own forthcoming union. After all, William junior earned extravagant praise within the *History*:

> The first son was called William,
> and I can tell you that in this kingdom,
> as I have heard said, there was nobody
> who so dedicated himself to performing noble exploits;
> that is what I have heard everybody say,
> and no man can help but acquire a great reputation
> and involve himself in a grand undertaking
> who has that sort of witness to his character.
> He became earl after his father
> and he was a fine and worthy knight.[56]

The *History*'s author was particularly careful to stress the nobility of the connections forged by the marriages of William senior's children, and especially his daughters.[57] Yet the text curiously neglected to mention the royal marriage, a

truly extraordinary oversight, which suggests either that the marriage had not
yet taken place when the text was written or that William junior and Eleanor
had not yet begun to live together as husband and wife, so that the future of the
union remained in the balance. What matters here is that those persons who
visited William junior's household in the 1220s might well have listened to the
poem in its entirety or to extracts from it; it is also likely that other members
of the Marshal family – William junior had four brothers and five sisters –
possessed copies of this text. Just one manuscript of the *History* survives today,
but there are references to others formerly in the possession of St Augustine's
Abbey, Canterbury, Westminster Abbey and Thomas, Duke of Gloucester (in c.
1397) that hint at its wider dissemination.[58] In glorifying his father, this work
promised to elevate William junior's reputation and that of his siblings at a
peculiarly sensitive period in the dynasty's history.

THE FRUSTRATED BRIDEGROOM

At the time of her betrothal in or around 1221 to William Marshal junior,
Eleanor was still just a six-year-old child and below the age of canonical
consent for betrothal approved by the church. The deliberations over the pros
and cons of the match by the English barons undoubtedly delayed matters.
By the summer of 1222, Pembroke was blaming the machinations of 'jealous'
parties for the failure of the marriage to come to fruition. Eleanor's extreme
youth might also have offered Hubert de Burgh, the justiciar, a convenient and
plausible reason to postpone the marriage, while at the same time guaranteeing
Pembroke's loyalty as a political ally, but without actually delivering William
junior's marital prize. A strong sense of Pembroke's frustration at having turned
down alternative brides in order to accept the match with Eleanor, only to
have her withheld from him, is conveyed by his decision to solicit support
by petitioning the pope in 1222 – the year in which Eleanor turned seven.[59]
William junior's representations secured a papal mandate in June that year,
whereby the Archbishop of Canterbury and the Bishop of Salisbury were both
ordered to ensure that the promised union between William and Eleanor went
ahead. The mandate stipulated, however, that their marriage ought only to
proceed if it was to the advantage of Henry III and his kingdom, and on the
express condition that it resulted in no great scandal, a clear reference to the
relative obscurity of Pembroke's birth in relation to that of his intended bride.
Indeed, the concerns expressed in this mandate might have reflected concerns
at the papal curia itself about Eleanor's possible disparagement, concerns that

prompted Henry III's detailed memorandum on the subject when the marriage finally went ahead in the spring of 1224.

By the early months of 1224, there were no reasonable grounds for delaying the union any longer. Pembroke had, after all, more than fulfilled his side of the bargain by surrendering Marlborough in 1221, and performing important services for the English crown during the Welsh campaign of 1223. The closing months of 1223 were also a momentous time for the royal government: Henry III, now sixteen, assumed control of governmental affairs and, with the assistance of his supporters, recovered his royal castles and sheriffdoms from those who had held them during his minority.[60] In Ireland, however, where the younger Marshal possessed extensive lordships and where his cousin, John Marshal, controlled Ulster for the crown, the situation was far less promising for the king. Hugh de Lacy, a former rebel and a former lord of Ulster, invaded Ireland and laid waste to lands in Meath.[61] These events placed a higher premium still on the value of retaining Pembroke's loyalty and, arguably, explain Henry III's readiness to see his youngest sister's marriage to Pembroke finally come to pass. In addition, the projected marriage, once again, offered a way of strengthening the position of Pembroke's ally, de Burgh, at the heart of government against the competing interests of des Roches and his associates, who had found their power base eroded by the resumption of castles and shrievalties.[62] The connection between affairs in Ireland and the conclusion of the Marshal marriage is implicit in the order of entries recorded on the patent rolls, a series of rolls containing copies of royal letters that were issued open or 'patent'. On 5 February 1224, the same day that the king informed the Archbishop of Dublin that he had awarded custody of Roscrea Castle to Theobald Walter, for whom Pembroke stood as surety, Henry III furnished his future brother-in-law with another letter. Significantly, this was addressed to Robert de Courtenay, the nobleman who then had charge of Eleanor's household, and instructed him to hand Eleanor over to Marshal, so that she might travel with him to the king.[63] In assigning Marshal the role of escort, the king, it seems, sought to reassure him that his long-anticipated union with Eleanor would stand.

THE MARSHAL BRIDE

When, in the spring of 1224, Henry III appointed William junior to escort the nine-year-old Eleanor to the royal court, he provided his youngest sister with a valuable opportunity to become acquainted with her future husband in advance of the couple's nuptials on 23 April 1224.[64] At the time her marriage was celebrated, Eleanor was probably no more than nine years old at most, three years below the canonical age of consent for marriage, and she had not yet reached puberty. Pembroke, her new husband, was, by contrast, in his mid-thirties. William junior had also experienced married life before. His first wife was Alice de Béthune, daughter of Baldwin, Count of Aumale, to whom he had been betrothed in 1203, and whom he had married in 1214. Alice, who bore William junior no surviving children, died in or around 1216.[65] William's transition from the husband of a count's daughter to the husband of the daughter and sister of a king stood as testimony to his rise in power and influence during the minority of Henry III. The value that he placed upon securing a royal bride explains why, initially at least, and in a departure from the usual social conventions of his day, William received Eleanor without a substantial marriage portion. As the king boasted to his proctors at the papal curia in 1224, 'without diminution of lands, castles, or money, we granted our younger sister to him'.[66] The marriage also, in the short term, secured a powerful and influential ally for the crown in Ireland. Indeed, the Dunstable annalist, in his account of the Marshal marriage, noted the contrast – while labouring his own political and moral point – between William Marshal junior, who 'took to wife the sister of Henry, King of England', and the behaviour of the rebel Hugh de Lacy in Ireland, who put aside his legitimate wife and lived in adultery, while the Marshal waged a just war against him and subdued Ireland on the crown's behalf.[67] The annalist was astute in linking the Marshal marriage so strongly with Irish affairs. Eleanor and Pembroke's marriage had been followed nine days later by William junior's appointment as justiciar there.[68] Marshal's extensive properties in Ireland, which included the lordship of Leinster, coupled with his new status as Henry's brother-in-law, made him an ideal candidate to represent the English crown in Ireland and bring the Irish rebels to heel.

But what did this union actually mean for Eleanor in personal terms? Throughout the negotiations between de Burgh, Henry III and the younger Marshal, Eleanor was treated as a valuable asset and pawn in the hands of the royal government. It is useful here to consider Eleanor's experiences in the light of those of other girls of similar rank. John Parsons's study of eighty-seven matrimonial alliances entered into by members of the English royal house and the noble families of Mortimer of March and Holland of Kent between 1150 and 1500 found thirty-eight brides who were fourteen or younger on marriage, but observed that it was more usual for Plantagenet brides to marry when they were fifteen or older.[69] Margaret Howell's research has modified this view for the thirteenth century: no fewer than eight of the twelve royal women who were associated with the courts of Henry III of England and Louis

IX of France as mothers, sisters, wives, daughters and daughters-in-law of the two kings married at twelve or a little earlier in order to cement advantageous political alliances.[70] This accords well with the experiences of the generation of royal women who preceded Henry III and his sisters. Eleanor's aunts on her father's side had married at similarly young ages. Born in 1156, Matilda, the eldest daughter of Henry II by Eleanor of Aquitaine, was betrothed in 1165 and married in 1168 to Henry the Lion, Duke of Saxony, a man twenty-seven years her senior.[71] Matilda's younger sister, Eleanor/Leonor, was just nine years old when she married Alfonso VIII (b. 1154), King of Castile, in 1170, with an eye to strengthening the Pyrenean frontier of Eleanor of Aquitaine's lands.[72] Matilda and Eleanor's youngest sister, Joan (b. 1165), was betrothed in 1176 to William II, King of Sicily, and married him in the Palatine Chapel in Palermo on 13 February 1177; William was more than a decade older than his bride.[73]

The relative youthfulness of Henry III of England's sisters, Joan and Eleanor, at the time of their first marriages to the King of Scots and the Earl of Pembroke sat well with contemporary practice at the level of the elite. Above all, it demonstrated the importance attached to their marriages as a means of bringing security and stability to the English realm. It is useful to think of the young princesses, Eleanor and Joan, as highly prized assets during the first, uncertain decade of Henry III's reign, at a time when the crown's position at home and abroad remained relatively weak. In such circumstances, there was little point in delaying the arrangement of their marriages, when they might secure immediate political advantages – Joan's marriage strengthened England's northern borders, while Eleanor's procured a powerful and wealthy English ally for the young king. This partly explains why Eleanor, in particular, found herself married to a much older man.

On the occasion of her marriage to William Marshal junior in 1224, Eleanor was simply too young and too inexperienced to play a role in the arrangements for the match. If, as a nine year old, she expressed an opinion on her future husband, it went unrecorded. We do not even know at which point Eleanor was informed that she would marry Pembroke. Her marriage to an English magnate, rather than a foreign potentate presumably exempted her from the custom for foreign ambassadors to 'view' her, that is, meet her and appraise her suitability as their master's prospective bride.[74] Yet we must be cautious of bringing modern values to bear on a thirteenth-century dynastic union and of painting too bleak a picture of the way in which Henry III and his counsellors regarded Eleanor and her marriage. There are clear signs that the young king was far from indifferent to the emotional and physical wellbeing of the young bride-to-be. In the first place, it is worth noting her connection with Robert de Courtenay during these formative years. Robert, in whose care Eleanor can be found early in 1224, was lord of Okehampton in Devon and the husband of Marion de Vernon, a daughter of William (d. 1217), Earl of Devon.[75] He was also, more significantly, a kinsman of the French lords of Courtenay from whom Eleanor was descended through her maternal grandmother Alice de Courtenay.[76] Furthermore, as sheriff of Devon, a county where the queen dowager held substantial properties in dower, Robert had witnessed a grant by his kinswoman, Isabella of Angoulême, of the fair of Exeter to St Nicholas's Priory on 29 May 1217, shortly before she departed from the realm.[77] The combined importance of this family connection and Robert's earlier association with Eleanor's mother should not be overlooked. It seems likely that Courtenay's distant blood relationship with Eleanor recommended him to the crown as a suitable custodian and gave him a strong personal interest in the upbringing of the king's youngest sister. It also potentially allowed Eleanor to maintain a connection with her maternal heritage in her mother's absence. If this was, indeed, the case, then it is not inconceivable that the queen dowager herself remained informed after all, via letters and messengers, of her youngest daughter's health, welfare and impending marriage throughout Eleanor's childhood.

In the second place, having made Pembroke wait three years for marriage, the king was perfectly prepared to make him wait quite a bit longer for the match to be consummated and for the couple to fulfil their conjugal debt to one another. It was possibly in recognition of the final consummation of Eleanor and Pembroke's union that the king decided on 18 October 1229 to make a special grant to William and his heirs of ten manors – Brabourne (Kent), Sutton (Kent), Kemsing (Kent), Luton (Bedfordshire), Norton (Northamptonshire), Foulsham (Norfolk), Wantage (Berkshire), Severnstoke (Worcestershire), Toddington (Bedfordshire) and Newbury (Berkshire), and half a manor in Shrivenham (Berkshire). This gift, made on the express condition that these manors would remain with Eleanor for life in the event of her widowhood, was clearly intended to provide the king's youngest sister with some form of future maintenance.[78] These lands were all former properties of the Count of Perche that Pembroke held already; Eleanor's long-term financial support was, thus, guaranteed at minimal cost and inconvenience to the English crown.[79]

The timing of the grant in 1229 was significant from the point of view of Eleanor's physical development. Delays between the wedding ceremony and the advent of regular conjugal relations between couples were, so Parsons argues, fairly common when royal brides were in their early teens or younger.[80] Eleanor's mother, Isabella of Angoulême, married King John in 1200 at the age of twelve, but bore their first child in 1207. Roger of Wendover blamed the loss of Normandy in 1203–4, in part, upon John's infatuation with his young bride, a comment that might indicate that it was widely believed that their union had been consummated by the time that Isabella reached the age of fifteen or sixteen.[81] Henry III's wife, Eleanor of Provence, was twelve at the time of her marriage in 1236, and gave birth to her eldest son, Edward, three years later.[82] Their eldest daughter, Margaret, married Alexander III, King of Scots, in 1251, when she was eleven, but only lived together with him as his wife after 1255. In the interim, and much to Margaret's frustration, the couple were kept apart by their Scottish guardians.[83] Royal daughters might be 'sacrificed' to the interests of national and international diplomacy through their early marriages, but not entirely without thought of their future health and welfare. A bride who was still too young to be nubile would be unable to bear an heir until she reached the age of menarche. Medical treatises indicate that contemporaries understood that once a girl reached the age of menarche, and was potentially able to bear an heir, the travails of pregnancy and childbirth might be particularly dangerous for a younger, rather than an older, woman. Brides who were in their early teens were less likely to carry a living child successfully to full term and were also less likely to survive delivering a child or to bear healthy sons or daughters in the future. The *Trotula* texts, for example, a compendium of work on women's medicine that originated in southern Italy in the late eleventh and twelfth centuries and which circulated throughout western Europe in the Middle Ages, observed that women usually menstruated between the ages of thirteen or fourteen and thirty-five to sixty or sixty-five.[84] The compilers of such texts believed that young women who gave birth in winter were more likely than others to encounter difficulties and were more likely to experience stillbirths due to 'a tight orifice of the womb', exacerbated by the cold weather.[85]

In the years between Eleanor and Pembroke's marriage in 1224 and its consummation in 1229, Eleanor was placed in the care of a governess, Cecily of Sandford, with a view to preparing her for married life.[86] The continuing value that the English crown placed upon the marriage in the meantime as a way of keeping one of the kingdom's wealthiest magnates in check is demonstrated nowhere more clearly than in a letter patent that the king sent to William junior on 10 July 1226. In this letter, the contents of which are suggestive of a certain degree of reluctance on the Marshal's part to become a mere cipher of the crown, Henry III admonished his brother-in-law for failing to meet with him; rumours had reached Pembroke that Henry regarded him with suspicion once more. Pembroke had apparently informed the king of his intention to undertake a pilgrimage but appears instead to have set off for Ireland. In seeking to reassure Pembroke of his continuing affection, the king reminded the earl that he had given him his own sister in marriage.[87] After all, what clearer statement of the king's continuing regard was needed than that?

Pembroke was frequently employed on royal business after his marriage to Eleanor was consummated in 1229. Even if the royal campaign overseas planned for 1229 was postponed, Pembroke and his knights were summoned to serve the king in Brittany in 1230.[88] Eleanor accompanied her husband and the royal court on the Breton expedition. Perhaps Pembroke was hopeful that by keeping his long-anticipated royal bride by his side, it would remind the king of his new ties of kinship and strengthen Pembroke's stature as a senior adviser on the campaign. Eleanor's attendance alongside her husband also increased the likelihood that the couple might conceive an heir. Her presence during the initial stages of the campaign is confirmed by a remarkable letter sent by Nicholas de Neville to Ralph de Neville, Bishop of Chichester and royal chancellor, which describes Henry III's crossing to Brittany.[89] The letter reported how Henry, with a retinue of about thirty ships, landed on the isle of Jersey before nine in the morning on 2 May. The rest of the great fleet, meanwhile, had diverted to the port of St Gildas. The king, however, remained on Jersey 'because his sister was just a little fatigued by the sea'.[90] Once Eleanor recovered, Henry and his ships set sail for St Malo at three in the morning on the following day, together with Eleanor's husband, the Earl Marshal, where they joined the remainder of the English fleet.[91] The king's sympathy for Eleanor's seasickness – that he stopped for her and then refused to leave her behind – provides yet another striking demonstration of the king's personal interest in his sister's welfare and hints at his affection towards her.[92]

On their arrival at St Malo in Brittany, the royal party prepared to receive their ally, the Duke of Brittany. The king and his retinue then proceeded to Dinan in the company of Isabella of Angoulême and from there made arrangements to travel on to Nantes for a family conference with his stepfather, Hugh (X) de Lusignan, Count of La Marche.[93] Eleanor's presence in Brittany on this occasion is intriguing. In accompanying her older brother, Eleanor was presented with an opportunity to meet with her mother for the first time in thirteen years, a further testimony to royal favour. Eleanor's presence was also not without its potential for political leverage from the crown's point of view. Henry might well have hoped that, in bringing his youngest sister with him and thus engineering a family reunion, her involvement would incline the queen dowager and her husband to lend their support to the king's campaign. It is, of course, possible that Isabella requested, and perhaps anticipated with pleasure, her youngest daughter's presence. Henry III's and Eleanor's maternal connections mattered – on both personal and political levels.

If there was any attempt to play upon Isabella's sentiment during the early part of the summer of 1230, it failed to secure a steadfast ally for the English crown. On 8 June 1230, Ralph fitz Nicholas, the steward of the king's household, informed the royal chancellor in England of the Count of La Marche's defection to the French crown.[94] One cannot help but wonder how Eleanor reacted to this news – with sadness or with a degree of cynicism at her mother's behaviour. Eleanor's role during the remainder of the Breton campaign went unrecorded, but her marriage to Pembroke, as well as the earl's extensive experience and wealth, undoubtedly holds the key to the king's subsequent decision to leave Pembroke, along with the Earl of Chester and Count of Aumale, to continue the campaign after his own return to England in October 1230.[95]

Eleanor's involvement in the Breton campaign raises the question of the personal dynamics within the relationship between Pembroke and his bride. English law, feudal custom and religious teaching expected and exhorted wives to be attentive, submissive and obedient to their husbands, who legally controlled their wives and their wives' property during marriage.[96] In practice, a husband's authority within marriage and a wife's level of subservience might be tempered by the personalities involved and by practical necessity; a long-running motif within medieval literature was the image of the wife who acted as her husband's deputy in his absence, managing the noble household and its administration when he was engaged in family business elsewhere or in service to his lord or the king.[97] The disparity in both age and experience between Pembroke and his royal bride strongly suggests that Eleanor was very much in her first husband's shadow. The fifteen-year-old Eleanor's presence alongside her husband on the Breton campaign, coupled with the existence of effective estate stewards on the Marshal estates, prevented Eleanor from assuming a role in the administration of Pembroke's extensive lordships as her husband's deputy or representative in his absence. Yet Eleanor's status as the king's sister might well have re-configured the sexual politics within their relationship in certain situations. Research into religious patronage by women in twelfth- and thirteenth-century England has illuminated the role of 'persuasive wives' as channels of benevolent influence and as active participants in religious patronage alongside their husbands.[98] Like other great nobles of his day, the younger Marshal was a patron of religious houses throughout his estates in England, Ireland and Wales. He was a keen supporter of the new orders of friars who arrived in the British Isles in the 1220s, founding a house for Dominican Friars in Kilkenny in Ireland.[99] He was a benefactor of Reading Abbey (Berkshire), where his father's body had rested on its journey to its final resting place at the New Temple in London.[100] William junior also made gifts to Tintern Abbey (Monmouthshire),[101] Mottisfont Abbey

(Hampshire),[102] St Paul's Cathedral, the resting place of his first wife,[103] and St Mary's Hospital, Roncevaux (in the Pyrenees).[104] William junior confirmed the grants made by his father to William senior's foundation of Cartmel Priory (Lancashire) [105] and Duisk Abbey (Ireland),[106] as well as making gifts in his father's memory to St Thomas's Abbey, Dublin.[107]

Useful points of comparison with William junior's activities are offered by William senior's religious benefactions and by mention of his wife, Isabella de Clare, in his charters. A striking feature of the charters addressed by William Marshal senior to religious houses was the way in which he sometimes, quite deliberately, associated Isabella with his grants by naming her in *pro anima* clauses – clauses concerned with the safety of the souls of the grantor and other beneficiaries after death.[108] Since Isabella was the great heiress through whom the elder William had secured vast estates, her appearance in her husband's charters was not only an expression of his concern for her spiritual welfare, but also a reminder of her importance as the conduit through whom the greater part of the Marshal family's wealth and influence had been secured and would be passed on to another generation. It reflected the importance attached to Isabella's Anglo-Norman and Irish ancestry, as well as, perhaps, the length of her marriage to William Marshal senior; she had, after all, thirty years to build up an adult relationship with her husband. When Isabella was eventually widowed on William senior's death, she secured control of her inheritance, fulfilled her commemorative responsibilities towards her late husband and, in doing so, associated William junior with her in her charters.[109]

Although William junior's wife, Eleanor, was not a great heiress like her mother-in-law, she was the English king's sister in an aristocratic society that valued royal birth, noble lineage and impeccable political connections. When William junior married Henry III's sister as his second wife, he deliberately associated Eleanor with him in at least some of his charters. This is clearly apparent in his patronage of the New Temple in London, his father's burial place. When William senior granted the church of Speen in Berkshire to the Templars there, the *pro anima* clause of his charter included his wife as a beneficiary.[110] When William junior confirmed his father's gift of the advowson (the right of patronage over the church) of Speen, it was his turn to state that he did so expressly for the salvation of his own soul and that of his own wife, Eleanor.[111] Admittedly, it is difficult to determine whether the association of a wife in a *pro anima* clause might simply have been a matter of form, rather than reflecting a desire on William junior's part to celebrate his wife's connections. It is, none the less, striking that the younger William's charter mentioned his new, royal, wife by name.

William junior's attitude towards Eleanor as his wife might well have been influenced by the example set by his parents in other respects. In the *History of William Marshal*, a work probably informed by the younger Marshal's personal testimony, Isabella de Clare emerges as a figure who was treated by her husband with the utmost respect. It is worth noting that, as was also the case with William junior and Eleanor, there was a significant age gap between the older Marshal and his bride. At the time of their marriage in 1189, Isabella was in her teens and William senior was in his forties; William received his young bride, who was, as we have seen, a substantial heiress, as a reward for his services to the crown.[112] If, however, the countess was less experienced in public affairs than her older husband, William senior acknowledged her superiority of birth and status, and valued the wealth and connections that she brought to him on marriage. Throughout the *History* William senior's wife, Isabella, is never mentioned by her personal name, but is referred to after her marriage simply as 'la contesse' as a mark of deference to her rank.[113] In spite of, or perhaps because of, Isabella's youth, she is portrayed as her husband's frequent companion and trusted confidante, especially in the management of her natal family's Irish lands. William senior, for his part, is clearly mindful of her personal importance both as the vessel through whom he holds many of his lands and as a figurehead for their tenants' loyalties, especially on the Clares' Irish estates. Hence the significance of the couple's trip to Ireland in 1207, where William senior presented the countess to his men in Kilkenny and announced his intention for his wife to remain behind with them as his representative when he was summoned away on royal business, with the words:

My lords,
here you see the countess whom I have brought
here by the hand into your presence.
She is your lady by birth,
the daughter of the earl who graciously,
in his generosity, enfeoffed you all,
once he had conquered the land.
She stays behind here with you as a pregnant woman.
Until such time as God brings me back here,
I ask you all to give her unreservedly
the protection she deserves by birthright,
for she is your lady, as we well know;
I have no claim to anything here save through her.[114]

Crouch has argued that the countess's stay in Ireland 'may have been by her own insistence, rather than for health grounds'.[115] Within the *History*, the countess certainly emerges as a woman who knew her own mind and offered frank advice that did not necessarily accord with her husband's own views. When, for example, Isabella suffers 'many a wrong and hurt' in her husband's absence, the *History* recalls her personal fury and desire for revenge against those persons who had committed these injuries to her lands and reputation; her husband, however, adopts a more moderate approach and shows mercy to those who come before him and restores their hostages to them.[116]

Secondly, the *History*'s portrayal of the marriages of William junior's sisters contains echoes of, and perhaps resonates with, Eleanor's experiences as his youthful second bride. The *History* records the arrangements in or around 1206 for the marriage of William's eldest sister Matilda (or Mahaut) with the Earl of Norfolk's son. The boy, who is described as 'worthy, mild-mannered and noble-hearted', is regarded as an eminently suitable match for the teenage Matilda, who was 'a very young thing … both noble and beautiful'.[117] The marriage, which allied two powerful comital families, was to the 'advantage and honour' of the two earls who negotiated the union, with the unspoken assumption that it also suited the personal interests and tastes of the bride and groom.[118]

There are also strong hints within the *History* of the feminine qualities and virtues that William junior might well have hoped to find, and perhaps encouraged, within Eleanor. In a passage where the author names and lists the attributes 'Of the Marshal's worthy children', Matilda, the eldest daughter, is praised in no uncertain terms as a young woman whose character was endowed with 'the gifts of wisdom, generosity, / beauty, nobility of heart, graciousness, / and, I can tell you in truth, all the good qualities / which a noble lady should possess'.[119] Isabella, the second daughter, was 'a handsome and beautiful girl', and Sibyl, the third, similarly possessed 'many fine qualities'.[120] Eva, the fourth daughter, made a fitting match with the son of the 'wise [and] powerful' baronial family of Briouze, while the youngest daughter, Joan, was married, after her father's death, to Warin de Munchensy, 'a powerful man' who was also of suitably 'high birth'.[121] The *History*'s apparent concern to emphasize that William junior's sisters had not married 'beneath themselves', but had, in the case of the elder three, acquired husbands of comital rank (the son of the Earl of Norfolk, the Earl of Gloucester and the son of the Earl of Derby) or, in the case of the younger two, married men of equivalent wealth and power, betrays a real concern to celebrate and publicize the nobility of birth and the exemplary social connections of William senior's offspring.[122] The powerful political alliances embodied with the marriages of William Marshal senior's daughters clearly made these women fitting sisters-in-law for Henry III's youngest sister, Eleanor.

The author of the *History* also waxed lyrical on the subject of William junior's first marriage to the daughter of the count of Aumale, recalling the negotiations that had attended this match and the universal praise the two fathers received for bringing successfully to fruition a union of 'two children from such very worthy fathers/and mothers' until 'Death' prematurely robbed William junior of his first bride.[123] Viewed against the existing network of Marshal marriages and the qualities and marital relationships constructed within the *History*, it appears that William junior expected his new, youthful, royal bride to be tutored to fill his mother's shoes in the long term; there might well have been an expectation that Eleanor, like Isabella, would play an active role in family affairs. The value of the connections – both personal and political – that Eleanor brought to William junior on their marriage were reflected by her presence on the Breton campaign of 1230.

THE DEATH OF WILLIAM MARSHAL JUNIOR

Eleanor returned to England from Brittany by the summer of 1230,[124] but was reunited with her husband once more in the autumn. On 18 September 1230, the same day upon which instructions were issued by the king to furnish William junior's messengers in England with a 'good boat' for their return to Brittany, Henry also saw to it that another 'good boat' was found to convey 'the sister of the lord king, the wife of the earl', overseas, presumably to rejoin her husband.[125] The timing of this request – a matter of weeks before Henry III left for England – was significant, and provides another strong indicator of Eleanor's importance to her new husband's position. In the king's absence, and with her husband continuing the war on Henry III's behalf, Eleanor provided the English crown with a figurehead and focus for personal ties of loyalty to the Angevin dynasty, and a visual reminder of Pembroke's marital relationship with the English crown.

It was not until 22 February 1231 that William and, presumably, Eleanor finally returned to England.[126] Pembroke was at Gloucester on 2 March 1231, when the earl witnessed a charter issued by the king.[127] At the beginning of April, the Earl and Countess of Pembroke attended the wedding of Eleanor's brother, Richard, now Earl of Cornwall, to William junior's second sister, Isabella. Isabella's first husband, Gilbert de Clare, Earl of Gloucester, had died at Penros in Brittany on 25 October 1230, leaving her free to marry again.[128]

Immediately after Gloucester's death, the custody of his estates and of Richard, his eight-year-old son and heir, had been granted to the justiciar, Hubert de Burgh.[129] This came at a time of growing resentment within England against de Burgh's influence over the king and his domination of royal patronage; it is therefore possible that Isabella's personal willingness to enter into a union with Richard of Cornwall suited her personal interests, as well as those of her brother and her future husband. Richard of Cornwall and the Earl of Pembroke had already joined together as part of a wider baronial alliance in 1227 against de Burgh. Richard, for his part, might well have resented surrendering his claims to the honour of Berkhamsted to de Burgh's nephew, Raymond.[130] The younger Marshal, on the other hand, opposed de Burgh's promotion of the claims of another nephew, Richard, in Ireland, and probably resented losing the justiciarship there in June 1226.[131] In 1231, therefore, Cornwall and Pembroke renewed their earlier association through marriage.[132] It is, unfortunately, impossible to know whether Eleanor played a role in negotiating this match behind the scenes, but she was certainly well placed to serve as a go-between between her husband and brother and between her future sister-in-law and her brother. Richard and Isabella were, as the Tewkesbury annalist recalled, subsequently married on 30 March 1231 by Peter, Abbot of Tewkesbury, at Fawley in Buckinghamshire, much to Henry III's dismay.[133] Within seven days of his sister's marriage, William junior was dead, dying from a swift and unexpected illness on 6 April 1231, and was buried a few days later at the New Temple in London, near his father.[134] This sudden turn of events left Eleanor a widow at the age of sixteen.

3

The Chaste Widow

'Woe is me! Is not the blood of the blessed martyr Thomas [Becket] fully avenged yet?'[1]

The death of William Marshal junior in April 1231 was greatly lamented in royal circles. The king, so the chronicler Matthew Paris recalled, was overcome with grief at the loss of his brother-in-law, attributing it to divine vengeance for Henry II's role in the martyrdom of Thomas Becket in Canterbury Cathedral on 29 December 1170. The depth of Henry III's sorrow was also strongly conveyed within the records of the English royal chancery. On 25 May 1231, a little over a month after Pembroke's death, a letter addressed to the king's subjects in Ireland spoke of the recently deceased earl, 'over whose death we violently grieved and [still] grieve'.[2] The date of this letter was significant. By the end of May, the recently widowed Eleanor was in a position to inform her brother whether or not she was carrying her dead husband's child, and thus a future heir to the Marshal estates. She was not.[3] This left as William junior's heir his younger brother, Richard, a liegeman of the king of France. His succession to the Marshal family's English, Irish and Welsh lands raised the spectre of a Capetian–Marshal alliance that threatened the security of the realm. The royal letter, therefore, announced the king's intention to take William junior's Irish lands into the crown's hands.[4]

Next, though, came a curious twist in the tale. When Richard crossed the Channel in the summer of 1231, the English king informed him that he had learned that Eleanor was pregnant after all. Henry refused to entertain Richard's claim to the Marshal estates until the truth of the matter had been determined.[5] Thus, Eleanor's potential, if not necessarily her actual, maternity offered the crown a convenient excuse for delaying Richard's succession.

Eleanor's personal reaction to William's death mirrored that of the king; a keen sense of sorrow and loss on her part is suggested by the young countess's subsequent decision to make a 'solemn vow' to live out the remainder of her days as a chaste widow.[6] In a formal ceremony presided over by Edmund of Abingdon, Archbishop of Canterbury, Eleanor took her vow alongside her erstwhile governess, Cecily of Sandford. Having received a ring 'in testimony of perpetual celibacy', Eleanor cast off her former finery and adopted clothes of russet, a relatively cheap and coarse cloth, as a mark of her new spiritual status.[7] In committing herself to such a vow, Eleanor effectively ruled out the possibility that she might remarry and bear children, a decision that was neither taken lightly nor rushed into. Although Paris assigned no date to the ceremony during which Eleanor took her vow – it appears in a passage in his *Chronica majora* that describes Cecily of Sandford's death in 1251 – the presence of Edmund of Abingdon as Archbishop of Canterbury is instructive. Edmund was elected archbishop by the monks of Christ Church on 20 September 1233 and subsequently consecrated in Canterbury Cathedral on 2 April 1234.[8] If Paris's dating can be trusted, the earliest that Eleanor took her vow was in the spring of 1234, three years after her husband's death. So what, then, had happened to Eleanor in the intervening period that persuaded her to become a vowess?

THE MARSHAL DOWER

William Marshal's death in 1231 left Eleanor, in theory at least, an extremely wealthy young widow. In addition to the ten and a half manors that Henry III granted William junior and Eleanor in 1229,[9] she was entitled to a third of her dead husband's lordships in England, Wales and Ireland as her dower (or widow's share). No figures survive that indicate the precise value of the Marshal estates in 1231, but by 1247 the English and Welsh properties alone were valued at £1,333 per annum, and the Irish estates at £1,715.[10] In 1247, Margaret de Lacy, the widow of another earl of Pembroke – Walter, a younger brother of William junior – stood to receive as her Marshal dower English and Welsh lands worth £444 per annum and Irish lands worth £572 per annum.[11] If allowance is made for changes to the overall value of the Marshal lands between 1231 and 1247, it is clear that in 1231 Eleanor was entitled to a life interest in a substantial portfolio of properties. As a result, Richard Marshal, William junior's next heir, stood to lose possession of a third of his lands to a young widow of just sixteen, who might very well live outlive him, as she had his older brother.

In thirteenth-century England, a widow's right to dower was safeguarded by the common law and effectively served as a woman's 'insurance policy' against penury in the event of a husband's death.[12] Yet dower and widows' property rights remained sufficiently controversial political issues to merit their inclusion in the successive re-issues of Magna Carta in the early thirteenth century. Cap. 7 of the 1225 version of the Great Charter, for instance, laid down that a widow ought to have her marriage portion and inheritance without any delay after her husband's death, and that she should pay nothing for her dower, inheritance or marriage portion. It recognized a widow's right to remain in her husband's 'chief house' for forty days after his death until her dower was assigned to her, unless her husband's 'chief house' was a castle, in which case she ought to be provided with an alternative residence.[13] This was all very well in principle, but, as Eleanor soon discovered, these provisions were unworkable in complex cases where large estates were involved and where the assignment of a substantial mass of lands to a widow might have weighty political implications for the crown.

In Eleanor's case, at least, her position as the king's sister, coupled with William junior's close proximity to the court at the time of his death, ensured that Magna Carta's initial 'insurance' mechanisms came into play straight away. On 15 April 1231, just nine days after William junior died, the king instructed his English sheriffs and the Irish justiciar to assist the dead earl's executors and took immediate steps to safeguard his sister's rights.[14] Henry also instructed his agents to ensure that Eleanor enjoyed reasonable estover (the right to cut and take wood) in the manor of Inkberrow (Worcestershire). Then, a day later, Henry III informed the sheriff of Worcestershire and other royal officials that Eleanor, Countess of Pembroke, was to reside in her late husband's castle at Inkberrow until she received her dower entitlement.[15] A fortnight after this, Henry III implemented further measures for his sister's maintenance; the young dowager countess was awarded custody of the manors of Badgeworth (Gloucestershire), Weston (Hertfordshire), Inkberrow (Worcestershire) and Wexcombe (Wiltshire) as a temporary assignment until her full dower settlement was handed over.[16] This, in its turn, was followed on 13 May 1231 – a little more than a month after William junior's death – with another royal order to see that Eleanor was placed in possession of her Irish dower estates.[17]

It was unfortunate for Eleanor that the process of assigning her dower from such a vast and scattered collection of properties was both complicated and challenging for the officials concerned. The Marshal properties needed to be surveyed and valued before an assignment might be made, a process that dragged on well into the summer of 1231.[18] Representatives of the countess or perhaps the countess herself visited the royal court at Oxford in July 1231, presumably in an attempt to hurry matters along. On 11 July, Henry III placed his sister in possession of the manor of Hamstead Marshall (Berkshire), the Marshal family's ancestral seat, while she continued to await her dower. The king also gave her some oaks from Chute Forest (Hampshire and Wiltshire) with which to repair her mill at Newbury (Berkshire), together with a gift of venison from the forest near Havering in Essex.[19] The gift of oaks, at least, suggests that Eleanor was taking an active interest in the day-to-day administration of those lands that were now directly under her management.

With the assignment of such a prestigious Marshal family property – Hamstead Marshall – to the countess, it might have seemed that it would only be a matter of time before Eleanor enjoyed her full dower. Such hopes were soon to be dashed by Henry III's apparent change of heart towards her brother-in-law, Richard Marshal, a change of heart that was seemingly prompted by the resumption of hostilities in the Welsh Marches. In the power vacuum created by William junior's death, Hubert de Burgh had attempted to intrude the king's men into the Marshal lands there, a situation that created confusion and which provided an excellent opportunity for the Welsh prince, Llywelyn, to pursue his own interests there once more.[20] In early August 1231, Richard Marshal performed homage to the English king and finally secured possession of his inheritance.[21] Not altogether surprisingly, once he had secured his estates, the new earl proved reluctant to address the outstanding issue of Eleanor's dower. In fact, Richard attempted to withhold the Worcestershire manor of Severnstoke – one of the manors specifically earmarked for Eleanor's upkeep in 1229 – from his royal sister-in-law. On 6 September 1231, Henry III stepped in and ordered Pembroke to allow Eleanor to enjoy this manor, otherwise the sheriff would intervene and eject the earl's officials by force.[22]

If Eleanor's rights were a thorn in Richard's side, the failure of the king and her brother-in-law to agree her dower allocation placed the countess in an increasingly difficult and, no doubt, stressful situation. Although some care was evidently taken on the crown's part to ensure that Eleanor's English manors were stocked with the oxen and ploughs necessary to sustain them in continuous cultivation,[23] not all the properties were in good repair, hence Eleanor's concern to renovate the mill at Newbury. This added burden of maintenance at a time when Eleanor possessed a limited pool of revenue-generating properties exposed her to financial hardship; she seems to have suffered from a lack of ready cash with which to meet her own expenses. By the winter months of 1231, if not earlier, Eleanor had turned to Jewish moneylenders as a source of personal finance. In doing so, Eleanor's experiences reflected those of other noble and gentle women who 'were most frequently drawn into credit relationships' with the Jews in their widowhoods, either through inheriting their husbands' debts or by contracting new bonds themselves.[24] On 15 November 1231, Henry III gave permission, 'at the instance of Eleanor, Countess of Pembroke, his sister', for three Jews – Deusaye, son of Isaac of Winchester, Bonevie of Bristol and Lynn of Bristol – to stay at the countess's manor of Newbury until 2 February 1232.[25] Bonevie was either still at Newbury or paying another visit there in April 1232, when, again at Eleanor's request, the king allowed him to extend his stay until Pentecost.[26] Perhaps Eleanor entered into, or contemplated entering into, a short-term mortgage of this manor while she awaited her dower. Henry III, for his part, was not unsympathetic towards his youngest sister's plight. On 7 January 1232, he ordered the knights and free men of Eleanor's manors of Luton, Sutton, Kemsing and Brabourne to pay her a 'reasonable aid' to discharge her debts.[27] The problem was that a measure such as this offered, at best, a short-term solution to Eleanor's financial problems. The much-needed long-term solution – the assignment of Eleanor's full amount of Marshal dower – still remained to be addressed.

If, as the spring of 1232 gave way to summer, Eleanor hoped to receive her final dower allocation, she continued to be disappointed. In Eleanor's case, the forty-day limit for dower assignments imposed by Magna Carta was simply unworkable. It was not until June 1232 that there was any significant headway. At the beginning of the month, Peter des Roches, Bishop of Winchester, prevailed upon the king to undertake what Nicholas Vincent has termed 'a root and branch overhaul of royal finances'.[28] As part of this, the king yet again attempted to settle the matter of Eleanor's dower. On 8 June, the king informed Richard de Burgh, the justiciar of Ireland, that Richard Marshal had appeared before him at Worcester. There, in the presence of the king's magnates, Richard agreed to surrender to Eleanor, the king's 'beloved sister', her Irish dower. The new earl of Pembroke nominated nine properties, including the castle and vill of Kildare, and promised to hand over further lands to Eleanor should these fall short of the full value of her entitlement.[29] Attentive to his sister's interests, Henry then dispatched six officials to inspect Eleanor's new lands and report their findings back to the English court.[30] It might finally have seemed to Eleanor that her widow's share of the Marshal estates in Ireland was at last within her grasp. This was not to be.

THE ROAD TO REBELLION

The political situation in England during the summer of 1232 was complicated by a dramatic coup at the very heart of Henrician government. Hubert de Burgh, the justiciar and leading architect of Eleanor's first marriage, and an early opponent of Richard Marshal's succession in 1231, fell from power.[31] Between August and November 1232, through the connivance of des Roches and others who were dissatisfied with de Burgh's regime, including Richard Marshal, the justiciar was stripped of lands and offices.[32] Among the more outlandish charges levelled against Hubert was the improbable accusation that he had murdered Eleanor's late husband, William Marshal junior, using poison.[33] Against the background of this coup, Richard Marshal – Eleanor's opponent – emerged, as Vincent has noted, as 'the most active figure at court', a situation that Eleanor might well have regarded with growing anxiety.[34] If Eleanor entertained any hope that Marshal's close proximity to Henry might encourage the new earl to regard her claims more favourably, she was sorely mistaken, as Earl Richard continued to block her interests. In fact, as the events of the final months of 1232 and opening months of 1233 unfolded, Richard Marshal's own resentment continued to simmer – against the crown over Eleanor's dower and against the crown over the king's handling of patronage when disposing of de Burgh's former lands and offices. Even now, Richard remained reluctant to surrender any of his Welsh and Irish estates to the king's youngest sister, so keen was he to preserve the integrity of his inheritance. Richard's reluctance might explain why, as early as 29 July 1232, when the king was at Woodstock, Richard had decided to offer the young dowager countess a cash sum of £400 per annum in lieu of her dower in Pembrokeshire and Ireland.[35] Eleanor, apparently at her brother's prompting, initially accepted this sum, driven perhaps by desperation at the length of time that had elapsed since William junior's death and by a desire to alleviate her financial difficulties.

It is, of course, perfectly possible that both the king and his youngest sister believed, perhaps on the basis of the Irish lands recently nominated by Richard Marshal, that £400 represented a fair deal. After all, Eleanor had already received a temporary dower allocation in England, which was presumably now made permanent, as well as those ten and a half English manors earmarked for her upkeep in 1229. A cash sum would save her from the trouble of managing her dower in south Wales and Ireland remotely as an absentee landlady,[36] and thereby provide her with a guaranteed source of income. Henry III and Eleanor's naivety on this matter would later return to haunt them.[37]

Richard Marshal, for his part, either experienced a shortage of ready cash with which to pay Eleanor £400 or perhaps hoped to use this arrangement as a bargaining counter in his subsequent relationship with the crown. The £400 sum was payable in two instalments at the New Temple in London: the first £200 was to be paid within a month of Michaelmas and the remaining £200 within a month of Easter.[38] In order to ensure that Eleanor would not be left out of pocket should Richard prove unable or just plain reluctant to pay, the threat of distraint (compulsory seizure) was placed upon Richard's English lands.[39] Yet even this safety clause proved inadequate to guarantee Marshal's loyalty. As he grew increasingly disillusioned with Henry III's court and resentful at the pre-eminence of Peter des Roches and his Poitevin allies, Pembroke's willingness to pay waned. Indeed, Pembroke's resentment against the crown threatened to boil over at the beginning of February 1233, when his kinsman Gilbert Basset was deprived of the Wiltshire manor of Upavon in favour of Peter de Maulay, the long-standing associate of Peter des Roches.[40] Marshal withdrew from Henry III's court, whence he initially travelled to Wales, and then on to Ireland.[41] By the summer, Eleanor's brother-in-law had allied himself firmly with a group of disaffected barons against the crown.[42]

Eleanor, as the king's sister, bore at least part of the brunt of Marshal's antagonism towards the English crown. On 6 June 1233, the king felt compelled to inform the sheriff of Gloucestershire that the earl had failed to meet his payments to Eleanor. The sheriff was ordered to seize Pembroke's goods in the county, so that Eleanor might thereby recover £150 in arrears.[43] This was followed on 30 June by further letters addressed to the sheriffs of Berkshire, Sussex, Gloucestershire (again) and Worcestershire that instructed them to furnish Eleanor with money from the earl's demesne properties to satisfy Marshal's debts.[44] Eleanor's agreement with Richard had not been worth the parchment upon which it was written, after all: Richard had defaulted upon the entire payment for the first year.

The agreement reached between Eleanor and Richard Marshal raises the question of Eleanor's agency and her personal level of involvement in the negotiations over her Irish dower. As a teenage widow under her brother's protection, it is tempting to dismiss Eleanor, once more, as a mere pawn who was excluded from the process of securing her dower by an older and more experienced brother. Eleanor was effectively packed off to Inkberrow and her other English Marshal manors to await the assignment of her Irish dower. This is certainly a view that found favour with M. A. E. Green, who claimed that 'This agreement [between Eleanor and Richard Marshal] was made without the knowledge or consent of the countess, although it was sealed with her seal.'[45] In Green's eyes, it was Henry who acted on Eleanor's behalf and Henry who, in his naivety, 'allowed himself to be woefully imposed upon.'[46] Admittedly, this was a line of argument that Eleanor herself adopted in the 1240s, when she attempted to apportion blame for the inadequacies of the £400 settlement.[47] Yet there are signs that by 1232, if not earlier, Eleanor enjoyed a significant degree of leverage over her eldest brother and therefore agency, perhaps, in the negotiations for her Irish dower. The privileged access to the king that Eleanor enjoyed as his sister gradually allowed her to mediate between her brother and third parties who sought privileges from him. On 5 November 1231, for example, Eleanor probably attended the royal court at Marlborough, where the countess – or officials charged with her business – successfully petitioned Henry to grant Mabel de Cantilupe a forge within the Forest of Dean (Gloucestershire).[48] Eleanor was also a regular recipient of royal patronage; the English chancery rolls are littered with gifts of venison that the king made to her from the royal forests near her English manors and which bear further witness to her high standing in her brother's favour, not to mention the king's brotherly concern that she partake of fare appropriate to her rank. Venison was widely regarded as a high-status and highly valued dish in thirteenth-century England, one which was often eaten on feast days and other special occasions, and one that was procured primarily through hunting within private deer parks and the royal forest. The recipients of royal gifts of venison were either permitted to hunt the deer within a designated royal forest themselves or were supplied by royal officials.[49] The gift to Eleanor of five deer from the forest near Havering park in July 1231 was followed by further gifts from the forests of Salcey (Northamptonshire), Chute (Hampshire and Wiltshire), Rockingham (Northamptonshire), Bernwood (Buckinghamshire) and Savernake (Wiltshire). In total, Eleanor had received no fewer than fifty-one deer by late August 1233.[50] She thus began to emerge as a figure of note at Henry III's court.

THE MARSHAL REBELLION, 1233–4

By the end of August 1233, Richard Marshal had entered into open rebellion against the crown, a situation that left Eleanor particularly exposed – financially and politically.[51] A truce between the warring parties in September 1233 was ended by the renewal of hostilities. Richard Marshal's alliance with the native Welsh prince, Llywelyn ap Iorwerth, resulted in Henry III's authorization of the wholesale resumption of his estates at the Westminster Council of October 1233.[52] In February 1234, the attacks on the Marshal Irish lordship of Leinster by the king's justiciar and other loyalist allies forced the Earl of Pembroke to go to the aid of his Irish tenants.[53] The fortuitous dismissal of Peter des Roches on a wave of anti-alien sentiment, however, paved the way for a critical political realignment at the heart of Henrician government, a move supported by none other than Edmund of Abingdon, Archbishop-Elect of Canterbury. Edmund's consecration on 2 April 1234 was followed immediately by the Bishop of Winchester's removal from court and, more dramatically, on 16 April by Richard Marshal's death from wounds sustained in Ireland.[54] In the month immediately preceding Richard's death and in the weeks and months that followed (May to July 1234), the new archbishop played a leading role in peace negotiations between the king and the rebels, and in orchestrating and effecting a lasting truce with the Welsh.[55] Chief among the rebels whom Edmund escorted in person to the king was Gilbert Marshal, Richard's younger brother and the new heir to the lands in which Eleanor claimed her dower.[56] Once Gilbert's inheritance was restored to him, it was Edmund who was appointed keeper of the Marshal castle of Striguil (Chepstow) during the king's pleasure.[57]

These events and the archbishop's central role in bringing about peace proved to be particularly significant for Eleanor. It was most probably against the political backdrop of negotiations to end the Marshal rebellion and to bring about Gilbert's succession to the earldom of Pembroke that Eleanor, Richard's and Gilbert's sister-in-law, made her vow of perpetual widowhood, a point hitherto neglected in the historiography of the Marshal rebellion and its aftermath.[58] The supervisory presence of Edmund at these proceedings reveals that Eleanor's action was not, as M. A. E. Green believed, the 'intense and passionate' act of a young widow 'in the first transports of her sorrow', but was perhaps a more measured decision taken by a young widow three or more years after her husband's death.[59]

Clearly, there were a number of forces at work that might well have prompted Eleanor to take such a step at this particular time. In the first place, the vow was made in the presence, and therefore with the compliance and potential influence, of Edmund of Abingdon himself. Paris's *Life* of St Edmund, written for Isabella, Countess of Arundel, paints a compelling picture of the archbishop as a tireless negotiator in the peace process of 1234.[60] In the second place, the £400 due to Eleanor from the earls of Pembroke for her Irish dower remained a highly contentious issue, as the ever-increasing arrears owed to Eleanor by Richard demonstrate, and one that posed a serious obstacle to the restoration of peace. Eleanor's vow of chastity offered Richard and, after his death, Gilbert an olive branch from Eleanor and, by implication, from the crown. In promising to remain a widow, Eleanor effectively removed herself, at the age of nineteen, from the marriage market and, in doing so, removed the possibility that she would convey her dower lands to a new husband, who might subsequently obstruct the Marshal family's smooth recovery of those properties upon Eleanor's death. The childless Eleanor's vow also made it likely that the earl would benefit, in the long term, from the reversion of the ten and a half English manors that the king had bestowed upon the couple and William's heirs in 1229.[61] As we have seen, Archbishop Edmund was a key agent in the process whereby the king was persuaded to accept Gilbert's accession to the earldom – it was Edmund who accompanied Richard's heir at his first audience with the king, making it highly likely that Archbishop Edmund was privy to Gilbert's personal concerns on this point.[62] It is, therefore, possible that Edmund actively encouraged or at least advised Eleanor to enter into such a vow during the summer of 1234.

Eleanor's vow, then, might be seen as an appropriate political concession to the Marshals, even if neither Eleanor nor Henry III were prepared to – or in Eleanor's case, could afford to – write off the arrears owing for the £400 sum. Yet there were other considerations that might have influenced Eleanor's decision. Perhaps her vow was also, in part, motivated by a personal desire to avoid repetition of the situation in which she had found herself as a young child, when her future had been decided for her in the years leading up to her first marriage. As a child she had enjoyed no say over her choice of marriage partner; as the widowed younger sister of the king, she might well be pressured to marry a candidate of Henry's choosing once more.[63] Eleanor had only to recall the example of her paternal aunt, Joan, Queen of Sicily, who had been widowed at the age of twenty-four in November 1189, and whose second marriage to Raymond (VI), Count of Toulouse, had been orchestrated by her brother, King Richard I, with a view to settling a long-term territorial dispute when Joan was thirty-one.[64] The death of William Marshal junior immediately after the marriage of her sister-in-law, Isabella, Countess of Gloucester, to Eleanor's second brother, Richard of Cornwall, served as another timely reminder of the pressures on aristocratic widows to remarry.

There was, furthermore, the additional danger that, should Eleanor remarry, her second marriage might be a source of personal unhappiness. Here, the experiences of her older sister, Joan, Queen of Scots, offered a contemporary and cautionary example. Jessica Nelson has argued that her childlessness had serious repercussions for Joan, who consequently preferred the company of her birth kin to that of her husband. Her failure to produce the all-important heir who might tie the interests of England and Scotland more firmly together 'resulted in her failure to be integrated fully into the Scottish royal family', whereby Joan was effectively marginalized from political life in her adopted kingdom.[65] Eleanor might also have wished to avoid the uncertain situation in which her older sister, Isabella, found herself. In the early 1230s, Isabella still lacked a husband altogether after a whole series of abortive marriage negotiations with different foreign potentates.[66] At least as a widow *and* a vowess Eleanor would retain possession of her property and, potentially, a measure of personal independence from the high politics of the Henrician court.

By the spring of 1234, Eleanor was also quite possibly faced with the growing realization that her position as Henry's widowed younger sister rendered her vulnerable to schemes for remarriage, especially at a court riven with faction between the Poitevin supporters of Peter des Roches and the disaffected allies of Richard Marshal. In the early months of 1234, rumours were apparently circulating at court that the royal women most closely connected with the king were vulnerable to the marital machinations of des Roches and his associates. According to Roger of Wendover, the English bishops feared that Eleanor of Brittany, the king's cousin, and one of the king's sisters, perhaps Isabella, might be compelled to accept unsuitable husbands at the hands of des Roches and his associates.[67] It is extremely likely that Eleanor heard these rumours and that this made her consider her own situation. The vow that Eleanor made with the spiritual counsel and guidance of Cecily of Sandford, her erstwhile governess, offered the young countess the chance to maintain her personal autonomy as a widow, while removing the danger that she might be disparaged by marrying an alien to further Poitevin interests. Yet this is not to deny the existence of strong religious motives on Eleanor's part. Eleanor visited religious houses during her widowhood and perhaps found solace within their precincts. She was, for example, a guest of the nuns of Wherwell Abbey in Hampshire on 20 January 1234, when the king granted her firewood for her stay there. Perhaps during this visit Eleanor paused to reflect upon her personal spiritual interests as well as the uncertainties that dogged her widowhood.[68]

Whatever the truth of the matter, Henry III remained interested in his youngest sister's welfare. The king himself was at Winchester in Hampshire on 25 January 1234, when he granted Eleanor the Sussex manor of Bosham during his pleasure and made her a further gift of venison from Chute Forest.[69] On 21 May 1234, and again on 14 June, Richard's executors were instructed to raise £550 from his goods and deliver the money to Eleanor for the arrears of her Irish dower.[70] Even in death, Richard Marshal was unable to escape his debts to Countess Eleanor.

4

The Countess as Lord

'saving to … Eleanor her dower …'[1]

With the accession in June 1234 of Gilbert Marshal, the younger brother and nearest male heir of Richard Marshal, Earl of Pembroke, it seemed that an end to the problems surrounding Eleanor's dower was once more in sight. The olive branch offered by Eleanor's vow and Gilbert's return to allegiance after his brother's rebellion potentially boded well for relations between this brother- and sister-in-law. Yet the matter of Eleanor's final English dower assignment and the outstanding arrears for her Irish share remained unresolved. On 12 August 1234, when the royal court was at Marlborough, Eleanor sued the new earl for the recovery of a third of the manors of Awre (Gloucestershire), Caversham (Oxfordshire) and Upper Clatford (Hampshire) and a third of half the manor of Long Compton (Warwickshire), all of which were intended to make good the shortfall in Eleanor's full entitlement in England.[2] It fell to Henry III to mediate between Gilbert and the young dowager countess. In the king's presence, the disputing parties reached a compromise, whereby the earl granted Eleanor an alternative manor, the manor of Weston (Hertfordshire), and a further £40 worth of land in Badgeworth (Gloucestershire) to supplement all the dower properties that Eleanor already held. Then another date was set so that the countess and the new earl might settle the issue of Eleanor's Irish and Welsh dower.[3] Eleanor's continued pursuit of her rights in the Marshal estates and her management of her affairs in widowhood form the focus for this chapter.

THE IRISH DOWER

Gilbert Marshal's willingness to address Eleanor's dower in August 1234 paved the way for more cordial relations between the new earl and the king. Gilbert was rewarded for his return to loyalty and for assigning Eleanor the remainder of her English dower with a substantial concession from the crown. On 22 August 1234, just ten days after the Marlborough settlement, Henry III finally confirmed Gilbert in possession of his English, Irish and Welsh inheritance. This included the castles of Striguil in south Wales and Dumas in Ireland, previously placed in the keeping of Archbishop Edmund of Canterbury and Archbishop Luke of Dublin to ensure Gilbert's continued co-operation.[4] Earl Gilbert and Countess Eleanor then turned their attentions to Eleanor's Welsh dower. On 26 September 1234, in the presence of Henry III and his council at Marlborough, Eleanor sued Pembroke for dower properties in Netherwent (Monmouthshire) and Tidenham (Gloucestershire). On this occasion another compromise was reached, whereby Gilbert conceded to Eleanor the manor of Magor (Monmouthshire), along with extensive rights and privileges there. The earl also formally acknowledged the countess's right to enjoy all the land previously assigned to her from the Marshal properties in Usk.[5] The future finally looked rosier – from a financial perspective at least – for Countess Eleanor.

If the second agreement at Marlborough drew a line under Eleanor's Welsh dower allocation, the problem of her Irish dower and its arrears rumbled on. On 28 September 1234, just two days after the Welsh settlement, Henry III was compelled, yet again, to dispatch instructions to the Irish justiciar. An impatient king ordered the justiciar to raise 'without delay' £500 by selling off the new earl's corn and goods for Eleanor's benefit.[6] In November, Earl Gilbert again appeared before the king, acknowledged that he owed Eleanor 400 marks, 300 marks for her Irish dower and 100 marks 'for the peace made between them at Marlborough', and agreed terms of payment. Henry III stood as surety for the earl and promised to pay the money directly to his sister should the earl default.[7]

By the following spring, however, it was becoming abundantly clear to both the countess and the king that Gilbert Marshal, like his older brother before him, was struggling, or was quite simply reluctant, to pay Eleanor's £400 annuity. Having defaulted upon the payments due at Michaelmas 1234 and Easter 1235, Gilbert himself now owed arrears of £400 to Eleanor. It was this situation that prompted Henry, presumably at Eleanor's insistence, to broker yet another new deal, whereby Gilbert assigned Eleanor income from the manors of Long Crendon (Buckinghamshire), Ringwood (Hampshire), Inkberrow (Worcestershire) and Upper Clatford (Hampshire) to satisfy the £400 owing to her.[8]

A keen sense of Eleanor and her brother's frustration emerges from the terms that accompanied this settlement. In an effort to ensure that £400 actually reached Eleanor, Gilbert's bailiffs, together with four men from each manor, were made to swear oaths to collect the money and deliver it directly to the countess.[9] In a further bid to compel the earl to abide by these arrangements,

Pembroke himself was required to pledge his word before Walter, Prior of the Friars Preacher of Bristol, in the presence of Eleanor and Henry's brother, Richard, Earl of Cornwall, as well as the earls of Kent and Norfolk, and Ralph fitz Richard and William Bluet, two knights in Eleanor's service.[10] There was, however, a significant reciprocal element to this new settlement. Eleanor, for her part, promised to relinquish her claim to money from these manors and to repay any sums received if the new earl discharged his debts by other means. To ensure that Eleanor fulfilled her side of the bargain, Henry III stood as her surety, and both the king and the countess attached their seals to the accompanying bond.[11]

Gilbert Marshal's return to loyalty and the steps he took to address the problems relating to Eleanor's dower placed him high in the king's favour. In July 1235, Henry III consented to Gilbert's marriage to Marjorie, the sister of Alexander II, King of Scots, noting his personal pleasure at this union.[12] Yet Eleanor's financial concerns did not disappear overnight. In October 1235, Henry III, presumably at the countess's request, pardoned her from paying £135 of a £141 debt owed at the Exchequer.[13] Financial uncertainty continued to cast a cloud over Eleanor's life as a widow.

THE COUNTESS AS LORD

On 19 August 1234, a week after Eleanor and Gilbert reached their agreement over the English Marshal properties, Henry III granted special protection to Richard Marshal's executors so that they might carry out their duties effectively and free from obstruction. The executors, though, were ordered *not* to interfere with Eleanor's Marshal properties.[14] Having finally helped Eleanor to secure her English manors at least, Henry III now took steps to ensure that his youngest sister enjoyed undisputed and untroubled possession of those properties.[15] According to a later roll that listed Eleanor's principal Marshal properties in or around 1275, the countess enjoyed the English manors of Weston (Hertfordshire), Luton and Toddington (Bedfordshire), Brabourne, Kemsing and Sutton (Kent), Newbury, Speenhamland and Woodspeen (Berkshire), Wexcombe and Bedwin (Wiltshire, together with Kinwardstone Hundred), Badgeworth (Gloucestershire) and Long Crendon (Buckinghamshire).[16]

As Eleanor entered her late teens and early twenties in the 1230s, her role as an estate and household manager gathered momentum. From the earliest days of her widowhood, much of Eleanor's daily life focused on her manors and castles, away from the royal court. Having accumulated property and established her authority over the men and women who staffed her domestic establishment and resided upon her lands, Eleanor took a strong personal interest in the governance of her estates. This was, by its very nature, a complex and potentially challenging task, and one that inevitably blurred conventional gender roles.[17] As a widow Eleanor expected to safeguard her own interests; the death of William Marshal junior transformed his wife from a lady under her husband's legal coverture into a sole woman and a lord. The *Rules*, a treatise that Robert Grosseteste, Bishop of Lincoln, compiled between 1245 and 1253 for Margaret de Lacy, the newly widowed Countess of Lincoln, offers a valuable, if idealized, impression of just what this might entail. Managing a noble household and its attendant estates involved the recruitment, employment, direction and co-ordination of a whole score of comital officials and servants. There was also a strong expectation that the widowed countess would possess or would quickly acquire a detailed knowledge of the farming year, its seasonal changes and the means by which her domestic establishment might be provisioned from estate produce – in both crops and livestock – supplemented by prudent purchases at local markets and fairs. A landholder needed a clear understanding of a whole range of legal rights and local customs that touched upon all areas of her lordship, or at least the services of trustworthy officials who were experienced and knowledgeable in these matters.[18] Only then might she stand a chance of effectively defending her rights and, most importantly, of preserving her estates, and, by implication, the good honour and reputation of her house.[19]

In the absence of surviving household rolls from this period of her life, tantalizing glimpses of Eleanor's activities feature in the records of the English royal government. Although the responsibilities that Eleanor assumed within the fields of estate and household management were similar to those of other comital widows, she enjoyed a privileged position as Henry III's sister and was, therefore, able to turn to her elder brother for assistance with greater ease than his other subjects.[20] Even in her teenage years, Eleanor was prepared to stand her ground. Eleanor's determination to ensure that wardships in her English manors came into her own hands, rather than those of her brother-in-law, presumably lay behind a royal order, dated 6 September 1231, whereby Richard Marshal was instructed to surrender to Eleanor the wardship of the heir of Roger de Clifford, a former tenant in Severnstoke.[21] Fifteen months later, a royal inquiry determined that Eleanor ought to enjoy the custody of the land and heir of Simon de Chelefeld' by virtue of her possession of the manor of Newbury.[22] On 1 September 1233, Henry III committed Ralph Bluet's former land in Daglingworth (Gloucestershire), which fell within the countess's dominion, to Eleanor, thereby removing it from the keeping of the king's faithful servant,

Mathias Bezill.[23] Later that month, Eleanor secured possession of another property in Wiltshire, which also belonged to her fee.[24] On 31 August 1234, the sheriffs of three counties – Bedfordshire, Berkshire and Buckinghamshire – were all ordered to ensure that Eleanor enjoyed the same liberties in their bailiwicks as those formerly enjoyed by her dead husband.[25] Eleanor readily and effectively solicited Henry III's help to enforce her position as lord.

In general terms, then, the widowed countess took her responsibilities as a landlord seriously. She also looked to the interests of those who served her. In this, her position as the king's youngest sister once again stood her in good stead: she was a conduit for royal favour. Richard of Havering, Eleanor's 'servant', discovered this to his advantage in 1234–5, when the king granted him land in Havering, Essex, at Eleanor's request.[26] It was not just members of local elites who benefited from Eleanor's benevolence. When, on 4 June 1234, the men from her manor of Kemsing were summoned by the Exchequer for a 'murdrum' or murder fine of forty shillings, Eleanor procured a royal pardon and her men were acquitted.[27] She stepped in on other occasions to clear the names of manorial officials who had fallen foul of royal justice. When the justices visited Canterbury in the spring of 1236, they heard how three men employed by Eleanor had defended her property when a group of malefactors broke into her park at Kemsing. One of the intruders was slain in the ensuing struggle, whereupon the countess subsequently petitioned the king and the killer, her servant, was pardoned.[28]

In the aftermath of Richard Marshal's rebellion, Eleanor occasionally served as a peace-broker for Marshal supporters caught on the wrong – the losing – side of the conflict. It was expressly 'at the instance of our beloved sister, Eleanor, Countess of Pembroke' that the king pardoned Robert de Grendon, who had previously fought against the king alongside Richard Marshal in Ireland, from paying a forty-mark fine to return to royal favour.[29] Eleanor's involvement here is significant in two respects. In the first place, it is striking that an Irish landholder, albeit one associated with the Marshal family, decided to approach the king through Eleanor rather than anyone else; Eleanor's reputation as someone with influence over the king, her brother, evidently extended to the Anglo-Norman lords in Ireland. In the second place, it raises intriguing questions about Eleanor's relationship with the tenants and officials of William junior, her former husband, and Richard, her disgraced brother-in-law. In his biography of Peter des Roches, Nicholas Vincent noted the difficulties faced by Richard Marshal, who had spent a considerable amount of time in France, in assuming effective control of the English, Welsh and Irish Marshal lands.[30] As William junior's widow, Eleanor offered an alternative focus for the loyalties of those Marshal followers with lands on or near her English manors. When the Marshal tenants were faced with an alien earl of Pembroke in Richard, the prospect of service to Eleanor as William junior's widow and the English king's sister was sometimes a more appealing proposition. Bartholomew de Crek, Eleanor's yeoman, had, for example, previously served William junior in Ireland in 1224 and yet apparently chose to remain in Eleanor's employment rather than enter that of Richard Marshal.[31]

A similar continuity in service can be traced in the cases of Ralph fitz Richard and William Bluet, both of whom witnessed the assignment of Eleanor's English dower by Gilbert Marshal in 1235 and both of whom were described as Eleanor's knights ('knights of the countess').[32] Prior to this, 'Lord Ralph fitz Richard' had attended William junior when he confirmed his father's gifts to Tintern Abbey in Wales.[33] The Bluets (or Bloets) possessed long-standing ties with the Marshal honour of Striguil in England and Wales, where they were important tenants. Ralph Bluet held lands in Gloucestershire, Hampshire, Somerset and Wiltshire from the honour. William, who appears to have been his younger son, had served William Marshal junior, acting as his banner-bearer at the battle of Lincoln in 1217.[34]

There was, naturally, a strong element of self-interest involved in such activities on Eleanor's part: it was important for her as a lord to be seen as someone who was capable of protecting the men and women who were connected with her.[35] Eleanor's dealings with the crown, though, betray an overriding concern to assert her seigneurial rights and prevent any further diminution of her revenues or properties. When Adam fitz Hugh, one of her men from the manor of Newbury, committed an offence and abjured the realm, Eleanor, through her brother's assistance, successfully recovered five and a half marks that the Exchequer had demanded from her as the value of the wrong-doer's chattels.[36] In a similar way, Eleanor's position as a landholder brought her into contact, and sometimes into conflict, with neighbouring landlords. In September 1232, for example, Eleanor found herself in dispute with Richard, Prior of Dunstable, over the customs of her manor of Toddington.[37] At Michaelmas 1233, Eleanor was the plaintiff in a property dispute centred upon her manor of Luton.[38] During the same term, her attorney brought another lawsuit on her behalf against the men of Collingbourne Ducis and Everleigh in Wiltshire.[39] On occasion, the activities of Eleanor and her officials landed the young dowager Countess of Pembroke in hot water. In June 1233, Henry instructed the sheriffs of Herefordshire and Worcestershire to restore forthwith to Hugh of Kinnersley lands that Eleanor had seized from him.[40] Eleanor's position as the king's sister did not render Henry III indifferent to her transgressions against others.

Eleanor's involvement in administration was motivated by a clear and practical purpose. By taking an interest in the day-to-day business of her estates, she might improve the profitability of her manors and thereby maximize her income from them. Eleanor attempted, for example, to invest, when possible, in her properties and ensure they were kept in good condition. Henry III's gift to his sister of twenty oaks from Chute Forest (Hampshire and Wiltshire) so that she might repair her mill in Newbury has already been discussed in chapter 3.[41] In April 1233, Eleanor received a further twenty oaks, this time from Tonbridge Forest, for rebuilding her houses at Kemsing, which had lately been damaged by fire.[42] It was yet another telling indication of the countess's or her officials' talent for estate management that the measures implemented in Eleanor's name looked beyond the immediate necessity of maintaining, provisioning and stocking her manors. With an eye to the commercial development of her manor of Seal, near Sevenoaks in Kent, the countess secured from the crown the right to hold a weekly market every Wednesday and an annual fair there.[43] Eleanor also saw to it that the royal licence to hold a weekly market each Thursday on the Marshal manor of Toddington was extended beyond her dead husband's lifetime to cover her life as well.[44]

Elsewhere, building work provided the countess with improved accommodation and allowed her physically to stamp her authority on those properties and the surrounding countryside. After all, new and renovated structures, which might be decorated with the armorial devices of Eleanor's blood and marital kin, served as visual reminders and markers on the landscape to tenants, neighbours, local communities and visitors of her position as their new lord.[45] On 22 August 1235, the countess secured a gift of yet another twenty oaks from the manor of Chute and forty oaks from its neighbouring forest of Savernake for the construction of a new hall on her Wiltshire manor of Wexcombe.[46] Such activities on Eleanor's part perhaps reflected a heartfelt desire to establish comfortable and well-maintained residences that might support the luxurious lifestyle appropriate for a woman of her rank. It was possibly with this in mind that Eleanor's estates from the Marshal marriage were enlarged by further grants of property from the king. When Eleanor turned twenty-one, for example, she was given a royal residence all of her own – the manor and castle of Odiham in Hampshire.[47]

Odiham, which was situated midway between the royal centres of Winchester and Windsor, offered Eleanor a residence convenient for maintaining contacts with her brother's court. Built near the River Whitewater, it was defended by a series of inner and outer moats. At the heart of its complex lay a great three-storey octagonal keep, which Eleanor's father, King John, had begun building in

1207; the surrounding park had been a popular hunting venue with the late king who had visited Odiham on no fewer than twenty-four separate occasions. The castle keep was home to a hall, which rose to thirty feet in height, and above that to the king's chamber.[48] Since the beginning of Henry III's reign the castle had undergone a series of repairs, at least some of which were for damage sustained during the civil war of 1215–17. The keep's chimney, one of the earliest in England, was repaired in 1226, and further work was carried out over two years on the castle chapel.[49] When Henry visited Odiham in the autumn of 1234, he had initiated a further series of renovations – the keep's windows were repaired with iron and the chapel redecorated and refurbished. With the completion of these repairs, he passed the castle to Eleanor.[50]

Eleanor's close relationship with her brother, the king, brought with it other tangible rewards that helped the countess to support a lifestyle appropriate to her station in spite of her personal indebtedness. By 1238, the king had loaned the countess no less than £1,000 to meet her expenses.[51] The dowager Countess of Pembroke divided her time between Odiham, her different Marshal manors and her brother's royal residences.[52] It is, of course, possible that by occasionally residing on her brother's estates, Eleanor sought to defray some of the cost of provisioning her household. On 30 May 1235, Eleanor was Henry's guest at Tewkesbury (although her brother was elsewhere), where the king's houses were placed at her disposal for as long as she wished, and the countess was provided with fodder for her horses and wood for her fire.[53] For most of the time, however, Eleanor's household was, in all probability, supplied from the produce of her manors and by purchases from local markets and fairs, along the lines envisaged in Grosseteste's *Rules*.[54] Yet regular gifts from her brother helped to ensure that the finest quality meat – venison – continued to reach her high table in the mid 1230s. Eleanor's taste for venison as well as, perhaps, her employment of huntsmen and her own enjoyment of hunting as a form of pastime suitable for a lady emerges clearly from the record evidence. As before, Henry III bestowed upon Eleanor the right to take deer from the royal forests at different times of the calendar year, presumably at locations that were most convenient for Eleanor or which reflected her current place of residence. Venison was a meat enjoyed particularly when it was fresh.[55] Nevertheless, the number of deer that Eleanor received from her brother was truly remarkable. In 1233, the year of Richard Marshal's rebellion, Eleanor was given thirty-eight bucks, including three roe-bucks, and two stags, from the forests of Savernake, Chute and Rockingham.[56] These were followed by a further thirty deer and two stags from the forests of Feckenham (Warwickshire and Worcestershire), Savernake and Chute in 1234,[57] twenty-six deer and a stag from the forests of Savernake, Dean, Rockingham and Chute in 1235,[58] twenty-one deer and six stags from Wychwood (Oxfordshire), Whittlewood (Buckinghamshire), Bernwood, Dean, Braden (Wiltshire) and St Briavels (Gloucestershire) in 1236[59] and thirty-one deer from Savernake, Bernwood and Clarendon (Wiltshire) in 1237.[60]

The king's kindnesses to Eleanor did not stop at gifts of venison. On 8 November 1236, Henry gave Eleanor a black palfrey, apparently anticipating the pleasure that such a beast might bring her.[61] Another guest at the English royal court at this time was Eleanor's older sister, Joan, Queen of Scots, who had been enjoying an extended stay in her brother's realm since the Anglo-Scottish conference at York in September that year. Joan's presence provided an opportunity for a family reunion between the sisters.[62]

The largesse shown by Henry III to Eleanor and the countess's presence at court in 1237 raise the question of how often she visited him. In all likelihood, Eleanor was probably in attendance on her brother at major religious festivals and state occasions, such as celebrations to mark anniversaries significant for her natal kin. One wonders whether Eleanor attended her brother's Christmas court at Winchester in 1231–2, where her former guardian, Peter des Roches, entertained the king and his followers.[63] When the body of King John was moved to a new tomb in Worcester Cathedral on 21 October 1232, the Tewkesbury annalist recorded Eleanor's presence at this ceremony, alongside that of the king, Hubert de Burgh, Ralph de Neville, the royal chancellor, the Prior of Worcester and Robert, Abbot-Elect of Tewkesbury.[64] Admittedly, a grant of venison to Eleanor for Christmas in 1232–3 suggests that the countess spent this festive season away from court.[65] Eleanor was also perhaps absent from the Christmas court at Gloucester in 1233–4, which was marred by Richard Marshal's rebellion.[66] Even so, she might well have participated in Henry's subsequent Christmas celebrations at Westminster in 1234–5[67] and at Winchester in 1235–6 and 1236–7.[68]

As Matthew Paris observed, the atmosphere at the Christmas court of 1235–6 was heavy with anticipation at the imminent arrival of Henry III's prospective bride, Eleanor, the daughter of Count Raymond-Berengar V of Provence by Beatrice of Savoy.[69] The couple's marriage at Canterbury on 14 January 1236 was followed by the new queen's coronation as Henry's consort at Westminster Abbey on 20 January.[70] Paris described in elaborate detail the pomp and ceremony that surrounded the latter occasion. Among the nobles who fulfilled their traditional roles at such events was Countess Eleanor's brother-in-law, Gilbert Marshal, Earl of Pembroke, who as 'grand marshal of England' carried a wand before the king and cleared the way before him in the church and banquet hall.[71] Paris praised the lavish dress of those who enjoyed these nuptial festivities and the abundance of meats and fish at the table, offering a valuable insight into the opulence and conspicuous consumption that surrounded such gatherings. Countess Eleanor, as the king's youngest sister and the only sister then resident in England, presumably witnessed this event and partook of the festivities.[72] Eleanor also probably witnessed the preparations for her older sister Isabella's departure from the realm in April and May 1235 on Isabella's marriage to Emperor Frederick II of Hohenstaufen.[73]

THE RHYTHMS OF DAILY LIFE

It remains, though, frustratingly difficult in the absence of letters, diaries or household accounts for these years to determine the precise rhythms and activities of Eleanor's daily life. Eleanor's education, examined in earlier chapters, indicates that she might have found comfort and enjoyment in reading religious and other works.[74] She very probably followed Henry III's example and the practice of other noble households by overseeing the regular distribution of alms to the poor.[75] This was certainly the case later in her life, in 1265, a year for which particularly detailed records survive, when she regularly provided bread for paupers.[76] In 1265, she also modified her diet on specific days of the week, like her cousin Eleanor of Brittany had done when in residence at Bristol Castle in the mid 1220s, so that she might adhere to the Christian regime of abstinence, whereby fish, rather than flesh, was typically consumed on Wednesdays, Fridays and Saturdays.[77] Important religious feasts, including Christmas, Easter and the Marian feasts, were usually marked in great households by fasts on their eves, as a prelude to the consumption of meats.[78]

In addition to observing restrictions on her diet, it is highly likely that Eleanor followed convention by observing a strict regime of liturgical celebrations that punctuated each day, beginning with the celebration of Matins by her household chaplain and concluding, perhaps, with Evensong and Compline.[79] She might also have engaged in other acts of piety, such as pilgrimages to holy shrines, like that which her eldest sister, Joan, Queen of Scots, and her sister-in-law, Queen Eleanor, made to Canterbury early in 1238.[80] If the main motivation for the visit by the two queens to Canterbury was to seek heavenly aid so that they might conceive children and strengthen their husbands' dynasties,[81] Eleanor's status as a widow carried with it strong commemorative responsibilities towards her dead husband so that she might help through, for example, religious patronage, to speed his soul in its passage through purgatory.[82] As

Malcolm Vale has aptly observed, 'The giving of alms formed a major part of the devotional life of any layman or laywoman of any substance.'[83] This was particularly the case with widows. Perhaps Eleanor marked the anniversary of William junior's death with masses for his soul and the distribution of alms to the poor, like those that Henry III subsequently arranged after the deaths of Joan and Isabella the Empress.[84]

When Countess Eleanor was not occupied by religious observances or estate and household affairs, she might have found time for recreational pursuits popular with other noblewomen. Eleanor probably passed at least some of her time engaged in embroidery and other forms of needlework, producing fine items of clothing, including vestments, as gifts for members of her family or churchmen.[85] In her *Life*, Countess Eleanor's contemporary, Isabella of France, is described sewing a cap 'with her own hands', which her brother, King Louis IX, requested from her and which Isabella, true to her saintly character, secretly bestowed upon a poor woman in his stead.[86] Henry III's youngest sister might also have played games for her amusement. Chess was popular in royal circles throughout the thirteenth and fourteenth centuries. At Easter 1235, Henry III bestowed a chess table and set on his sister Isabella, which she carried into the Empire on her marriage.[87] The wardrobe books of Henry III's son, King Edward I and his second wife, Margaret of France, reveal that they both possessed a chess set of jasper and crystal.[88] Beyond the confines of her household, falconry, like hunting deer, was another pursuit popular with royal and noble women, some of whom were depicted on their seals holding birds of prey.[89]

As part of her daily life, Eleanor enjoyed the company of others, most notably the damsels of her household who served as her female attendants. Of lesser noble status than their mistress, it was these young women who provided companionship and who saw to Eleanor's personal needs. In the thirteenth century and later, it was fairly common for noble daughters to be placed in service in other households so that they might acquire an education appropriate to their gender and rank.[90] Service within the household of a queen or a countess offered a number of advantages beyond the acquisition of feminine manners and womanly skills. A damsel who pleased her mistress might benefit from personal gifts. Furthermore, a young woman might expand her social connections and friendship networks, thereby allowing her to advance her own interests and, through her, those of her family. Such service might help her to reap the benefits of patronage by securing an annuity or a materially advantageous marriage, arranged with her mistress's blessing. On 12 January 1238, for example, Countess Eleanor persuaded Henry III to grant Mabel de Druval, one of her damsels, an annuity of ten marks until the king was able to find Mabel a husband or provide for her maintenance in another way.[91] When Henry was unable to find Mabel a suitable husband, this initial grant was followed by a further grant of £10 worth of land for the remainder of her life.[92] Just as Countess Eleanor benefitted from the king's generosity, so too did those who served her by virtue of Eleanor's proximity to, and privileged contact with, the Henrician court.[93]

5

The Montfort Marriage

'the clandestine marriage'[1]

On 7 January 1238, 'in the very small chapel of the king, which is in the corner of the [king's] chamber' in the palace of Westminster, Eleanor Marshal, Countess of Pembroke, married as her second husband Simon de Montfort, one of the king's leading counsellors. The ceremony took place in Henry III's presence and was presided over by Walter, a royal chaplain.[2] If the clandestine marriage of a widowed vowess was not shocking enough in its own right, Eleanor's new choice of bridegroom was highly controversial. Simon de Montfort might well have been a prominent figure at her brother's court, but he was also an alien and, at the time of their union, an alien of inferior status to that of his new royal wife. Simon's natal kin were of comital rank and subjects of the kings of France; his birth family took their name from the lordship of Montfort l'Amaury, situated to the west of Paris. If this was not potentially embarrassing enough in itself, Eleanor's new husband was also a younger son, the third son, in fact, of the Albigensian crusader Simon de Montfort senior and his wife, Alice de Montmorency.[3] What had prompted Simon to set his sights on Eleanor, the English king's sister, and what had prompted Eleanor to renege on her earlier decision to live out her days in perpetual widowhood?

SIMON DE MONTFORT

Simon de Montfort the younger came to England at the beginning of the 1230s, ostensibly to make his fortune. The Montfort dynasty was not unknown in England: Simon's paternal grandmother, Amicia (d. 1215), had been the eldest sister and co-heiress of Robert (IV) de Beaumont, Earl of Leicester, and it was this claim that provided Simon with his entrée to the English court.[4] Simon's older brother, Amaury, resigned his rights to the English earldom in favour of his younger brother probably in return for a substantial sum of money, allowing Simon to embark upon a campaign to secure Henry III's recognition of his claim to the lands of the honour of Leicester. [5] After Simon junior performed homage to Henry III for these properties (worth around £500 per annum), he set about establishing himself on his new estates and at the English court.[6]

If the English king remained, for the time being, reticent about recognizing Simon's succession to the title of earl, Simon gradually established himself as one of Henry's leading advisors during the course of the next five years. John Maddicott has calculated that Simon was one of the most regular witnesses of the king's charters between May 1236 and December 1237.[7] Simon was present in January 1236 at the coronation of Henry III's new queen, Eleanor of Provence, at Westminster, during which he fulfilled the earl of Leicester's hereditary ceremonial role as steward of England in the festivities by providing the king with water basins in which to wash before the wedding feast.[8] Yet, in spite of Simon's meteoric rise in royal favour, his future remained highly insecure. As Maddicott astutely observed, 'A limited endowment, debt, and the residual claims of Amaury' all posed serious and ever-present threats to his new found position as a royal counsellor.[9] Yet we must not forget that Simon, as a younger son of a French nobleman, had done remarkably well for himself in a relatively short space of time. It is, therefore, of no great surprise that he looked to increase his wealth still further through marriage to a well-connected aristocratic woman. He did not, though, alight immediately upon Eleanor as a prospective bride. In fact, from Simon's earlier choices of brides, we gain a strong sense of his personal political ambition and sheer audacity. Simon, who was still no more than the lord of Leicester, paid court first in 1235 to Mahaut (II), *suo jure* Countess of Bolougne and the widow of Philip Hurepel, a younger son of King Philip Augustus of France by Agnes of Meran. Then, during the early months of 1236, his attention switched to Joan, *suo jure* Countess of Flanders and the widow of Ferrand, the son of the king of Portugal.[10] Not only were both prospective brides important heiresses of comital rank, but they both possessed ties with the ruling houses of France and Portugal through their first marriages to the sons of kings. Although Simon failed to realize his goal in marrying either of these women – his plans fell victim to suspicions at the French royal court about the strength of his attachment to the English crown – his subsequent interest in Eleanor, the widowed sister of the English king, suggests that his ego remained unabashed.[11] By comparison with the other two women, Eleanor proved to be a more realistic 'catch'. True, she was of royal birth and the widow of one of the wealthiest English earls, but she was no great heiress in her own right. The landed endowment that she brought to her new husband was one that was a life, rather than a permanent, interest. Henry III's recent marriage to Eleanor of Provence and the possibility of future heirs issuing from that union also made it seem increasingly unlikely that Eleanor and her sisters would find themselves as heiresses to the English throne.[12] Even so, marriage to Eleanor still carried with it, as Matthew Paris noted, manifest attractions – 'her beauty, the rich honours contingent to her, and the excelling and royal descent of the lady'.[13] Marriage to Eleanor meant marriage to the sister of an English king, an empress and a queen of Scots.[14]

Simon's relatively swift climb to a position among the king's inner circle of counsellors inevitably provided the dowager Countess of Pembroke and the Lord of Leicester with numerous opportunities to become acquainted with one another. Simon was, for example, in attendance upon Henry III when the court was at Worcester on 24 July 1236 and the king gave his sister four stags in the Forest of Dean. On this same day, the sheriff of Buckinghamshire was instructed to see that Simon received a forty-shilling rent that pertained to the honour of Leicester.[15] Simon's position as a royal confidante might have ensured his presence at a number of royal occasions at which Eleanor was required. Yet a history of meetings at the English royal court offers what is, at best, a partial explanation for what followed. The circumstances surrounding Eleanor and Simon's marriage were remarkable. What motivated the king's youngest sister to marry de Montfort? Paris offers a simple and straightforward reason for Eleanor's remarriage and one which has a ring of truth about it: 'Wishing to become a mother, she married the earl of Leicester.'[16] Eleanor desired a child and wished, perhaps, as Margaret Howell commented, to experience 'the sexual and personal satisfaction involved in procreation'.[17] Faced with the enthusiasm of Simon's suit and personal feelings of attraction, the twenty-three-year-old Eleanor regretted her earlier vow of chastity to such a degree that she was prepared to incur ecclesiastical censure and imperil her immortal soul by marrying again.

The prospect of marriage to a candidate of Eleanor's own choosing was not, of course, one lacking in other, practical attractions. A new husband might prove to be an invaluable ally in Eleanor's ongoing struggle with Gilbert Marshal and perhaps a more effective and forceful ally than her brother the king, if only in the level of personal support that a new husband might give her. Remarriage promised Eleanor a potential solution to her immediate financial worries. Yes, she might lose a measure of the independence that she enjoyed as a widow – after all, her lands and property would come under the legal authority of her new husband – but she would gain a share in her new husband's wealth, in the sense that responsibility would fall to him to provide for her maintenance. The drawback here was that Simon's financial situation, like that of his bride, was somewhat insecure: he had already incurred heavy debts in his pursuit of the

Leicester inheritance.[18] Even so, it is perfectly possible that at the time of their courtship Eleanor was not fully aware of the uncertainty surrounding her new bridegroom's financial affairs. Indeed, Eleanor might have looked upon Simon's enjoyment of the king's favour as something that was to be valued in itself, especially at a court in which a new queen was beginning to establish her place in Henry's affections.[19]

In agreeing to become Simon's wife – or in letting him know that she was willing to accept his suit – Eleanor made a conscious decision to marry a new husband who was beneath her in social rank. She would not, like her sisters, acquire crowns through marriage or, in her case, remarriage. Rowena Archer's study of women as landholders and administrators in the later Middle Ages observed that marriages between countesses and, from the fourteenth century onward, duchesses and the officials or estate servants of their deceased husbands were not entirely uncommon.[20] No such earlier relationship under-pinned Eleanor's union with Simon, but Eleanor is unlikely to have been blind to the difference in status between her and her new husband. Even if Simon was seven years her senior, Eleanor might well have hoped that she would retain if not necessarily the upper hand, then a measure of equality or degree of influence in her relationship with her new husband. In anticipating her second marriage, perhaps Eleanor had learned from her own past experiences, as well as from those of her sisters and, indeed, her mother. In effectively selecting her own bridegroom, Eleanor deliberately placed herself in a very different situation from that in which her older sister, Isabella, for example, had found herself three years earlier. Isabella's marriage had been entirely negotiated and agreed between Henry III and the representatives of her new husband, Emperor Frederick II, whereupon the new bride was dispatched to the Holy Roman Empire to marry a much older man of dubious reputation, if exalted rank, whom she had never met.[21] It was also a very different situation from that in which Eleanor had spent much of her own childhood as a bride promised, but not delivered in good time, to William Marshal junior in a bid to guarantee his loyalty to the crown. Eleanor might also have paused to reflect upon the circumstances of her mother Isabella of Angoulême's marriage to Hugh (X) de Lusignan. After all, the queen dowager's remarriage to a man of her own choosing, who was closer to her own age and of lesser social rank than her first husband, and whose terri-torial interests in the south of France were tied closely to her own, had allowed Isabella to forge a more assertive political role in widowhood than had ever been possible during her first marriage to King John.[22]

Even if, as King Henry III later alleged in anger, Simon seduced Eleanor, it seems unlikely that Eleanor's participation in the seduction was carried out without a measure of calculation on the part of the bride, as well as that of the groom. Henry III's personal role in overseeing the legitimization of their union was also incredible. According to Paris, the king himself had placed Eleanor's hand in Simon's. It was exceptional for a thirteenth-century king to have a clandestine marriage, a *matrimonium clandestinum* as Paris described it, contracted in his presence, with the accompanying mass celebrated in his own private chapel.[23] The arrangement of the marriage, apparently with the king's connivance, or at the very least his tacit approval, was a very striking indication of Eleanor and Simon's close relationship with the monarch. Henry not only condoned but effectively colluded in this marriage, a marriage of which even his younger brother, Richard, Earl of Cornwall, initially remained ignorant.[24] Perhaps the couple did successfully 'pull the wool' over the eyes of Eleanor's older brother. Perhaps Henry was a romantic whose heart was softened by Eleanor's love affair.

If anything, though, Henry's initial approval of the Montfort–Marshal match makes it unlikely that Eleanor and Simon had, in fact, risked consummating their union before their marriage. Henry was a monarch who was noted for his religious devotion and his spirituality, and he might well have taken a dim view of an illicit sexual liaison by his youngest sister.[25] Furthermore, the monastic chroniclers who recorded the marriage and from whose pens we might have expected vitriolic criticism of any irregularities in sexual conduct were silent on the matter. The Worcester annalist simply noted that 'Lord Simon de Montfort took to wife the sister of the lord king, who conceived for him a son.'[26] The Waverley annalist similarly observed, without critical comment, that 'Simon de Montfort took to wife Eleanor, Countess of Pembroke, relict of William Marshal, sister, namely, of Henry IV [i.e. III], King of England.'[27] Even Paris, who provides the most detailed description of Eleanor's second marriage, made no allegations of sexual impropriety before the match, but noted the bride's earlier vow of chastity and the need for special dispensation to be sought from Rome.[28] Paris's initial silence on this matter assumes added significance when it is borne in mind that this same chronicler had artfully blackened the reputation of Eleanor's mother by casting her as an adulteress during her marriage to Eleanor's father, King John.[29]

The clandestine nature of Eleanor's second marriage held the key to its successful outcome. Had Eleanor's willingness to renege on her vow and consider remarriage become public knowledge, then her freedom of choice in the matter and her personal happiness might well have been jeopardized. In its early days, news of the Montfort marriage was carefully concealed. It apparently escaped the attention of the royal clerks, who continued to describe Eleanor as the Countess of Pembroke.[30] The need for secrecy was, to some extent, justified by the ferocity of the reactions of the king's other counsellors once news of the marriage became public. Frustratingly, the means by which knowledge of the marriage was disseminated remains unclear. What is clear is that the news came as a great shock to many at court and that it found little favour with those closest to the king. In a short passage that was subsequently marked up for deletion from his *English History*, Paris noted that the marriage was expressly made 'against the counsel of Archbishop Edmund [of Canterbury]'.[31] The archbishop's opposition was understandable, as the churchman and peace-broker who had presided over Eleanor's earlier vow of chastity. The remarriage of the dowager Countess of Pembroke posed a direct threat to the earlier agreements over her dower, which had bound her Marshal in-laws into a closer relationship with the English crown. Some contemporary writers made a strikingly accurate connection between the Montfort–Marshal marriage and a short-lived rebellion led by Eleanor's other brother, Richard, Earl of Cornwall, and her brother-in-law, Gilbert Marshal.[32] Both men had been left in the dark about the union, presumably in anticipation of their opposition.

The timing of Eleanor's second marriage and her choice of groom was unfortunate. It came at a time when the English baronage was highly sensitive to the presence of foreigners at the Henrician court, to the possible disparagement of royal wards through marriages to them and to the more general issue of the disposal of valuable wardships to the king's favourites without wider baronial consultation on the issue.[33] Henry III's decision, later in January, to support the marriage of Richard de Clare, the heir to the earldom of Gloucester, to the daughter of Montfort's fellow counsellor, John de Lacy, Earl of Lincoln, was seen as a particularly controversial move.[34] The king himself acknowledged Richard of Cornwall's anger at Eleanor's marriage in letters that he dispatched to the barons of the Cinque Ports on 3 February 1238: Henry III thanked the barons for their services and instructed them to be on their guard against false instructions from Richard, which might harm the king's interests.[35]

Interestingly, it has been the actions of Henry III in endorsing his youngest sister's alliance, rather than those of Eleanor or Simon, which have incurred the criticism of modern writers. For Maddicott, 'The marriage exemplified all Henry's most characteristic shortcomings: his failure to consult the magnates on important political matters, his patronage of aliens, his promotion of family interests above those of the kingdom, [and] his lack of judgement in lightly entering into the most far-reaching commitments.'[36] The marriage also reveals a great deal about Eleanor and Simon's hopes and aspirations, and their self-interest. Yet, were those hopes and aspirations subsequently realized, or did the political fallout from Richard and Gilbert's rebellion dim their stars? In spite of the rebellion, both Simon and Eleanor profited personally from Henry III's continuing benevolence towards them. On 3 February 1238, as the king took steps to limit the potential damage caused by his younger brother's rebellion, he arranged for the payment of a loan of £120 to Simon and Eleanor.[37] The precise purpose of this loan was not recorded. It might have met the couple's immediate expenses at court or the demands of their various creditors. Some of this money was possibly intended to help Simon amass funds for his journey overseas to secure a papal dispensation for his marriage to Eleanor. Paris informs us, in a passage notable for its dramatic tone, how in the spring of 1238 Earl Simon, fearing for the validity of his marriage, collected together a great sum of money and set sail, with great stealth, for Rome.[38]

Although Paris might well have over-exaggerated the furtive nature of Earl Simon's departure to enhance his narrative, Eleanor's earlier position as a vowess might by now have become the unwelcome subject of common gossip. This, together with the wider political fallout from their marriage, made a papal dispensation to validate their union in the eyes of the church and the wider political community all the more necessary. On 27 March 1238, the king furnished Simon with royal letters, addressed to the Pope and his cardinals at the Roman curia, which asked them to support his new brother-in-law's representations.[39] It is just possible that extra urgency was also leant to Simon's departure in these final days by his wife's suspicions that she had recently become pregnant – a son was subsequently born to the couple on 28 November 1238, eight months after Simon set out on his journey.[40] It is, nonetheless, striking that Simon chose not to travel directly to Rome. Instead, he visited the court of his brother-in-law, Emperor Frederick II, whose wife, Isabella, had recently been delivered of a child, and from whom, after entering the emperor's service, he solicited further letters of support, trading no doubt upon his marital connection with the empress.[41]

During Simon's absence from the realm, Eleanor dwelt at Kenilworth Castle, where she 'lay concealed', so Paris tells us, 'in a state of pregnancy ... awaiting the issue of the event'.[42] Her seclusion and the uncertain status of her marriage did not, though, prevent Eleanor from attempting to protect her own and her husband's financial interests. She remained a recipient of the king's generosity and favour. On 23 April 1238, Henry III wrote off a long-standing debt of £60 that Eleanor owed him and, two days later, dispatched five tuns of wine from Southampton for her enjoyment.[43] Further gifts of venison and wine followed during the course of the summer.[44] Yet the king's bounty did not protect Eleanor's purse from the resentment that Gilbert Marshal bore her over her remarriage. Gilbert, like his brother Richard before him, seems to have expressed his displeasure by withholding the payments for Eleanor's Irish dower. In May 1238, the king, who had agreed to stand as Gilbert's surety when the settlement of 1234 was first hammered out, paid Eleanor £200 to cover the sum that Gilbert should have paid to her at Easter.[45] When the Earl of Pembroke failed to compensate the king for this sum, Henry threatened to recover the £200 directly by seizing the earl's lands and chattels.[46] At the beginning of September, presumably in response to a plea for help from his sister, Henry granted the Montforts permission to seek an aid, a form of financial levy, from their tenants to help cover their expenses.[47] Simon's visit to Rome and the delays over Eleanor's dower placed a severe financial strain on the countess.

ROME

While Eleanor remained in England, Simon de Montfort faced the arduous task of securing a papal dispensation for their marriage. The letters of support from his royal and imperial brothers-in-law offered him an entrée to the papal curia, but it was, so Paris claimed, only by making a substantial offer of money that Simon finally secured Pope Gregory IX's approval for his marriage.[48] The Pope made separate declarations to Eleanor and Simon that their marriage might stand in spite of Eleanor's earlier vow, and issued a further letter to the papal legate, Otto, Cardinal of St Nicholas in Carcere, to ensure that their marriage was now recognized.[49] Yet this did not silence opposition within the English church to the match. Edmund of Abingdon, Archbishop of Canterbury, did not hold back from expressing his concerns to the Pope about Eleanor's decision to renege on her vow.[50] The Dominican friar William of Abingdon was another vociferous critic of the Montfort marriage.[51] William and his supporters drew on the work of the twelfth-century theologian and bishop, Peter Lombard, whose *Four Books of Sentences* was a particularly influential text in the cathedral schools of Western Europe. The friar argued vigorously that 'the woman in question [i.e. Eleanor] may not have assumed the habit with the veil, yet she has taken the ring, with which she has devoted, or rather betrothed herself to Christ, and is, therefore, indissolubly united to Christ her spouse'.[52] According to Lombard, a widow who had taken a 'vow of continence' could not, therefore, marry again.[53] In the face of such vehement disapproval, it is, however, noteworthy that in his account of these affairs Paris himself was cautious in his treatment of Eleanor, neither demonizing her nor passing his own judgement upon her. Perhaps he sympathized with her motives for remarriage or wished to avoid overt criticism of the wife of a man, Simon, whom he admired.[54]

SIMON'S RETURN

Simon de Montfort returned triumphant from Rome on 14 October 1238, whereupon he visited the English royal court before hastening to join Eleanor, who was then in the final stages of her pregnancy at Kenilworth.[55] It was at Kenilworth that Eleanor spent her lying in and gave birth to a son, possibly on 26 November, two days earlier than Paris reported.[56] The roll of the king's almoner for 1238–9 indicates that it was on this day that the king made a hasty and apparently unscheduled trip from Woodstock, where the royal court was then in residence, to Kenilworth.[57] Just as Henry had rushed to attend the deathbed of his older sister, Joan, on 4 March 1238, he now rushed to attend his youngest sister when she was safely delivered of her first child.[58] As well as giving another 'small' but nonetheless significant 'glimpse of the warm relations which existed at this time' between Eleanor, Simon and Henry III, the king's visit strongly suggests that he gave his blessing to the couple's decision to name their son Henry in his honour and presumably acted as godfather to their child.[59] The baby was baptized by Alexander de Stavenby, Bishop of Lichfield, who was apparently eager to secure the king's favour by performing this service.[60] Amid what would prove to be unfounded fears that Queen Eleanor might be barren, the birth of Henry de Montfort was particularly welcomed in royal circles as an event that promised to strengthen the ruling dynasty and lend comfort to the realm.[61]

For six weeks or so after the birth, Eleanor remained in relative seclusion at Kenilworth, once her brother had departed and while she recovered from her delivery. Her absence from the king's Christmas court at Winchester did not, however, mean that the welfare of his youngest sister escaped the king's notice. On the contrary, the king ordered a luxurious new gown for Eleanor at Christmas, a robe she might well have received in time for her churching. This fine new robe and surcoat were made from cloth of gold and gold baudekyn cloth (a type of figured silk). They were trimmed and lined with miniver, easily rivalling the splendour of the robes with which Henry III had furnished Isabella the Empress before her marriage in 1235.[62] These clothes were accompanied by further gifts in the form of a quilt and a mattress of baudekyn and a coverlet of scarlet cloth and the best 'gris' (grey fur), again made expressly for Eleanor's use.[63] These gifts, packaged in waxed canvas and other materials intended to protect them on their journey, were dispatched from London to the countess at Kenilworth in the safekeeping of Roger the Usher and his assistant, Taillefer.[64]

The countess's churching had apparently taken place by 13 January 1239, when Simon returned to court.[65] The purpose of Simon's attendance on this occasion was to secure the collection of the arrears of his wife's Irish dower. Henry III, in keeping with his earlier agreement to stand surety for Gilbert Marshal, the errant debtor, stepped into the breach once more: Simon received £200 from Henry's coffers to cover the arrears for Michaelmas term 1238.[66] Papal support for their marriage and the birth of a son placed the Montforts in an apparently unassailable position and entrenched them firmly in the king's affections. There was no clearer indication of Henry's regard for this younger sister and his new brother-in-law than his decision to allow Simon to realize his long-term ambition and elevate him to a rank comparable with that of his wife. On 2 February 1239, in recognition of his family's long-standing claim, Henry III finally granted Simon the earldom of Leicester.[67] Simon's new-found status was given ceremonial prominence later that year when he participated in the baptism of the king's eldest son, Edward, born on 17/18 June 1239. During the splendid state occasion that accompanied the baptism of the new heir to the throne, Earl Simon numbered among those appointed to receive Edward from the font.[68] As the only one of the king's sisters then resident in the realm, Eleanor very probably numbered among 'the noble ladies' whose presence at these celebrations was noted by Paris.[69]

Then, without warning, the Montforts' fortunes experienced a sudden and dramatic change for the worse. Within just a matter of weeks after Edward's baptism, the fragility of the edifice upon which their position at the Henrician court had been built was exposed for all to see. The peculiar circumstances of Eleanor and Simon's marriage, the outcry that followed and the uncertainties surrounding the couple's financial situation (Simon's earlier debts, the outlay for his trip to Rome and the recurring problem of Eleanor's Irish dower) placed them in a vulnerable situation: their position and lifestyle were secure only so long as they retained Henry's goodwill. As Eleanor and her husband now discovered, the king's benevolence was far from unlimited, all the more so now that there were new strings pulling on his purse. In the first place, the king had his own son and heir, as well as a wife, for whom he needed to provide. In the second place, visits by Eleanor of Provence's Savoyard uncles to the English royal court allowed them to secure positions of influence and thereby compete with Henry's blood kin and the English nobility for royal patronage.[70] In the third place, Henry had recently been channelling large sums of money towards the crusade to the Holy Land planned by Richard of Cornwall in alliance with the Emperor.[71] In such circumstances and in view of the sheer level of support that Henry had previously shown towards Eleanor and Simon – support that had jeopardized Henry's relationship with Richard of Cornwall – it is perhaps easy to understand how Henry's affection towards the couple came to be tinged with resentment.

The Montforts were certainly adept at taking from the crown. By the summer of 1239 Henry might well have felt justifiably aggrieved at the continual financial drain that Eleanor and her husband placed upon him, especially if there were those around him, like perhaps his younger brother, Richard, who were ready to point out to him the problematic nature of his relationship with the Montforts. The final straw came early in August 1239, when Henry III learned that Earl Simon had named him as a surety for a large debt (2,000 marks) he owed to the queen's uncle, Thomas of Savoy, without first seeking Henry's permission.[72] This was a step too far. Henry was fed up with being treated as a bottomless pit from which to draw money. On 9 August 1239, in full view of the royal court, Henry III rounded on his brother-in-law and accused him of seducing his sister.[73] It was a very public confrontation and one that betrayed the full measure of the king's anger, albeit in a typically familial setting. The Earl and Countess of Leicester were turned away and barred from attending the purification of the queen, Eleanor of Provence.[74]

What is particularly striking about this episode is the way in which it was staged so as to make it clear that Henry's rage was directed against his sister as much as her husband: Eleanor and her husband were equally culpable in the king's eyes, a situation that strongly hints at Eleanor's own political agency. According to Paris, 'the noble ladies' of the Henrician court assembled in London so that they might accompany the queen to Westminster Abbey for her purification.[75] When Earl Simon arrived with his wife, Henry expressly forbade the couple from attending the ceremony. A furious king then threw a series of insults at his brother-in-law. In the presence of numerous witnesses, Henry called Simon 'an excommunicant' and claimed that he had 'wickedly and secretly defiled' Eleanor before their marriage.[76] This public attack on Eleanor's sexual reputation by her own brother, the man who had hitherto championed her remarriage and, indeed, protected Eleanor's financial and personal interests even against their closest kin, was remarkable. For Eleanor, it was deeply humiliating. To make matters worse, when the Montforts fled and sought refuge at the Southwark palace of the former Bishop of Winchester, a residence loaned to them by the king, they found themselves rudely ejected from the premises. In an attempt to salvage the situation, the couple approached the king once more 'with tears and lamentations', but to no avail. In the bitter exchange of words that followed, Eleanor and Simon were rebuffed by the king, who repeated the accusation of his sister's seduction and claimed that he had possessed prior knowledge of their affair before the couple's marriage. In anger, the king now claimed that he had only approved Eleanor's union with Simon in order to avoid a scandal.[77]

In general terms, Paris's account of these dramatic events sits comfortably with those that Earl Simon and Eleanor later recalled for the benefit of the French king, Louis IX, in 1261.[78] Such was the king's wrath against the Montforts that they felt compelled to leave the realm, fearing for their safety. After the king unsuccessfully attempted to imprison Earl Simon within the Tower of London, Earl Simon and Eleanor, who was pregnant again, fled by boat to France, attended by their small *familia*.[79] If the scale of the couple's fall from favour can, in part, be measured by the ignominious nature of their departure from Henry III's realm, it can also be measured by the subsequent silence of the English government records that document no gifts offered to Eleanor or her husband in the aftermath of their flight.

When, during the winter of 1237–8, Eleanor and Simon had solicited Henry III's support for their marriage, in the face of opposition from the church on the grounds of Eleanor's earlier vow and in the face of opposition from Richard of Cornwall, they had taken a tremendous political gamble. Initially, once Henry III had at great personal and financial cost rebuilt his relationship with Earl Richard and supported Simon's mission to Rome, it might well have seemed to the couple that their actions had paid off. Yet, in the summer of 1239, they fell victim to their own ambitions, to the scale of their continued indebtedness in a fast-changing political climate, and, inevitably, to the enemies that they had made in contracting their *matrimonium clandestinum*. In the end, it was the Montforts' troubled finances that finally pushed Henry over the edge; Eleanor's supposed seduction merely provided grist to the mill.[80] By late August 1239, Earl Simon had secured various royal loans amounting to no less than £1,565, a vast sum of money, in addition to the more modest sum of £15, which Eleanor had received, expressly by the king's order, from the royal wardrobe.[81] Enough was enough, for the time being at least.[82] From their exile in France, it remained to be seen how long it would take for Henry III's anger against the Montforts to wax and then wane.

6

Family, Faction and Politics

'Against the designs of malicious people take care'
[Friar Adam Marsh to Eleanor de Montfort][1]

During the 1240s and 1250s, Eleanor de Montfort and her husband, Earl Simon, came to rely increasingly upon the advice of their closest friends and allies at the Henrician court as they weathered the political storms that came their way. In the aftermath of their flight into exile in August 1239, it was not until April 1240 – eight months after their departure – that Earl Simon dared to set foot in his brother-in-law's kingdom again. When he came, he came alone. Countess Eleanor, who was then pregnant again, remained overseas, a guest perhaps of her French in-laws at Montfort l'Amaury.[2] Simon's decision to leave his wife behind might well have reflected the couple's personal concerns about the warmth of their reception in England, as well as the countess's state of health.

The reason for Earl Simon's visit was a money-raising expedition and one whose ultimate purpose was unlikely to anger his brother-in-law, King Henry III. Before his marriage, Simon had vowed to go on crusade, and the departure of his older brother, Amaury, for the East in 1239 might well have helped to focus Simon's mind on the need to fulfil his own vow.[3] Perhaps Simon and Eleanor attributed their own run of bad fortune in England to divine displeasure at the circumstances surrounding their marriage and sought to make amends. Now, Simon attempted to raise the funds for his crusade through the sale of lands to the canons and hospitallers of Leicester, and others.[4] The crusade, the political rehabilitation of the Montforts in years immediately following Earl Simon's return and their relationship with the English crown during the 1240s and 1250s are explored within this chapter.

THE CRUSADE

In 1240, there were others among Eleanor's close kin who entertained similar crusading ambitions to those of her husband. Richard of Cornwall also actively planned to go to the East. In the spring of 1240, Earl Richard and Earl Simon departed for the Holy Land in two separate contingents.[5] Earl Simon found the time first, though, to restore 'his very small son' to Eleanor in France; Henry de Montfort, who was not yet two years old, had been left behind in England in the wake of his parents' flight in August 1239.[6] The pregnant Eleanor then travelled with Earl Simon and his contingent of crusaders over land through Lombardy and Apulia, as far as Brindisi, where the earl took ship for the East.[7]

Eleanor remained behind in Apulia, where she awaited her husband's return and her latest confinement in a castle with great lands, which Frederick II had placed at his sister-in-law's disposal.[8] Earl Simon's crusade came at a personal price – once the countess bade her husband farewell, she did not see him again for more than a year. In the East, Simon acquitted himself with dignity, apparently earning the regard of the inhabitants of the kingdom of Jerusalem to such a degree that they sought, unsuccessfully, his appointment as governor. When Simon decided to journey home in the autumn of 1241, he was finally reunited with his wife and with their growing brood of children. The Earl of Leicester travelled first to Burgundy, before he was recalled to English royal service for Henry III's disastrous Poitevin campaign of 1242.[9]

It was a measure of Simon and Eleanor's dramatic fall from Henry III's favour that, apart from the earl's brief visit during the spring of 1240, they effectively chose to absent themselves from the Henrician court for nearly three years. This was, perhaps, a reflection of the personal hurt that the king's accusations against the couple had caused them; Simon and Eleanor might still have felt deeply aggrieved by their treatment at Henry's hands. Although, as the price of his military support in Poitou, Earl Simon secured compensation for the lands seized by the king to discharge his debt to Thomas of Savoy, he harboured bitter feelings towards Henry.[10] Only in the autumn of 1243 did the Montforts consider it safe to return to England.

The fracturing of Eleanor's close personal relationship with Henry III naturally undermined her role as an intermediary between the king and her husband in the early 1240s. When the queen's mother, Beatrice of Savoy, Countess of Provence, visited England in November 1243, it was Beatrice rather than Eleanor who approached the king on the couple's behalf. Fortunately for the Montforts, the Countess of Provence, who had escorted the queen's younger sister, Sanchia, to England so that she might marry Richard of Cornwall, proved to be an extremely effective negotiator. Matthew Paris recorded her friendly reception by Henry III and Beatrice's kindness and consideration towards her royal son-in-law.[11] It was in the midst of, or a little while after, the family celebrations for Richard and Sanchia's marriage in late November 1243, that the

Montforts secured the Countess of Provence's help as an ally in a bid to alleviate their ever-increasing financial woes.[12] As a result of Beatrice's intervention and a renewed warmth of feeling towards Eleanor and Simon, Henry III made a fresh series of financial concessions. First, on 7 January 1244, he pardoned debts to the value of £1,000 that the Earl and Countess of Leicester owed to the king 'from the time of her [Eleanor's] widowhood'.[13] At Beatrice's insistence, Henry also, so the Montforts later recalled, agreed to bestow upon Eleanor a long-awaited dowry of 500 marks in lands or rents.[14] Countess Beatrice then turned her son-in-law's attention to the ever-thorny issue of the arrears still due to Eleanor from her Irish dower.[15]

In the event, Henry III made good his promises, perhaps wishing to save face with his mother-in-law. With regard to Eleanor's Irish dower, the situation surrounding the payment of the £400 fee owing to her from the earls of Pembroke had been complicated by Gilbert Marshal's sudden and unexpected death in June 1241 from wounds sustained in a tournament.[16] Walter Marshal, Gilbert's younger brother, stood next in line to succeed to the earldom of Pembroke, but Walter's succession was delayed until October 1241 by Henry III's refusal to recognize his claim. In fact, the king was angered by Walter's presence at the fatal tournament, a tournament Henry had expressly prohibited from taking place.[17] Once Walter became earl, he inherited the obligation to pay Eleanor the £400 fee in lieu of her Irish dower. Eleanor and Simon's prolonged absence from England had made it easy for Walter to ignore this payment.

Eleanor and Simon's return to England in 1243, with a family of young sons to support, made them particularly eager to pursue Eleanor's dower rights once more. One immediate problem that the couple faced was that the king's agreement to stand as a surety for Gilbert Marshal's payments had expired on Gilbert's death, alleviating the pressure on Walter to honour payments to his sister-in-law. On 9 January 1244, just two days after he pardoned Eleanor's debts to the crown, Henry III announced his agreement to stand as surety on Walter's behalf to Eleanor and Simon. Henceforth, the king undertook to make good any dower payments that Walter missed.[18] The arrangement was augmented by a bond which confirmed that on the first default of payment by Walter, the king would step in to assign the Countess of Leicester's dower directly from her late husband's lands in Ireland and south Wales.[19] This, as Maddicott has argued, represented a potentially momentous undertaking by the king; it suggests not only that the couple 'had complained about the inadequacy of the dower', but 'that they had broached the possibility of a full settlement in land, that Henry had recognized their case, and that he was even prepared to contemplate giving them what they wanted by assigning Irish land to Eleanor at Walter Marshal's expense'.[20] On 2 May, the king compensated Eleanor and Simon with 200 marks to cover the losses the Montforts had sustained because Eleanor was 'not fully dowered of the lands of W. Marshal formerly her husband'.[21]

Admittedly, it took a little longer for the king to provide Eleanor with her promised dowry. It was not until 28 May 1244 that Simon and Eleanor received an annual grant of 500 marks from the Exchequer for the remainder of both their lives. Henry promised to substitute the cash for lands to the same value as soon as he was able. He also agreed to give the Montforts' heirs 300 marks from the Exchequer after their parents' deaths.[22] On the face of it, this might have appeared like a generous grant, had not the king decided to reduce the sum payable to Eleanor and Simon's heirs. Had Henry provided Eleanor and Simon with a grant of land as a marriage portion, then that land might, according to custom, have descended to their heirs in its entirety.[23] Once again, Henry sold the interests of his youngest sister short.

Further favours were, however, on the horizon. Throughout 1244, the Montforts pushed for further concessions from Henry III that promised to place them on a firmer financial footing. In February, for example, the Montforts had been provided with another suitably royal residence for the king's sister, her husband and their sons, when Henry III granted Earl Simon the custody of Kenilworth Castle in Warwickshire, the royal residence where Eleanor had stayed in 1238 during Simon's trip to Rome.[24] In June, Henry III pardoned Eleanor for a debt of £100 that she was bound to pay to the Jewish moneylender, David of Oxford, indicating the Eleanor had once again resorted to the services of Jewish financiers when faced with a lack of ready cash to meet her expenses.[25] A month later, another debt of £110 that the Montforts owed to David of Oxford was effectively written off and the king instructed that they were to be protected from prosecution by David's widow, Licoricia.[26]

The year 1244, therefore, represented a relative high point thus far in the Montforts' standing at Henry III's court. The couple remained, for the time being, on relatively warm terms with the king. Simon did not, for example, number among those barons who protested at the harshness of the king's government and denied Henry III's request for taxation at the November parliament.[27] The earl also served the king during the Welsh campaign of 1245.[28] Henry III, for his part, allowed Eleanor occasional favours that hint at the renewal of their earlier relationship. Significantly, the resumption of more cordial relations between Henry III and his youngest sister can be traced through the renewal of royal gifts to her. These presents often accompanied other grants intended to alleviate some of the couple's financial woes. On 8 November 1244, the same day that Henry III granted Eleanor the right to tallage (impose a tax on) the men of the manors of East Stoke and Garbeton in Nottinghamshire, for example, Henry instructed the keeper of the royal wines at Clarendon Palace to send the countess a tun of wine.[29] The king also began, once more, to send her venison. In December 1244, Henry arranged for a cart and horses to convey fifteen does to the Countess of Leicester's manor of Sutton in Kent.[30] On 17 August 1246, the king gave his sister seven bucks from Rockingham Forest in Northamptonshire.[31] The summer of 1247 found Eleanor a willing recipient of her brother's bounty: two stags from Feckenham Forest in June were followed by ten bucks from Rockingham Forest in July.[32] Some of these gifts were clearly intended to stock the Montforts' properties. It was, for instance, with a view to replenishing the herds in the Montforts' park at Hungerford that the Countess of Leicester secured a total of thirty does and ten bucks from the royal forests of Melksham and Chippenham in January 1248.[33] These gifts from Melksham and Chippenham were accompanied by another concession from the king that addressed, more directly, the couple's financial situation, whereby Henry promised to relieve his sister of the burden of paying an annual rent of £50 for her manor of Odiham.[34]

The royal patronage directed towards the Montforts hints at the extent to which Eleanor traded upon her kinship with the king to provide for her expanding family. The most striking indications of Eleanor's influence, though, were the privileges which she began, once more, to secure for third parties through her personal intervention with the king. In December 1248, the Countess of Leicester approached the king to secure an exemption from service on assizes, juries and recognitions for her servant, Adam de la Brech.[35] Eleanor also effectively petitioned her brother to pardon felons convicted of a variety of offences.[36]

The year 1248 marked a pinnacle in Earl Simon's public career: on 1 May, Simon was appointed governor of Gascony for seven years, whereupon he took up residence there with a view to restoring the authority of the English crown within the duchy.[37] Paris attributed the Earl of Leicester's Gascon appointment to Simon's reputation as a warrior.[38] His natal family's position in France and Earl Simon's experiences as a diplomat on the international stage also recommended him for the post.[39] In view of Henry III's increased generosity towards Eleanor, it is also possible that the king wished to please his sister and her husband by providing Earl Simon with a weighty role in government, an almost vice-regal role that signified the scale of the couple's political rehabilitation. From his point of view, Henry might have felt that his brother-in-law was ideally placed, through his marital ties to the crown, to act as Henry's trusted lieutenant in Gascon affairs.[40] It was unfortunate, to say the least, for the Montforts, that Earl

Simon's sojourn in Gascony was, ultimately, fraught with controversy.[41] At the same time, the matter of Eleanor's Irish Marshal dower returned, ominously, to the fore.

ELEANOR'S IRISH DOWER

The death of Walter Marshal, Earl of Pembroke, at Goodrich Castle on 24 November 1245 was followed just eleven days later by that of his younger brother and heir, Anselm Marshal.[42] This left the great Marshal estates in England, Ireland and Wales to be divided between the five sisters of William Marshal junior or their descendants as co-heirs. By the time that the final partition was made in May 1247, there were thirteen co-heirs with claims to the Marshal lands. Of the five sisters, only Matilda, the widow of Hugh Bigod, Earl of Norfolk, and of William de Warenne, Earl of Surrey, was still alive. Of the remaining sisters, Joan, the wife of Warin de Munchensy, was succeeded first by her son John (who died in 1247) and then by her daughter, Joan, while Isabella was succeeded by her son from her first marriage, Richard, Earl of Gloucester and Hertford, Sibyl by her seven daughters from her marriage to William de Ferrers, Earl of Derby, and Eva by her three daughters from her marriage to William de Briouze.[43] Furthermore, there were now two other Marshal widows with claims to dower in the Marshal lands in addition to those of Eleanor: Walter's widow, Margaret de Lacy, *suo jure* Countess of Lincoln, and Anselm's widow, Matilda de Bohun.[44]

The main problem with this situation from the point of view of the Montforts and, indeed, the crown, was essentially twofold. In the first place, the existence of other Marshal widows raised the question, once more, of whether Eleanor had, in fact, received a fair share of William junior's estates in dower. Under the common law, Eleanor ought to have received lands or property valued at a third of her dead husband's estates. As we have already observed in chapter 3, figures derived from the documents detailing the partition of 1247 indicate that Walter's widow, Margaret de Lacy, was entitled to English and Welsh lands worth £444 per annum and Irish lands worth £572 per annum.[45] It would, therefore, appear that Eleanor had been short-changed in accepting the £400 fee at the king's urging in 1232. The speed with which Eleanor and Simon reached this realization, or at least decided to act upon it, and just how much it rankled with them, was reflected by their decision at Easter 1247 to launch a legal challenge against the Marshal co-heirs. Eleanor, so the Montforts claimed, had been dowered with a third of all William junior's lands in Ireland and Wales, and they now demanded Eleanor's full dower entitlement. When the agreement between Eleanor and Richard Marshal, whereby Eleanor had agreed to accept her £400 fee, was produced in court, the Montforts claimed, quite simply, not to recognize its force. According to Eleanor and Simon, it was invalid. It had been made, so they argued, when the countess was underage and in the king's custody and power. In a bitter courtroom drama, this line of argument was, not altogether surprisingly, completely rejected by the Marshal co-heirs. According to them, the countess had possessed independent legal power at the time of the original settlement.[46] The case dragged on into 1248, a day was appointed for judgment, but no verdict was apparently reached, much to the Montforts' deep frustration.[47]

In the second place, the king was faced with the task of collecting the £400 fee for Eleanor's Irish dower from each of the co-heirs in turn, many of whom were married to Henry III's greatest earls and barons.[48] This state of affairs was far from ideal and had all the makings of an administrative nightmare. For the first years, though, the Montforts were able to collect their money directly from the crown as they had done in the recent past. On 1 May and 20 October 1246, for example, Henry III authorized two separate payments to Earl Simon of the £200 he was due to receive on his wife's behalf at Easter and Michaelmas.[49] The same arrangement continued in 1247–54.[50] Having issued instructions to his officials to pay the money owed to the Montforts, the king was then faced with the tricky task of recovering the sum from the Marshal co-heirs himself.[51] Yet the king proved reluctant to force those co-heirs who defaulted to compensate the crown. In January 1249, for example, Henry III allowed three defaulters – the Earl of Gloucester and Hertford, William de Valence (Henry III's Lusignan half-brother and the husband of Joan de Munchensy) and the Earl of Norfolk – to escape the threat of distraint on their lands for non-payment until Easter.[52]

As the crown lurched towards a severe financial crisis in the 1250s, however, the king's orders for payment to the Montforts from his own funds might not always have been honoured in practice.[53] By 1254, crown finances were in a parlous state. The payment of Eleanor's fee was no longer forthcoming after Michaelmas 1254.[54] By May 1256, the Montforts were still owed £400 to cover the payments due at Easter and Michaelmas in 1255, a situation the king attempted to remedy by authorizing an emergency payment of £600 to cover the period up to and including Easter 1256.[55] Henry appears to have come to rely increasingly upon funds received directly from the Marshal co-heirs. Yet even these funds, when they were forthcoming, might, on occasion, have been directed elsewhere to meet other, more pressing obligations. In August 1256, the king solemnly promised Earl Simon that the money received by the crown for the yearly arrears of £400 owed by the Marshal co-heirs to the Montforts would be used for no other purpose than to pay off the outstanding sum.[56]

With a degree of irony, by 1256, the greatest defaulter of all the Marshal beneficiaries was another widow, Margaret de Lacy, Countess of Lincoln, who owed the crown seven years in arrears for her contribution towards Eleanor de Montfort's £400 fee. When pressure was brought to bear on Margaret during the summer of 1256, the Countess of Lincoln came good and agreed to pay £1,066 directly to Eleanor and Simon.[57] This sum was apparently enough to cover the money owing to the Montforts for Michaelmas 1254 to Michaelmas 1256, according to the royal clerk who compiled the memoranda roll.[58]

GASCONY

Between 1248 and 1252, Simon de Montfort's political career was dominated by his governance of Gascony and Eleanor, as his wife, also experienced the highs and lows of his time there. Earl Simon's initial triumphs in 1248, whereby he negotiated and reached agreements with the kings of France and Navarre, were quickly overshadowed by Gascon complaints about the earl's administration and by the huge expenses he incurred in attempting to bring order to the duchy.[59] Furthermore, the earl's commitments in Gascony placed extra strain on the Montforts' finances as the crown struggled to divert adequate funds to support Simon's regime.[60]

The Countess of Leicester's activities during her husband's Gascon years are difficult to trace. Even Paris, who describes, in some detail, Simon's role in Gascony after his appointment, is often silent on the subject of Eleanor's movements during this period of her life. It seems, however, likely that the countess had accompanied the earl on his first visit to the duchy after his appointment in 1248 and was, as the English king's sister, an informal party to her husband's dealings with the kings of France and Navarre. According to Paris, Simon de Montfort returned to England in December 1248, whereupon the king received his brother-in-law with joy.[61] This date for his return, perhaps in his wife's company, is confirmed by a series of royal grants that served Simon and Eleanor's mutual interests.[62] The earl and countess were certainly in England together during the spring of 1249, when Simon, 'after discussing the matter with the lady countess', made arrangements for the education of the couple's eldest son, Henry, in anticipation of his return to Gascony.[63] In the event, the earl's departure was delayed until early June 1249.[64] Eleanor and Simon were in Gascony in the autumn of 1249 when the friar Adam Marsh regretfully informed the couple's friend Robert Grosseteste, Bishop of Lincoln, that he was 'unable to dispatch letters' for 'the earl and countess of Leicester in time for them to reach [the bishop's palace at] Buckden' in Cambridgeshire. Marsh asked if Grosseteste's messenger, who was destined for Gascony, might visit him en route to collect his letters for the Montforts.[65] The countess's presence in the duchy, holding court alongside her husband, is also confirmed by another letter, written by a clerk of Count Alphonse of Poitiers, whose master had been asked to visit the couple at La Réole.[66]

Earl Simon was in England again, according to Paris, during Rogation (May) in 1250.[67] Although the earl departed for Gascony by the middle of May, his wife was almost certainly in England in July 1250, when the king gave her ten bucks from the New Forest.[68] In 1251, Paris noted that Simon had returned from Gascony to his brother-in-law's court by Epiphany (6 January);[69] the earl departed again for the duchy in March.[70] Eleanor's presence overseas in 1251 is supported by Paris's story of a crossing to England which the earl and countess attempted to make that year in the company of Eleanor's half-brother, Guy de Lusignan. This chronicler described how the couple set out from the port of Wissant, only for their ship to be driven back by the wind, before they were able to cross safely to Dover.[71] One hopes that Eleanor had, by this time of her life, overcome the seasickness that plagued her teenage years.

The earl and countess were not constant companions that year. In October 1251, Marsh wrote to Earl Simon with news of the countess, whom he had visited in England.[72] In December 1251, Earl Simon attended the king's Christmas court at York, where the marriage of Henry's daughter, Margaret, to Alexander III, King of Scots was celebrated, and where he quarrelled with the king over a Gascon revolt, a revolt provoked, so the Gascons claimed, by the harshness of the earl's government.[73] Earl Simon returned, briefly, in the spring of 1252 to the duchy to deal with the situation before coming back to England, this time to answer the charges relating to Gascon affairs as political pressures mounted.[74]

The royal inquiry into Earl Simon's governance of Gascony inevitably brought to a head long-standing tensions between the Montforts and the king over Simon's lieutenancy. Marsh, in a letter dated 15 June, summarized affairs for Grosseteste's benefit. Writing from Eleanor's Kentish manor of Sutton, Marsh described how Earl Simon 'frequently suffered reproaches and vociferous abuse from the lord king in front of many great persons'.[75] 'It must be a long time', the clearly partisan Marsh reflected, 'since any nobleman or private individual has been so harshly and insensitively treated.'[76] Such was the Earl of Leicester's isolation at the English court, once the full fury of the king's rage became apparent, that only a few men were initially prepared to speak up on his behalf or offer him 'loyal protection', apart from Walter de Cantilupe, Bishop of Worcester, Peter of Savoy, the queen's uncle, and Peter de Montfort.[77] Fortunately for Simon, the prelates, Richard of Cornwall, the Lusignans and 'the barons of the kingdom' stepped in as well to defend Earl Simon's reputation.[78]

The king's anger against the earl ultimately remained unabated. Eleanor as Simon's wife shared in her husband's troubles and anxieties. Alongside him, she felt the weight of the king's displeasure once more. Dismissed from court, Earl Simon sent letters reaffirming his loyalty to Henry III before crossing the Channel to France on 13 June 1252, 'safe and cheerful, with Henry, his eldest son'.[79] The precariousness of the Montforts' position, Eleanor's deep sense of unease with the situation and her concern for the immediate future all were conveyed by a message which Marsh added, expressly at her bidding, to the end of his letter to Grosseteste:

> The illustrious lady countess sends her greetings to your lordship [Grosseteste] by this letter, with respectful thanks, and embracing the feet of your fatherly goodness in humble supplication, in this time of fear and danger, she commends to you in the blessed Son of God through the Mother of God, her lord, herself, with her children and her house and all those connected with it.[80]

It was a moving missive, but one with a clear political purpose. Eleanor urged Grosseteste, through Marsh, to assist and protect her husband's interests, her own interests and those of their offspring, their household and their followers. In expressing herself thus and in mentioning 'her lord' (i.e. Earl Simon) first, Eleanor or perhaps Marsh employed a form of address that observed patriarchal conventions in a way which might be pleasing to the addressee, but which, at the same time, subverted patriarchal norms by exercising political agency. If the Montforts' relationship with Henry III remained unstable, then the Montforts' wider network of courtly contacts, a network Eleanor helped to foster, offered them alternative routes for influence.

HOUSEHOLD, RELIGION, ESTATES AND FAMILY

Eleanor's activities during the time of Simon's Gascon lieutenancy are, as we have seen, difficult to determine with any degree of certainty. What is, however, striking is the decision apparently taken by the earl and countess that Eleanor should often accompany her husband overseas, rather than remaining behind in England to oversee the couple's estates there. Initially, at least, it might well have been hoped, both by the earl and by his brother-in-law, the English king, that Eleanor's presence in the duchy would strengthen the legitimacy of the earl's administration there and perhaps foster loyalty to Henry III through her close kinship with the king/duke. The latter connection was, after all, one that the countess was happy to advertise; on the seal that Eleanor used during her second marriage, she was styled 'countess of Leicester', and on her counterseal, she was styled 'sister of the king of England'.[81] Even Eleanor's close friend, Marsh, acknowledging the difference in rank between them, addressed her deferentially as 'the noble lady Eleanor, countess of Leicester', 'the illustrious lady Eleanor, countess of Leicester', 'the illustrious Countess of Leicester' and 'the most excellent lady Eleanor, countess of Leicester', and referred in his letters to 'your excellency's royal heart'.[82]

In Gascony, it presumably fell to Eleanor to assist in running the Montfort's great household in the duchy. When Earl Simon was called away to counter the various military threats that arose there, Eleanor was ideally placed to act as her husband's representative. Marsh certainly believed Eleanor capable of influencing the earl in political affairs. In one letter, which dates from the time of Simon's lieutenancy, the friar advised the countess that if the earl met with failure in Gascony, she might assist her husband 'with quiet advice'.[83]

When the couple were in England during the 1240s and 1250s, Eleanor took a keen interest in the day-to-day administration of the Montforts' household and estates, and in the domestic needs of her growing family. It was Eleanor, for instance, rather than Simon, whom Grosseteste thanked for lending him the services of her cook, John of Leicester.[84] Eleanor responded by reassuring Grosseteste that 'if she had the best of servants, however indispensable they might be to her, she would joyfully and promptly grant them to … [him] to minister to … [his] lordship', a generous gesture of friendship, intended to find favour with the bishop.[85]

Eleanor also looked to the spiritual welfare of her family. The countess and the earl actively attempted to recruit spiritual advisers into their service, including Brother Gregory de Bosellis, a friar well known to the Franciscan Marsh, whom Marsh praised for being 'well versed in mystical language'.[86] On one particular occasion, Marsh counselled Bosellis on the appointment of a suitable priest to serve Eleanor's Kentish manor at Kemsing.[87] On another, he rebuked Earl Simon after he learned from Eleanor that he had taken the vicar of the chancellor of Salisbury who served the church of Odiham with him overseas, thereby depriving that church of its priest.[88] In 1250, while Simon was in Gascony, Marsh extended to the earl his commiserations for the death of

Master Ralph of Canterbury, another cleric who served the earl overseas. Eager to find someone to fill Ralph's place, Marsh asked Simon whether 'your discreet lordship together with the lady countess, if you please' could advise him on how to proceed with this business.[89]

The couple's special devotion to the Mendicant Orders was one that the Montforts shared with Henry III and his queen, Eleanor of Provence. The English king was a generous patron of the friars, who regularly provided financial support and gifts in kind, such as fuel and clothing, to the houses at Canterbury, London, Reading and Oxford.[90] Throughout the 1230s, 1240s and 1250s Dominican and Franciscan friars were constantly in attendance upon Henry and his wife, fulfilling a pastoral role as confessors and preachers.[91] The friars exerted an important influence on Earl Simon's religious life beyond his friendship with Marsh. In his daily devotions, Simon's prayers and vigils mirrored those of the early Franciscans, and he favoured the same russet cloth for his clothes as that from which the Franciscans made their habits, in contrast to the jewellery and luxurious fabrics adopted by his wife.[92] It is likely that the earl founded the house for Black Friars (Dominicans) in Leicester, perhaps with his wife's support.[93] After all, the couple selected the chapel of St Peter the Apostle in the Dominican priory at Bordeaux as the final resting place for an infant daughter in or around 1248–51.[94] Eleanor used her relationship with the king to secure gifts for communities of friars who resided on or near the Montforts' English estates and who might otherwise have missed out on her brother's bounty. In November 1255, for example, at Eleanor's special request, Henry III granted the Friars Minor of Leicester eighteen oaks from the 'hay' (forest enclosure) of Alrewas in Staffordshire for making their stall and wainscoting their chapel.[95]

Contact with the friars shaped Eleanor's piety in a highly personal way. A strong sense of her religious outlook, or at least of the way in which it was sculpted by Marsh, emerges from the Franciscan's correspondence with the countess. A postscript added by Marsh to an undated letter to Eleanor of Provence urged the queen to receive the countess, her sister-in-law, with sympathy and encourage her towards a spiritual conversion: 'Lady, if at this Easter you wish to have a serious discussion with the Countess of Leicester about the salvation of souls ... I hope in the blessed Son of God that by the power of his glorious resurrection, he will give you counsel for the occasion to the glory of his name.'[96] In another letter addressed to Earl Simon, written in October 1251, Marsh recalled the countess 'speaking to me about matters relating to both your eternal salvation and hers and your temporal situation'.[97]

Eleanor's spiritual interest did not begin and end with the friars; it also extended to the patronage of the Cistercian Order, an affection for which she shared with her father and her brother, Richard of Cornwall.[98] On Palm Sunday (1 April) in 1245, so the annalist of the house recalled, the Montforts – Eleanor, who as a woman had secured the Pope's special permission to enter a Cistercian monastery, Simon, and two of their sons, Henry and Simon junior – all paid a special visit to Waverley Abbey.[99] Once at the abbey, the couple heard a sermon in the chapter house, watched the procession and observed the celebration of mass. Eleanor, a 'most sincere lover' of the abbey, presented its monks with a precious cloth for its high altar, perhaps one that she had sewn herself.[100] The ceremony obviously made a deep impression on the countess, as she later gave the abbey sixty-eight marks, eighteen of which were donated to the fabric of the church. The monks used the money to buy 150 acres of land in Neatham in Hampshire.[101] The Waverley Abbey annalist placed Eleanor's piety firmly within a family context – her husband and sons shared in the uplifting religious experience of visiting the abbey, apparently at their mother's behest.

Eleanor's participation in other acts of religious benefaction during her marriage is suggested by her occasional appearance in her husband's charters. When, for example, the earl was in London on 21 October 1255, he granted the abbey of St Mary de Pre in Leicester plots of woodland. Simon's charter, documenting this gift, stated that he did so expressly for the salvation of his own soul 'and the soul of Eleanor our countess'.[102] Eleanor also supported, alongside her husband, the wealthy Benedictine abbey of St Albans, which was also the home of Matthew Paris. The remnants of the Montfort family archives, now in the Bibliothèque nationale de France, preserve confraternity letters addressed to Earl Simon and his wife that outline a complex series of arrangements for their posthumous commemoration by the monks there, accompanied by a schedule of almsgiving to the poor.[103] Significantly, these letters were issued in November 1257 at Eleanor's manor of Luton in Bedfordshire,[104] and were, perhaps, intended to reciprocate a charter, issued jointly in the names of both Simon and Eleanor, a year earlier, which had granted the abbey the tithes from their demesne in Luton parish.[105]

The management of the Montforts' English estates, so that they might support the great household, also absorbed Eleanor's energies. According to Maddicott's calculation, the couple's income from their estates – Earl Simon's own and those acquired through marriage to Eleanor and by royal grant – stood at around £1,950, placing them in the second rank, but still within the wealthiest half dozen, of English earls and countesses.[106] Gifts of venison, although less frequent than they had been during Eleanor's years as a widow, were still authorized by the king in order to provide fresh meat or increase the stock of the earl and countess's parks.[107] Gifts of wood that Eleanor secured from Henry for building work convey the countess's continued interest in maintaining and improving the family properties. This was a concern that Earl Simon evidently shared with his wife. Even before Simon's departure for the East in 1239, he had overseen the construction of a new hall and kitchen at Odiham Castle.[108] When the royal court visited Canterbury in Kent in May 1246, Eleanor, for her part, secured a personal grant of ten oaks in Savernake Forest, that were presumably destined for one of her southern dower manors.[109] Three months later, Eleanor received another forty oaks from the king in the forests of Savernake and Chute to assist in rebuilding her chapel of Everleigh in Wiltshire.[110]

In an age when visual displays of wealth might enhance a family's prestige and function as outward indicators of their status and influence, such expenditure might, as discussed in chapter 4, have served a valuable political purpose.[111] When the king granted Earl Simon custody of Kenilworth Castle in 1244, he effectively provided the couple with a royal residence fit for the king's sister and the king's nephews.[112] By the time the Montforts took possession of Kenilworth, it had undergone extensive restoration work to turn it into a luxurious and more comfortable residence worthy of a royal palace and fortress. Eleanor's father, King John, had, for example, spent £1,115 on improvements to Kenilworth's living quarters and its defences.[113] The castle included a great oblong hall-keep, built in the twelfth century, inner and outer baileys and a series of water defences in the form of artificial meres or lakes.[114] Under Henry III, the work continued. In 1233, for example, the king ordered the sheriff of Warwickshire to supervise repairs in lead, wood and stone to the tower there.[115] In February 1241, the king had issued detailed instructions for the refurbishment of the castle's main chapel. The interior was to be wainscoted, whitened and painted, a wall was erected to separate the chancel from the main part of the chapel, and special wooden seats installed for the king and the queen. The queen's own private chapel, situated in the castle tower, was to be furnished with another seat, where she might say her private devotions. The porch of the tower was also rebuilt, the great chamber roofed, the gaol and gutters repaired, and a castle wall, which was falling into the fish pond, was knocked down and rebuilt.[116] In September 1241, when Henry III inspected the castle in person, he ordered substantial improvements to the queen's accommodation there, accommodation his sister Eleanor very probably occupied subsequently. The queen's chamber was wainscoted, whitened and lined. Its windows were made larger. The fireplaces in both the queen's and the king's chamber were enlarged. The queen's privy chamber was repaired, as was another chamber near the castle wall. A new porch was added to the queen's chamber, a new window was added to the north side of the castle chapel, a swing-bridge was installed, although it is not clear precisely where, and the castle's defences were improved by the construction of a new wall between the inner and outer walls of the fortress.[117] It was, indeed, generous of the king to hand over such a splendid residence to his sister and brother-in-law so soon after these works were undertaken.

Kenilworth was a far more appropriate and spacious residence for Eleanor and her growing brood of children than that which they already enjoyed at Odiham. Henry III appreciated this, if we can judge from his subsequent decisions to place the couple's possession of the castle on a firmer footing. In 1248, the year of Earl Simon's appointment to Gascony, the king granted Eleanor personal custody of Kenilworth Castle for life.[118] In 1253, in the aftermath of the debacle over Gascony, the couple's enjoyment of both Kenilworth and Odiham was extended further so that henceforth both Eleanor *and* Simon held these properties for the remainder of their lives.[119]

It was no mean task for a noblewoman like Eleanor to assist her husband in the day-to-day maintenance of such properties. Eleanor even appears to have issued charters in her own name during her second marriage. An undated charter is deposited in the Shakespeare Centre Library and Archives that records a grant made by Eleanor, styled Countess of Leicester and Pembroke, of property in Desford to a man named Walter, which was endorsed by her husband, Earl Simon.[120] At times, Eleanor almost seemed to cut a semi-autonomous figure within her marriage. Earl Simon was not always happy with this situation. The letter that Marsh wrote to Eleanor in or about 1250, wherein he urged her to moderate her behaviour towards her husband and learn to act in a more meek and submissive, and a less angry and argumentative manner, certainly supports this impression. One wonders what particular action by Eleanor compelled Marsh to remind her, in no uncertain terms, of her wifely duty of obedience to her husband.[121] There were other potential sources of tension, apart from Eleanor's behaviour to her husband, within their relationship – financial pressures and the couple's continuing anxiety about the legitimacy of their marriage. According to Paris, it was this latter reason that prompted the earl, with the full support of his wife, to take the cross in 1247.[122] In the event, neither husband nor wife set out for the East, but this did not deter Earl Simon from taking the cross yet again in 1250.[123]

MOTHERHOOD

Perhaps the most important role that Eleanor de Montfort fulfilled within her marriage to Earl Simon was that of a mother. As Barbara Harris observed in her exemplary study of English aristocratic women in Yorkist and early Tudor England, 'Motherhood was a crucial dimension of aristocratic women's careers as wives. Their success in bearing children, particularly sons, ensured the survival of their husbands' lineages and constituted a crucial service to their spouses and in-laws.'[124] A similarly high premium was placed on motherhood in thirteenth-century England for similar reasons.[125] Eleanor de Montfort's marriage to Earl Simon proved to be extremely fertile – the countess bore her husband five sons and one daughter who are known to have survived infancy. After the birth of the couple's eldest child, a son named Henry, in November 1238,[126] Eleanor quickly became pregnant again. In fact, she was already pregnant when she fled the kingdom with her husband in August 1239.[127] Eleanor was either still pregnant or possibly pregnant for a third time when the couple set off on crusade in 1240.[128] The birth of the couple's second son, who was named Simon, after his father and grandfather, was presumably the result of Eleanor's second or third pregnancy. Next to Simon in age was his younger brother, Amaury, who was most probably conceived after the earl's return from the East and who was born, by his own account, between spring 1242 and 1243.[129] The births of Guy, whom Maddicott has suggested was born in 1244, Richard, who was perhaps the child born to the couple in 1252, and Eleanor, who might have been born as late as 1258, followed.[130] Eleanor's time in Gascony, between 1248 and 1251, also witnessed the burial of another daughter, who either died soon after birth or in early infancy.[131]

The small amounts of time that typically elapsed between the end of one of Eleanor's early pregnancies and the conception of another child suggests that the Countess of Leicester, like other women of her wealth and status, handed over the wet nursing of her newborn children soon after birth. This was perfectly in keeping with contemporary expectations; it allowed Eleanor to resume her role in governing the Montforts' household and estates, and assisted in the recovery of her fertility.[132] Although we do not know the names of the nurses who cared for the Montforts' children, noble mothers often played an active role in their recruitment, and were encouraged to keep a close eye on their health and character, to ensure the quality of their milk, their attentiveness to their charges and their moral fibre, since the latter would rub off on the children in their care.[133]

The placing of Eleanor's sons and daughters in the charge of wet nurses during their early infancy did not necessarily mean that they spent particularly long periods of time apart from their mother. A possible exception was the Montforts' eldest son, Henry, who appears to have been left behind in England when the couple were forced, unexpectedly, to flee in 1239. The fact, though, that Earl Simon collected this son, so that he might convey him to his mother in time for the family to set out on crusade in 1240, suggests that that the Montforts were concerned to see their son restored to their household.[134]

Admittedly, the large amount of travelling in which the Montforts engaged, especially during their time overseas in France and Gascony, might have proved unsettling to the children as well as their parents. There is no evidence to suggest that the Montforts deviated from the relatively widespread practice among the English and French nobility of sending their sons away at around the age of seven and placing them in the households of high-ranking churchmen or barons.[135] Two of the Montforts' sons, Henry, their son and heir, and Amaury, their third surviving son, who was destined for a career in the church, spent part of their childhoods in the household of Robert Grosseteste, Bishop of Lincoln.[136] The quality of the education that Henry received there – 'in learning letters and … good manners' – were, according to Marsh, important considerations behind the decision of the earl *and* countess that he should return there in 1249.[137] Earl Simon clearly valued and respected Eleanor's opinion on this matter.

If practical necessity as well as contemporary expectations sometimes dictated that at least some of the Montfort sons received their education in other households, then Eleanor still had an important role to play in super-vising their care in early infancy. It was presumably into his wife's capable hands that Simon placed the wards whose custody he received from the crown, like the infant heir of Gilbert de Umfraville, a wealthy northern baron,[138] and who were subsequently raised alongside the couple's younger children within the Montforts' own establishments. Furthermore, the removal of Eleanor's sons from their parents' household did not prevent the earl and countess from solic-iting regular reports on their progress. Marsh's letters to Eleanor and Simon are littered with frequent reports on Henry and Amaury: 'The lord bishop of Lincoln is well, blessed be the Son of God, and your noble children are also well and continue to make good progress';[139] 'The lord of Lincoln is well and your noble children are well';[140] 'The lord bishop of Lincoln is well, blessed be God, and your distinguished children, whose outstanding talents give us great hopes of them, daily progress in virtue';[141] 'Your dear children are also well and are, I hope, advancing in both age and grace';[142] and 'Your illustrious children are well, blessed be our Saviour'.[143] From Marsh's letters, both Montforts emerge as parents who bore a deep affection for their offspring.

FRIENDS AT COURT, 1251–3

Although Eleanor's personal feelings about her recurring pregnancies are not recorded, the letters of Adam Marsh convey the sense of trepidation with which she approached her confinements. A letter he sent to the earl in October 1251, for example, began with a report of a false alarm: 'On the feast of St Denis [9 October] the countess [who was then heavily pregnant] conjectured that she was going into labour, although the day of birth had not arrived as she supposed.'[144] Eleanor, like many of her contemporaries, sought spiritual comfort at such a dangerous time for mother and child. Another letter in 1252, this time addressed to Eleanor, celebrated the safe arrival of her child, giving 'Blessing and glory to the Lord, who has not despised your devotion and has heard your prayer, and granted you delivery from anxiety and danger and joyfulness for a beloved offspring.'[145] News of this child was also greeted with joy by the queen, Eleanor of Provence, herself the mother of four surviving children by 1252.[146] During the early 1250s, the Countess of Leicester remained on friendly terms with her sister-in-law, the queen, perhaps on friendlier terms than she and her husband were, at times, with the king. As Countess Eleanor awaited the birth of her child in the late summer and early autumn of 1252, Queen Eleanor sent her messenger, John, presumably to bring her news of how the final stages of her sister-in-law's pregnancy were progressing.[147] When Peter, Earl Simon's barber, brought the queen 'rumours of the birth' of the countess's long-anticipated child at Michaelmas, he received forty shillings, a sizeable gift that reflected the queen's personal pleasure.[148] The queen immediately dispatched one of her own nurses, Lady Alice, to Kenilworth to care for her sister-in-law.[149] Queen Eleanor remained in close contact with the Countess of Leicester throughout the autumn, sending another messenger from Winchester to Kenilworth at the beginning of November.[150] Further messengers were exchanged by the two women over the coming months and into the New Year, when Countess Eleanor was resident at Kenilworth and Odiham.[151] One messenger, William de Gardin, was enlisted to convey a gift of jewellery to the countess on 1 December 1252.[152] During the summer of 1253, the Countess of Leicester paid a visit to the queen, travelling from Kenilworth to Windsor and back again with an entourage mounted on 28 horses.[153]

Further and, at times, rather touching evidence of the close relationship enjoyed by these two women is provided by the royal jewel rolls for 1252–3, which record gifts made by the queen to members of the countess's household. On 1 January 1253, Clemencia, Countess Eleanor's damsel, received a brooch worth 2s. 10d., while another Montfort servant, Walter de Fauconberg, a knight of the Countess of Leicester, received another brooch valued at 2s. 9½d.[154] Significantly, other recipients of brooches from the queen at this time were associated with the Montforts. They included, for example, Lady Agnes, the wife of Richard of Havering, a close associate of Countess Eleanor and Earl Simon, and the Haverings' daughter.[155] Such personal tokens of esteem reinforced and gave visual expression to the ties of friendship that existed between Henry III's wife and his younger sister.

POLITICAL TENSIONS

The years 1252–3 were fraught with political upheavals and pressing financial concerns for the Montforts. Earl Simon's return to Gascony in the immediate aftermath of his trial, coupled with his renewed military activities there, threatened a truce the king had secured with the Gascons in an attempt to restore peace. In October or November 1252, the king finally removed Simon from his command by means of an agreement negotiated with the king's oldest son, the Lord Edward, which promised to compensate the Earl of Leicester for the losses he had sustained there in royal service.[156] By the summer of 1253, however, the king was courting the earl's assistance in Gascony in order to assist a royal campaign to subdue the province in the face of renewed rebellion. Although the earl was understandably reluctant to return, he finally arrived to assist the king in October that year, and he remained in royal service until the early months of 1254.[157] It is interesting, though, to note that Paris credited Grosseteste, rather than Eleanor as Simon's wife, with persuading the earl to set aside his resentment at his treatment by the king and join his brother-in-law in Gascony after all.[158] In the event, it was wise advice. The earl's change of heart paved the way for a reconciliation between Henry III and Earl Simon, which provided the Montforts with further opportunities to try to settle their financial affairs and resolve the ongoing matter of their family's debts. The result was a generous series of royal grants made in November 1253 which attempted to redress the matter of the expenses previously incurred by the earl in the king's service in Gascony. Henry did this by promising to pay the earl £500 and by bestowing an annual fee of 600 marks (£400) on Earl Simon, Eleanor and the couple's heirs that the king would substitute for lands in the future.[159]

The concessions that the Montforts secured in 1253 also represented a financial coup at a time when competition for the king's patronage was, arguably, at its peak, and at a time when the crown was increasingly strapped for resources. With the arrival of Henry and Eleanor's Lusignan half-brothers and half-sisters (the children of Isabella of Angoulême's second marriage) in England in 1247 came another group of relations, in addition to Henry III's siblings, his wife and her Savoyard kin, and the royal children, for whom the king might be expected to provide, and who appealed to his personal generosity.[160] William de Valence, the eldest of the king's half-brothers, became one of the leading defaulters for Eleanor's Irish dower after he secured the marriage of Joan de Munchensy.[161] Bitter and public confrontations between William and Simon in 1257 and in April 1258 on Welsh affairs helped to alienate the Earl of Leicester from Henry III's regime.[162]

The high cost of the war in Gascony also left Henry III short of funds. This, coupled with the king's decision in March 1254 to accept an offer made by the Pope to bestow the crown of Sicily on Henry's second son, Edmund, placed unprecedented strains on the crown's finances and stretched them to breaking point. The papal offer came with strings attached: an English army to reconquer Sicily from the Hohenstaufens and a promise to pay off debts incurred by the papacy there to the tune of more than £90,000.[163] For the Montforts, who relied for so much of their cash income on the crown, and who still awaited the conversion of some of the fees owing to them into land, the outlook might well have appeared understandably bleak. We have already noted how, by 1256, Henry III was struggling to safeguard and satisfy the payments for Eleanor's Irish dower. He was, as Maddicott has shown, also becoming increasingly tardy when it came to repaying the sums owed to Earl Simon under the terms of the settlement agreed for his past services in Gascony, so that some debts remained unpaid for more than two years.[164]

Although the Montforts' debts provided Eleanor and Simon with a shared sense of grievance against the English crown, it did not, as the 1250s progressed, prevent the earl from serving Henry III on diplomatic missions overseas. The outcome of affairs in Gascony did not dent Simon's reputation as a skilled diplomat and politician. In 1253, shortly before he joined Henry III's campaign to Gascony, the French nobles asked the Earl of Leicester to assume the office of seneschal of France; the death of Blanche of Castile had left the Capetian kingdom without a regent in Louis IX's absence on crusade.[165] One cannot help but wonder whether Eleanor influenced the earl's decision to decline this offer. Paris observed that the Earl of Leicester had no wish to serve two royal masters.[166] It is easy to understand why his wife's blood tie to the English king, together with the degree to which the couple were beholden financially to Henry III, might also have helped to determine Simon's choice. As it was, Simon's cross-Channel connections proved invaluable to the English king, who dispatched him to negotiate with the French in 1255 and 1257. Simon's advice was also sought on an abortive English mission to Rome, as well as in the crown's dealings with the kingdom of Castile.[167] It was Simon who was selected, in September 1254, to visit the Scottish royal court, with the sensitive mission of ascertaining the wellbeing of his royal niece, Margaret, Queen of Scots.[168] In the end, though, the loyalties engendered by such ties proved far too fragile to last; they could not withstand Simon and Eleanor's shared financial grievances against the crown and the resentment provoked by the Lusignans. Enough was enough.

7

Reform, Revolution and War

the lord king and the Lord Edward his son... submitted themselves,
for the correction and reform both of their own affairs
and of the state of the realm.[1]

By the spring of 1258 it was not just the Montforts who were disillusioned with Henry III's personal rule. The king's ill-considered handling of patronage and the favouritism shown to his arrogant Lusignan half-brothers provoked widespread discontent. On top of this came the king's involvement in costly schemes abroad, most notably the 'Sicilian Business' in 1254, whereby he attempted to secure a throne for his second son, Edmund, which contributed further to the parlous state of royal finances. The weight of royal government came to feel particularly burdensome and oppressive to the knights and free tenants in the localities, where the Exchequer attempted to raise ever-greater sums of money through the machinery of royal justice. In addition to this, the sheriffs, the crown's chief local agents, were now expected to pay much higher cash increments over and above the county farms, so that many resorted to extortion to raise funds. The crown exploited the Jews to a much higher degree than before, with the result that the Jews, in their turn, placed greater pressure on their debtors in order to meet their more onerous obligations.[2] It was against this backdrop of popular disenchantment with Henry III's regime that Simon de Montfort, Earl of Leicester, became involved in the baronial movement to reform the government of the realm. As his wife, Eleanor inevitably became involved in the events that unfolded in 1258–9.

At a parliament held at Westminster in April and May 1258, a group of seven magnates, including the Earl of Leicester, banded together and met the king, head-on, with demands to expel the aliens, especially the king's detested half-brothers, and create a committee of twenty-four to overhaul royal government.[3] Left with little choice other than to acquiesce, Henry III consented to the appointment of the committee, drawn from twelve royalists and twelve baronial supporters, which met at the Oxford parliament in June 1258.[4] Earl Simon's position on the committee ensured that its remit addressed two matters close to his heart and that of his wife: first, the issue of whether their annual fee of £400 that they had secured in 1253 ought to be replaced with land, and second, the settlement of outstanding debts now owed to the Montforts by the crown.[5] This was rather surprising business, perhaps, for a committee concerned with a nationwide programme of governmental reform.

It remains frustratingly unclear just what feelings Countess Eleanor harboured about the reforming mantle that her husband assumed in the late 1250s. There are signs that she supported her husband's actions. An awareness on her part that some of the Leicesters' servants were vulnerable to the money-raising initiatives employed by the crown is, for example, suggested by her activities at this time. In 1256, the king decreed that all persons in possession of lands worth £15 per annum or over should be compelled to become knights, and thereby become liable to hold a range of unsalaried offices in local government.[6] It is striking that it was Eleanor, and not her husband, who in June 1257 secured exemption (or respite) from knighthood for the Northamptonshire landholder William de Torvyle.[7] Furthermore, as a woman who had had recourse to the financial services of the Jews, Eleanor might have felt sympathy for other Jewish debtors who now found themselves in more straightened financial circumstances. Eleanor's involvement in politics in the era of reform raises intriguing questions about her role on both the national and international stage.

THE TREATY OF PARIS

As Maddicott observed, 'the most important external issue confronting both the king and barons in 1258' was that of concluding, successfully, a critical series of negotiations with the king of France for a permanent Anglo-French peace.[8] This peace was intended to end the years of fighting punctuated by truces which had shaped Anglo-French relations since the loss of Normandy, Anjou, Maine and Touraine under King John.[9] Under its terms, Henry III prepared to surrender all his claims in his dynasty's former continental possessions to King Louis IX, who, through marriage to Margaret of Provence, was Henry III's brother-in-law. In return, Louis allowed Henry to retain Gascony as a fief of the French crown. As a native French man with strong family ties to the English court and contacts at the French court, it was, perhaps, inevitable that Simon de Montfort served as Henry III's agent at various stages in the negotiations. Henry's decision to employ Simon in this capacity at a time when the earl was disenchanted with him was, at best, naive, and provided the earl and his wife with a perfect opportunity to secure leverage over the English crown.[10]

One of the remaining obstacles to the successful conclusion of the treaty in 1258 was Louis IX's demand that Henry III's surviving siblings, Richard, Earl of Cornwall and King of the Romans,[11] and Eleanor, Countess of Leicester, should resign their claims to the same territories.[12] In May that year, Henry III wrote to the French king to reassure him that he would do as much as was in his power to persuade his brother and sister to meet these terms. He even appointed Eleanor's husband as one of his proctors in this matter.[13] Yet Earl Simon might well have been, as Henry himself later claimed, directly responsible for persuading the French king to seek Eleanor's resignation of their rights. Among the charges subsequently brought against Simon by the English king at a later trial in 1260 was the accusation that 'the earl, both personally and through his agents, arranged and caused to be arranged, and put it into the mind of the king of France, that renunciation should be asked from the countess and her children'.[14] Admittedly, the earl rebuffed this charge, but it is easy to understand why Henry III suspected his brother-in-law of duplicity. It was certainly curious, as the English king observed, that no mention was made during the negotiations of the comparable rights of Henry III's daughters, those of Richard of Cornwall's second son, and those of the children of Isabella the Empress, all of whom might have been considered alternative claimants to the former Angevin dominions.[15] Although Earl Simon rigorously denied it, Louis's decision to prioritize Richard's and Eleanor's claims might well have originated in the machinations of the Montforts.

Admittedly, it is not clear just how far Eleanor was implicated in all of this, but it seems likely that, at the very least, she endorsed Earl Simon's activities. After all, the enduring strength of the couple's marriage and the high esteem in which Simon held his wife at this time was demonstrated when, on 1 January 1259, Simon de Montfort's eldest son, Henry, drafted his father's will. In this document, Simon announced his decision to make Eleanor his chief executor in the event of his death. In a personal note, he urged Eleanor to act as his attorney in settling his affairs 'in such a way as a good lady ought to do for her lord who trusts in her'.[16] Eleanor's appearance in this document is a strong indication of her husband's belief in her capabilities; it also implies recognition, on Simon's part, that Eleanor shared his personal, political and spiritual objectives to a sufficient degree for him to entrust her with overseeing his posthumous bequests.[17]

The question of Eleanor's rights in the continental possessions claimed by Louis of France under the terms of the so-called Treaty of Paris placed the Countess of Leicester firmly at the centre of events. Earl Simon was in France in May and early June 1258, and again between November 1258 and February 1259.[18] The peace settlement and the Montforts' personal, financial grievances against the English crown became intertwined when the couple refused to renounce Eleanor's claims to her natal family's continental possessions in a blatant attempt to obstruct the Anglo-French talks.[19] It was a measure of Eleanor's strength of character and her obstinacy that she stood firm in the face of mounting pressure to acquiesce to her brother's wishes. At his trial in July 1260, Earl Simon remembered how:

> he was not in England when the countess was asked for the renunciation, and that the countess was unwilling to make it until the king had assigned the land to her as he had agreed. And the earl says that the countess showed the king that she was not bound to make the renunciation of her hereditary right unless she received compensation.[20]

The land in question on this occasion related to the £400 fee settled on the couple in 1253.[21]

In February 1259, Richard of Cornwall and his eldest son, Henry, followed by the king's younger son, Edmund, all formally renounced their rights in Normandy, Anjou, Touraine, Maine and Poitou. Henry III surrendered his own claims on 24 February.[22] All that now remained was for the king's eldest son, the Lord Edward, and for Eleanor and Simon to follow suit. Edward reluctantly conceded in May, but the Montforts held out.[23] Chief among the stumbling blocks that Henry encountered in seeking to secure their co-operation was Eleanor's Marshal dower. Hence a royal order issued on 10 March 1259, whereby Henry announced that he intended to send Earl Simon to France in the company of Peter of Savoy, Richard de Clare, Earl of Gloucester, John Mansel and Robert Walerand. Henry assigned Simon's companions the express task of making peace with the Montforts in their actions against the crown, including that touching Eleanor's dower.[24] In 1260, the king later recalled 'that the earl [of Leicester] granted by his letter that he would make his wife and his children make the renunciation if the king paid to the countess what he owed her, and made good the wrongs done to her if he had done any'.[25] The earl, for his part, recollected that 'the king put himself on arbitration regarding the countess's dower in Ireland'.[26]

Eleanor and Simon's obstinacy and their sheer determination to press home their own interests proved an effective, if not insurmountable, obstacle to Anglo-French talks: the Montforts' refusal to renounce their rights delayed the ratification of the Treaty of Paris for nine months.[27] Yet their actions came at a high political price, as not only did their behaviour sour relations irrevocably between Eleanor and her brother, but their tactics drew criticism from members of the English baronage. Matthew Paris recounts a dramatic episode that took place in 1259, in which he placed the blame for the breakdown in friendly relations between Earl Simon and Richard de Clare, a fellow reformer and negotiator, squarely on Eleanor's refusal to resign her rights in Normandy. Richard and the Earl of Leicester argued so violently that they had to be physically restrained.[28]

Faced with the Montforts' intransigence, Henry III's hand was forced into making a series of concessions to Earl Simon that were clearly intended to purchase his youngest sister's co-operation. In May 1259, the king ordered that the earl was to be repaid the money that he had expended in the crown's service in Gascony, and Simon and his wife were subsequently granted nine English manors 'in tenancy' to replace the £400 fee.[29] More than a hint of Henry III's mounting annoyance at the couple's and, in particular, at Eleanor's behaviour was betrayed by another royal directive issued on 20 May 1259: the king instructed Simon's fellow negotiators, who now numbered John de Balliol among their ranks, that if Eleanor continued to refuse to resign her rights, they were to find another way to satisfy the king of France.[30] On the same day, the English king wrote to Louis, describing how, in the presence of the great men of his realm in London, he had offered to submit himself to an award negotiated on his behalf at Saint-Germain-des-Prés in France and give security to his sister that he would honour this intention. This was all to no avail – Eleanor still declined to fall in with his plans.[31]

On 24 May 1259, as a result of intensive discussions to which Eleanor and Simon were both party, Henry III empowered Richard, Peter, John de Balliol, John Mansel and Robert to make an award provided that they examined the Montforts' claim that the king had used force to persuade Eleanor to make peace with William Marshal junior's heirs.[32] The matter of whether Eleanor had been in the king's power and authority when she accepted an annual cash sum in place of her Irish dower had, of course, already been raised in the late 1240s.[33] The Montforts' decision to resurrect this earlier accusation on an international stage betrays the level of resentment harboured by the couple towards the English crown. Once more, the king of France was kept closely abreast of matters in this intensely personal, and now increasingly bitter, family dispute between Henry III and the Montforts. When, on the same day, the English king informed Louis that he had personally authorized the payment of all debts owed to the earl and countess by the English crown,[34] it seemed as though the Montforts' gamble had finally paid off.

Yet the matter of Eleanor's dower refused to go away. Eager to secure a new valuation of Eleanor's dower and a new assignment, the couple pushed for further concessions. On 26 June, news arrived in England from Henry's agents at the French court that Eleanor had agreed to a settlement.[35] Spurred into action, Henry III's officials worked hard to secure the Treaty's ratification in July, only to have their ambitions thwarted yet again by those of Eleanor and her husband.[36] Simon and Eleanor now demanded that the king should pay what the Montforts considered to be the true value of Eleanor's dower in Ireland and Wales – 2,000 marks per annum. The couple also demanded that the crown should compensate them for twenty-six years' worth in arrears, an impossibly large sum for a cash-strapped English king to pay, let alone collect from the Marshal co-heirs.[37] The couple had overstepped the mark and overplayed their hand. In the face of their inflexibility, Henry III was left with no other alternative but to negotiate the Treaty of Paris around them. When, in October 1259, Earl Simon returned to England he had no other choice but to consent to an amended form of the Anglo-French treaty that the French king had finally approved and which omitted all mention of Eleanor's rights.[38] Outmanoeuvred, Earl Simon demanded Eleanor's share of the former Angevin lands in parliament before the representatives of the French crown.[39] When, on 24 November 1259, Henry III finally visited Paris to ratify the Treaty, Earl Simon again managed to delay proceedings for at least another eight days. It was finally agreed on 3 December 1259 at Saint-Germain-des-Prés that 15,000 marks which Louis was supposed to pay to Henry under the Treaty's terms were to remain in the French king's hands until the quarrels between the Montforts and the English crown were resolved. Henry III promised to settle these differences within the next two years.[40] In the short term, this change of tact worked well for the English crown; Countess Eleanor fell in with Henry III's wishes. On 4 December 1259, the Countess of Leicester renounced her claim to the Angevin lands before Earl Simon, King Henry and King Louis and their respective courts, and the Treaty of Paris was published.[41]

The deal that Henry III brokered with Louis in December 1259 marked the beginning of renewed attempts to settle the issue of Eleanor's dower. In reality, and much to the Montforts' frustration, this new arrangement achieved little. A year passed before the English king gave serious consideration to the Montforts' grievances. On 7 January 1261 and again on 11 January 1261, Henry III issued letters in which he promised to submit to the arbitration of the king of France, or to that of Queen Margaret or of Peter the Chamberlain.[42] On 14 March 1261, the king again expressed his willingness to submit his quarrels with Earl Simon and Countess Eleanor to the French king's judgement, and secured the earl's agreement, presumably with the support of his wife, to do the same.[43] With the matter still progressing slowly, two new teams of negotiators were appointed on 5 July 1261 – Philip Basset, the royal justiciar, and John Mansel, treasurer of York, for the king and Walter de Cantilupe, Bishop of Worcester, and Peter de Montfort for the Earl and Countess of Leicester. On this occasion the Duke of Burgundy and Peter the Chamberlain were appointed as intermediaries.[44] When, however, the duke and Peter the Chamberlain refused to act, Henry III wrote to Louis IX, requesting that Queen Margaret might become involved.[45] The fast-moving political events in England, however, meant that matters had still yet to reach a satisfactory conclusion in 1263.[46]

If controversy over Eleanor's refusal to renounce her rights had placed her and her husband at the centre of Anglo-French negotiations, it remains difficult to trace her movements with any precision during the months preceding the final ratification of the Treaty of Paris in December 1259. Although it is likely that she accompanied her husband in England and France, the couple also experienced time apart. In August 1259, for example, it was Simon alone who paid a brief visit to Archbishop Odo Rigaud of Rouen, one of the chief French intermediaries, in a break from the talks.[47] When in England, Eleanor's formal attendance was not presumably required, as a woman, at the great councils or parliaments of this time. Nevertheless, there is good reason to believe that, even if her gender prevented her from attending these meetings, she was familiar with much of the business discussed there. In July 1259, for example, Eleanor apparently secured royal assistance for Thomas of Ash, a Kent landholder who was heavily indebted to the Jews. 'At the instance of the countess of Leicester', the king ordered a survey to be made of Thomas's lands and tenements, a move that brought Thomas a temporary respite from repaying his Jewish debts.[48] Eleanor was almost certainly at court again when Simon attended the Westminster parliament of October 1259. The affairs of this parliament were dominated by the publication of the Provisions of Westminster, a series of wide-ranging legal and administrative measures intended to reform the government of the realm.[49] On 15 October, just two days into this reform-dominated parliament, the reformer and justiciar, Hugh Bigod, authorized a royal pardon for Ralph de Burstal, a man who had killed in self-defence 'at the instance of Eleanor, countess of Leicester, the king's sister'.[50] Ralph's pardon was issued on the same day that Simon entered into a momentous agreement with the Lord Edward to uphold the reform movement and secure his aid to enforce support for the settlement of Eleanor's dower.[51] On 12 November 1259, when the royal court visited Canterbury en route to the Kent coast, Henry III turned his attention once more to the Jewish debtor Thomas of Ash. On this occasion, Henry III, who was keen to encourage his youngest sister's cooperation – whatever their personal differences – before they reached Paris, again conceded that Thomas's lands and tenements should be surveyed and valued, so that Thomas's lot might be alleviated further by paying a reasonable fine at reasonable terms.[52]

THE FORTUNES OF THE REFORM MOVEMENT

The years that immediately followed the Treaty of Paris were of momentous political importance for Eleanor, her husband and their eldest sons, who were now approaching adulthood. The events of these years in England and France are well known and need recounting only briefly here. After the ratification of the Treaty, Simon de Montfort travelled to Normandy and then to England, where he arrived in January 1260. The English king, however, delayed his return from France until April. Relations between the king and the reformers fractured further, so that when parliament gathered in London, both the Earl of Leicester and the Earl of Gloucester, with whom Montfort was at odds, arrived with armed retinues. Countess Eleanor's other brother, Richard of Cornwall, stepped in to act as a mediator. It was Richard who, in May 1260, secured an important political victory for the royalists when he persuaded the Lord Edward, Eleanor's nephew and Henry III's heir, to break with the Montforts and return to his father's side. It was a measure of the resentment that the king now felt towards the Montforts that he attempted to bring his brother-in-law to trial in the summer of 1260.

Relations between the king and the Montforts softened in the autumn of 1260; Henry and Simon, the Montforts' two oldest sons, were among the young men who were knighted by the Lord Edward during the court celebrations that marked the feast of St Edward the Confessor (13 October). The king's overarching concern, however, to revoke the Provisions of Oxford, the key piece of reforming legislation of 1258, finally paid off. In April 1261, his agent at the papal curia secured a bull which revoked the Provisions and paved the way for the king to recover power. One result of the rapidly changing political situation was Simon and Eleanor's decision to leave England and, in effect, enter exile in France during the early autumn of 1261, a little while after the Earl of Gloucester deserted the reformers for the king's party. The Montforts were to remain in France until late April 1263. Henry himself followed Earl Simon to France in the summer of 1262, where he amassed evidence to support his charges against the Earl of Leicester. This leant further impetus to the quarrel between the English king and the Montforts, greatly diminishing the chance of a settlement between them; the attempts of Louis IX at arbitration ultimately proved to be fruitless.[53]

The Earl of Leicester's return to England in April 1263 was apparently prompted by a visit from a delegation of English magnates, who sought his help to aid the reformers. Following a secret meeting of the king's chief opponents at Oxford, at which the reformers renewed their commitment to the Provisions of Oxford, Earl Simon assumed the leading mantle of the reform movement. It was Simon who headed the baronial sympathizers in opposition to the king in May, after which the quarrel between Henry and the barons erupted into violence. By June the Earl of Leicester had assumed control of the baronial army in the west, whence he proceeded to advance on Henry III in London. En route to London, Simon secured Kent, where Eleanor held a small collection of dower properties, and, in particular, the royal castle of Dover, in order to prevent Henry III from fleeing abroad. Fragile peace terms were agreed between the warring factions, but the Lord Edward subsequently stirred up trouble for the reformers; Henry III, for his part, remained in regular contact with Louis IX in France. It was the French king who summoned the English king and his baronial opponents to the French court later in the summer, in an unsuccessful attempt to settle their differences.

In December 1263 Henry III broke the truce between the two sides by laying siege to Dover Castle. At this point, Louis IX stepped in, once more, in an attempt to manufacture a peace settlement. In late December a party of baronial supporters, which included the Montforts' oldest son, Henry, but not Earl Simon, who was then recovering from a broken leg, departed for France, where both sides presented their complaints against the other. In the Mise of Amiens, issued on 23 January 1264, Louis IX made his judgement against the barons and roundly condemned the Provisions of Oxford. During the spring of 1264, England descended into civil war, as the royalists and baronial sympathizers vied to take control of key castles and ports. On 5 April 1264, Henry secured a significant victory for the royalists when he captured the town and castle of Northampton from the Montfortians. It was, however, the king's own defeat and capture at the battle of Lewes on 14 May that changed Simon and Eleanor's fortunes most dramatically. In one fell swoop, the Earl of Leicester and his supporters effectively secured control of royal government and Henry III was reduced to a mere cipher as a captive in their hands. The Mise of Lewes, an agreement hammered out between the two sides on 14–15 May, helped to secure the persons of the Lord Edward, Henry III's eldest son and heir, and Henry of Almain, Richard of Cornwall's eldest son and heir, who surrendered themselves as hostages on behalf of their fathers; Richard of Cornwall had also fallen prisoner to the barons at Lewes.[54]

ELEANOR, 1260–3

So what was Eleanor de Montfort's role in all these events? For much of the early 1260s, Eleanor was active in France, alongside her husband, where she pushed for the further enrichment of her family by pursuing a claim to a share of her mother's inheritance in Angoulême. In September 1242, Henry III had, at his mother's behest, renounced all his rights in Angoulême, and promised that Richard of Cornwall and Eleanor would follow suit.[55] Eleanor, who had not resigned her claims, seized upon the opportunity in the latter part of 1260 to sue her Lusignan half-brothers, Geoffrey and Guy de Lusignan and William de Valence, as well as her nephew Hugh (XII), Count of La Marche, for a share of her mother's lands.[56] There was certainly little love lost between the Montforts and the Lusignans. Furthermore, as Margaret Labarge astutely observed, Eleanor might well have looked to add to the Montforts' French properties in response to the difficult situation faced by Simon at the English court.[57] Following the failure of arbitration between the two sides, Eleanor and Simon pursued their case to Paris in the latter part of 1262, where they were both active in soliciting support from figures such as Louis IX's brother, Alphonse of Poitiers.[58] Although the return of William de Valence to England in 1261 had ended the countess's litigation against him, she was still in arbitration with Guy de Lusignan six years later, and her suit against Geoffrey and Hugh also failed to reach a speedy judgement.[59] In the pursuit of Eleanor's maternal rights, the earl and countess were partners in litigation. It was a measure of the value that the Montforts attached to Eleanor's claims in southern France that they continued to pursue their rights there during their self-imposed exile from England in 1262.[60] The couple's French lands offered a potential safe haven from their troubles in England, should their relationship with the English king breakdown irrevocably.

When the couple visited England in 1263, Eleanor's attendance at the English royal court was expected in spite of the highly charged political climate. A letter of safe conduct issued at St Paul's Cathedral in London on 16 June 1263 made provision for Simon, in the company of Eleanor and their children, to visit the king, provided that they came without arms.[61] The timing of this safe conduct was significant. It was during the late spring and summer of 1263 that Montfort strengthened his position at the head of the reform movement, against a background of mounting violence towards prominent royalists.[62] The king's safe conduct should be seen as part of his wider and, ultimately unsuccessful, attempts to curb the growing disorder, which found expression in a whole series of royal letters issued between 12 and 15 June, appointing new castellans and military commanders in the northern and south-eastern counties, and reissuing the earlier Provisions of Westminster as a sop to his critics.[63] His inclusion of Eleanor and her children in the safe conduct reflected Eleanor's importance as Henry's sister and as the crucial familial link between the king and the earl. In spite of the impact of Eleanor's intransigence on the progress of the Treaty of Paris, and in spite of the bitterness that Henry III clearly harboured towards Earl Simon as one of the architects and subsequent enforcers of the Provisions of Oxford, the king retained at least a vestige of outward respect for his youngest sister.

AFTER LEWES

In the aftermath of the battle of Lewes in May 1264, Eleanor de Montfort, Countess of Leicester, was pre-eminent in status among the highborn women who remained in England. Henry III's queen, Eleanor of Provence, was overseas, and Eleanor of Castile, the young bride of the Lord Edward, was in Montfortian hands. The countess was soon to prove adept at safeguarding and promoting her own, as well as her husband's and children's, interests.[64] It was a measure of Eleanor's close relationship with her husband, as well as her competence in estate and household administration, that the most important royal captives after the king spent time, so the London annalist observed, 'under the custody of the countess of Leicester' at Wallingford Castle in Berkshire.[65] First, Eleanor's nephew, the Lord Edward, was transferred in May from Dover Castle in Kent to Wallingford, along with his cousin, Henry of Almain, Richard of Cornwall's eldest son and heir. A little later, Richard of Cornwall himself was also transferred from the Tower of London to Wallingford.[66] The royalist chronicler Thomas Wykes commented upon the harsh treatment of royalist captives at Dover, while under the guard of its recently appointed constable, Henry de Montfort.[67] Although the Lord Edward's modern biographer, Michael Prestwich, found 'no solid evidence' of Edward's poor treatment, it is curious that Earl Simon apparently decided to transfer his royal nephew from Dover into his wife's care at Wallingford, rather than into that of any of his other close supporters or kin.[68] There were, admittedly, excellent reasons for removing the Lord Edward from Dover and Richard of Cornwall from the Tower on the grounds of security. In the summer, news reached the barons that the English queen was actively recruiting mercenaries and soliciting the support of her allies – the king and queen of France, her uncle Peter of Savoy and other royalist exiles – in order to mount an invasion of England to rescue her husband.[69] The

Dunstable annalist noted the barons' efforts to fortify the English coast against this threat.[70] Dover Castle's situation on the English Channel rendered this great fortress and its royal hostages vulnerable to the queen's potential military operations. Richard of Cornwall's residence in London, the kingdom's capital, might have left him similarly exposed should an invasion force land in the south east.

There might also have been other more personal reasons for transferring the Lord Edward, Henry of Almain and Richard of Cornwall into his wife's care. Simon needed to ensure that his most important captives, the men at the core of the royalist party who were closely related to Henry by blood, were held by someone who had the interests of the Montforts and of the baronial reformers at heart, and by someone whom the earl could implicitly trust. His wife was the ideal candidate. It is not inconceivable that news had reached Eleanor's ears about the treatment meted out by her eldest son and others to the royal captives and hostages. In spite of the grievances between Eleanor, her husband and the king, the countess might well have wished to ameliorate the discomfort of her captive kin, perhaps regarding it as her Christian duty to do so, and repay their past kindnesses to her. This might explain Earl Simon's decision to transfer into her care her other brother, Richard of Cornwall, the previous holder of Wallingford.[71] After all, by virtue of her position as a wife and hostess, not to mention her status as the king's sister, she was ideally placed to provide for her husband's reluctant 'guests'. It is possible that Eleanor requested or suggested that one or more of her kinsmen be placed in her charge.[72]

Admittedly, the captives' time at Wallingford was short lived. By the end of July, the Lord Edward and Henry of Alamain had been transferred to Kenilworth Castle.[73] Although the royal hostages were moved around during the summer and autumn 1264 – Henry of Almain, for instance, undertook a brief diplomatic mission to France in September before returning to captivity at Dover – Edward, Henry and Richard were all at Wallingford again later that year.[74] They were there in November when an attempt was made by the Lord Edward's followers to free him from Montfortian custody. As a direct result of this, the Earl of Leicester determined to move all three men to the greater security afforded by Kenilworth Castle. According to the chronicler Robert of Gloucester, Countess Eleanor might well have accompanied the captives there.[75]

Mindful of her obligations to reward those persons loyal to her family, Eleanor's activities in 1264–5 extended beyond the care of royal hostages and captives. Her husband's military success did much to resolve the couple's financial woes. The matter of Eleanor's Marshal dower looked like it might be resolved. On 18 November 1264, some of the Montfort's closest political allies and supporters, namely Walter de Cantilupe, Bishop of Worcester, Henry of

Sandwich, Bishop of London, Hugh Despenser, the justiciar, and Peter de Montfort, were appointed to a commission to investigate the case of Eleanor's Irish and Welsh Marshal dower, which had, so it was claimed, long been detained from her by the king. The commissioners were empowered to assign Eleanor her dower and ensure that she received due reparation for her losses.[76] The countess also secured profitable royal grants of properties and rights for men and women in her service. In December 1264, John of Havering, a yeoman of the countess, who was either the son or another relation of Richard of Havering, was awarded the wardships and marriages of the heirs and lands of Richard of Arden.[77] On 13 June 1265, royal letters issued at Hereford recorded that the services and customs of Christiana of Odiham, an unfree tenant of the Countess of Leicester, had been valued at 14s. 4d. a year, and that henceforth Christiana and her heirs were to be quit of all customs and services and were to pay an annual rent instead. The scribe who drew up the letters carefully noted that this grant had been made with the assent of both the Earl and Countess of Leicester in special recognition of Christiana's long service to Eleanor.[78]

As an experienced political operator, one cannot help but suspect that Eleanor also endorsed Simon's efforts to enrich their sons through grants of lands and offices across southern England. In the aftermath of Lewes, Earl Simon's role as leader of the baronial party allowed him to place his sons and his closest supporters in the key offices of royal government, and to profit from the estates confiscated from their defeated royalist opponents, including those of Richard of Cornwall.[79] Some of the Montforts' tactics were more than a little dubious in their execution. Their second son, Simon junior, resorted to a series of underhand measures to seize the Sussex lands of William de Briouze, a royalist who had attacked Simon junior's estate at Sedgwick.[80] Simon junior's stratagem involved a substantial claim for damages against Briouze in a court packed with Simon junior's sympathizers, including his older brother, Henry. Until Briouze paid up, the younger Simon retained custody of both Briouze's lands and his young son and heir, also named William.[81] A year later, Simon junior's mother was in charge of her son's hostage, providing for his maintenance and making payments to his groom and to Isabella his nurse.[82] Since Simon junior was unmarried, it was perhaps only fitting that his mother should care for young William. Even so, Eleanor's involvement raises the possibility of an element of complicity in her son's plans. Eleanor might also not have been entirely in the dark about the matrimonial ambitions Simon junior harboured towards Isabella de Forz, Countess of Devon and lady of the Isle of Wight. It is solely down to the chance survival of Eleanor's household accounts for 1265, which are discussed in the next chapter, that we know that she exchanged letters with Isabella, a wealthy young widow with baronial sympathies, throughout the spring of 1265 and entertained her at Odiham in April.[83] Earl Simon sold the royal rights to Isabella's remarriage to Simon junior during the summer of 1265 and, in a later lawsuit, Isabella claimed that she had been the victim of an attempted abduction by Simon junior, which forced her to seek refuge in Wales.[84] If Isabella's later claim can be trusted, one wonders whether Eleanor once again had a hand in encouraging her son.

8

1265

'the conflict of Evesham'[1]

In April 1267, Henry III wrote to the sheriff of Northamptonshire, ordering him to restore the lands confiscated from William de St Philibert, a former rebel, during the recent disturbances within the realm. These disturbances, the letter recalled, had drawn to a partial close after the battle of Evesham in 1265 with an 'ordinance and form of peace' made at Dover Castle between the Lord Edward, the king's eldest son, and Eleanor de Montfort, Countess of Leicester, widow of his fallen opponent Earl Simon.[2] This fairly innocuous phrasing concealed the full horror for the Montfort family and their supporters of the disastrous events of that year. If the Montforts' fortunes had been riding high after their success at Lewes in 1264, the summer of 1265 was nothing short of disastrous for Eleanor, Earl Simon and their children. Within the space of less than three months, between late May and the beginning of August, Eleanor witnessed Earl Simon's hold on government slip away, following the Lord Edward's dramatic escape from Montfortian custody at Hereford, his rapprochement with Gilbert de Clare, the new Earl of Gloucester, and the rapid collapse of the Montfortian regime in the Welsh Marches.[3] The resurgence in royalist fortunes culminated in a pitched battle at Evesham on 4 August 1265, where many Montfortians were slain, including Eleanor's husband and her eldest son.[4] In December 1264, Eleanor presided over her husband's splendid Christmas court at Kenilworth; by December 1265 she was a widow in exile in France.[5]

An invaluable insight into Eleanor's role in 1265 and her response to her family's changing political fortunes is provided by a large fragment of her household accounts for this year (British Library, Additional MS 8877), the only household roll of Eleanor's or Simon's that has survived down to the present day. Eleanor's household roll was preserved until the early nineteenth century in the archives of the Dominican nunnery of Montargis in France that she entered in widowhood. It is an important source not only in terms of its chronological coverage, but also by virtue of the fact that it is one of the earliest surviving private household accounts from England and it was produced for a woman.[6] The thirteen extant membranes, carefully compiled by Eleanor's clerks Christopher and Eudes, and possibly another, illuminate the functioning of the Montforts' domestic establishment at a critical stage in the Barons' War. They itemize the day-to-day expenses of the countess's household from 19 February to 29 August 1265 on the face, detailing Eleanor's place of residence, the names of visitors she received and the household's provisioning, including the numbers of horses for whom fodder and hay had to be found. Lists of wages and other miscellaneous expenses, including messenger accounts covering the period up to 1 October, appear on the dorse. This chapter offers a fresh appraisal of these accounts and the light that they shed on Eleanor's activities in 1265.

THE MONTFORT HOUSEHOLD IN 1265

Eleanor's household roll indicates that she spent most of 1265, apart from a brief visit in March,[7] separated from her husband, Earl Simon, who was preoccupied with the Hilary parliament and with later developments in the Welsh Marches. In the meantime, the Countess of Leicester presided over her own domestic establishment, which had 207 people present on average, including household officers, servants, guests and poor, and which was, in common with other great households of her day, a peripatetic institution.[8] For much of February, Eleanor stayed at Wallingford Castle, then in Montfortian hands, before moving later in the month to Odiham Castle via Reading in Berkshire at a relatively leisurely pace of fifteen miles a day.[9] The countess remained there throughout the spring until news of the Lord Edward's escape uprooted the household again.[10]

In view of Eleanor's attendance behind the scenes at earlier councils and parliaments in the reign, it is curious that she did not accompany the earl to the Hilary parliament. This was the longest of all the reforming parliaments and sat from 20 January until the middle of March 1265, discussing, amongst other weighty matters, the arrangements for the relaxation of the Lord Edward's custody.[11] Now that the aggrandizement of her husband and sons had alleviated her family's financial predicament, perhaps Eleanor felt that there was little to be gained by accompanying her husband there in person.

Another far more compelling explanation for Eleanor's absence from these proceedings is that she was already fulfilling an important role for her family at Wallingford and Odiham. Eleanor's residence at these castles during these months might arguably, as her later entertainment Isabella de Forz, an important local landowner,[12] suggests, have helped to strengthen her husband's political position in the south. Odiham, after all, was located in the heart of southern England. Eleanor's presence there made sound strategic sense within the context of her sons' recently acquired lands and offices. It meant that she resided, geographically, at the centre of a recently formed Montfortian network of influence, which stretched, if at times somewhat shakily, across southern England. In the south east, her eldest son, Henry, was constable of the royal castle of Dover and warden of the Cinque Ports.[13] Simon junior, Eleanor's second son, was constable of Portchester Castle in Hampshire,[14] and active in Surrey and Sussex.[15] Meanwhile, in the south west, Eleanor's fourth son, Guy, enjoyed custody of Richard of Cornwall's lands in Devon and Cornwall,[16] while her third son, Amaury, who was forging a career in the church, had been awarded the rectory of St Wendron (Cornwall), one of the wealthiest benefices in this region and formerly in Richard's gift.[17] In the midst of this Montfortian sea, and in Earl Simon's absence, there was no one better placed than Eleanor as a wife and mother to act as an intermediary and communication point for her family.

Eleanor's household accounts confirm that she maintained contact, via letters and messengers, throughout the spring with her husband, who, on one occasion, thoughtfully sent her a gift of porpoise for her table.[18] Furthermore, Eleanor's absence from proceedings at Westminster might not necessarily have inhibited her talents as an intermediary; her accounts reveal that the countess sent letters to the Lord Edward on 25 February.[19] Earl Simon's first action when the Hilary parliament dispersed was to set out immediately for his wife's residence at Odiham, where he arrived on 19 March for a family conference.[20] His arrival was preceded, two days earlier, by that of the Lord Edward and one of Richard of Cornwall's sons, escorted by the Montforts' eldest son, Henry.[21] Another son, Guy, had reached Odiham on 13 March.[22] Something of the scale of this conference and the hospitality that Eleanor was expected to provide emerges from her household roll. The number of horses in Eleanor's stable, all of whom were provided with hay from the castle stores, rose from 44 to 172 with the arrival of Henry and her nephews, and from 172 to 334 with the coming of the earl.[23] On the same day (17 March) that the Lord Edward arrived, the enlarged household consumed no fewer than 1,000 herrings, and the countess felt compelled to purchase no fewer than 1,000 dishes, presumably for the use of her newly arrived guests and their entourages.[24] It was clearly no small undertaking to house and feed the retinues of the visiting nobles.

Eleanor's central importance within the Montfort family, her continuing concern for the welfare of her sons, and her personal interest in their wider affairs was reflected elsewhere in her accounts. They firmly reinforce the impression that Eleanor enjoyed a particularly close bond of affection with Simon junior, a bond that undoubtedly holds the key to Simon's subsequent actions later that summer. On 6 April, for example, a few days after the earl's departure from Odiham, and again on 14 April, Eleanor dispatched letters to her second son, who had been engaged since the previous year in the siege of Pevensey Castle.[25] Admittedly, in the absence of any payments to messengers received from him in the interim, we cannot help wondering whether, on this occasion, Simon junior had been perhaps a little tardy in replying to Eleanor's missives. This son was back in touch by 30 April when his messenger received 12d. for conveying his master's news to the countess.[26] It was subsequently to Simon junior whom Eleanor turned for an escort in her flight across southern England in June 1265 after the Lord Edward's escape, thereby temporarily diverting this son from moving directly to assist his father against the resurgent royalists in the Welsh Marches.[27]

ELEANOR'S WIDER CONTACTS

Eleanor's household accounts are revealing not only of the personal support that she lent her husband and sons, but also of her role, more generally, in underpinning the Montfortian regime. They suggest that Eleanor was instrumental in upholding her family's position by fostering a range of contacts, many of whom were Montfortian sympathizers. During the seven months covered by the extant roll, she received more than fifty visitors[28] and sent numerous letters and messengers to a whole host of other people. She corresponded, for example, with Margaret de Lacy, the widowed Countess of Lincoln whose manor of Caversham was situated just fifteen miles from Odiham.[29] Margaret had enjoyed close dealings with the Montforts in the recent past: the Countess of Lincoln was Eleanor's sister-in-law through her second marriage to Walter Marshal and Earl Simon had helped to negotiate the marriage of Margaret's grandson in 1256.[30] Eleanor communicated with Margaret's daughter, Matilda de Clare, the dowager Countess of Gloucester.[31] On 12 and 13 March, another lady, Margery de Crek, the widow of a former servant of William Marshal junior, enjoyed the Countess of Leicester's hospitality, accompanied by her retinue of twelve horses.[32] Eleanor similarly entertained the Countess of Oxford and her somewhat larger retinue of twenty-one horses on 20 May, sending her away with a gift of wine when she departed on the following day.[33] This countess's husband, Robert de Vere, was a loyal adherent of Earl Simon and was among the Montfortians who were later captured at Kenilworth.[34]

There were other women who visited Eleanor or who were recipients of her favour: ladies such as Lady Catherine Lovel, the widow of John Lovel and sister of the royalist Philip Basset,[35] and the lady of Mauley, who was possibly Joan, the widow of Peter de Maule and daughter of Peter de Brus, the sixth lord of Skelton in Yorkshire.[36] At the beginning of August, Eleanor paid for the expenses incurred by her younger son, Amaury, in sending letters to the wife of Hugh Despenser, the baronial justiciar.[37] Overall, it is hard not to be impressed by the number and social standing of Eleanor's female acquaintances. Perhaps some of these women were petitioners who hoped, through Eleanor, to secure Earl Simon's and his sons' influence or allay possible concerns about the direction of their loyalties. It is certainly striking that on the same day (30 April) that the countess paid a messenger whom she had received from Lady Margery de Crek, another groom was dispatched by the countess from Odiham to Simon junior at Pevensey 'for the business of the said lady'.[38]

Women religious visited Eleanor and sought her aid. Not only did the Prioress of Amesbury in Wiltshire, a house with strong royal connections, enjoy Eleanor's hospitality at Odiham,[39] but it is quite possible that she secured the countess's intercession on her behalf with key figures in the Montfortian government. The record of a payment made by Eleanor to the prioress's messenger on 13 April was immediately followed in Eleanor's household roll by another note, detailing further expenses the countess had incurred in dispatching letters to the chancellor and Peter de Montfort, Earl Simon's close political ally, on the prioress's behalf.[40] Such entries offer intriguing glimpses of Eleanor's wider reputation for influence at the peak of her husband's political career.

Amesbury was not the only female religious community that came within Eleanor's orbit during the spring of 1265. Eleanor's accounts record a one-off payment of 6s. 8d. to Avicia de Fauconberg, a nun at the Benedictine abbey of Wherwell in Hampshire, who was possibly a member of the Fauconberg family, the lords of Rise in Holderness (Yorkshire), and a relation of Eleanor's knight, Walter de Fauconberg.[41] The prioress and nuns of Wintney in Hampshire, a Cistercian house situated approximately five miles from Odiham, often dined with the countess; Eleanor made their prioress regular gifts of wine and at Easter commissioned from them a cope for a priest.[42] Although Eleanor's generosity to these nuns might have accorded well with her spiritual interests and responsibilities as a local religious benefactor, the ties fostered through such relationships proved invaluable to her when she needed to call upon them as the events of the summer of 1265 unfolded. The prioress of Wintney later repaid Eleanor's generosity by lending her cart to aid the countess's flight to Portchester Castle when news of the Lord Edward's escape reached Eleanor.[43]

Eleanor's hospitality and the carefully measured demonstrations of generosity recorded in her accounts offer excellent examples of female networking through the domestic and gendered setting of the great household. Yet it is important to stress that men also occupied a central place within the countess's circle of influence. She communicated regularly with leading male political associates of her husband. Eleanor sent messengers, for example, to Simon's close ally Richard Gravesend, Grosseteste's successor as Bishop of Lincoln,[44] as well as entertaining Ralph, Abbot of Waverley (Surrey), the Cistercian monastery situated near Odiham long associated with Eleanor and the Montforts.[45] She apparently enjoyed cordial relations with the baronial chancellor, Thomas de Cantilupe, who had been appointed to office with her husband's backing; Eleanor sent him a gift of wine on 1 March.[46] During the summer, she corresponded with his uncle, Walter de Cantilupe, Bishop of Worcester, one of Simon's mentors and closest allies,[47] and another mutual acquaintance of the late Adam Marsh (d. 1259).[48] Eleanor also entertained her husband's tenants like Hereward de Marisco and Anketin de Martival, both of whom visited her at Odiham.[49] The manors of Hereward and his wife Rametta at Shapwick in Dorset and Chalton in Hampshire had been acquired by exchange with Earl Simon in 1255–6 in return for the barony of Embleton in Northumberland.[50] Anketin, who held the Leicestershire manor of Noseley from Earl Simon, had served as a baronial sheriff and as Earl Simon's steward in 1261.[51]

As had also been the case in 1264, some responsibility for the day-to-day care of the prisoners in Earl Simon's custody, including royal captives, fell to Eleanor. On 8 March 1265, two weeks after Eleanor's household had taken up residence at Odiham, following a sojourn at Wallingford, the royalist baron, Sir Robert de Brus of Annandale, who had been captured by her husbands' forces at Lewes, joined the countess's establishment. He was escorted there by Sir Thomas of Astley, a Warwickshire knight and Montfortian supporter who was later slain at Evesham.[52]

Various expenses were incurred by the countess throughout the spring and summer of 1265 in helping to maintain her kinsmen imprisoned in Montfortian strongholds. Her officials paid the Lord Edward's barber, both before and after the relaxation of the Lord Edward's custody as part of the settlement agreed in March 1265.[53] Eleanor sent both her brothers gifts of food and spices. During March, the countess dispatched a barrel of sturgeon and some whale meat to the king at Wallingford Castle.[54] A further 20lbs of almonds, 5lbs of rice, 2lbs of pepper, 2lbs of cinnamon, ½lb of galingale, 1lb of ginger, 2lbs of sugar and

20 pieces of whale were dispatched to her other brother, Richard of Cornwall, who was then confined at Kenilworth.[55] This was followed on 30 March 1265 by another gift of spices to Richard and, during the week of Pentecost, by yet another that comprised almonds, pepper, ginger, galingale and cloves.[56] In May, the countess's agents purchased twelve ells of high-quality ruby scarlet cloth in London for Richard's robes, together with other fine cloths, including rayed – or striped – cloth from Paris for new robes for Edmund his son.[57] Eleanor's generosity on this occasion extended to Henry III and the Lord Edward, for whom her representatives purchased hoods of the finest linen from an Italian merchant.[58] These gifts were strongly reminiscent of Henry III's earlier gifts to her of fine clothing and food,[59] and are strongly suggestive not only of Eleanor's generosity to her kin in captivity, but also of her personal concern that the captives might still enjoy some of the luxuries and clothing appropriate to their rank and dignity. There was, after all, the practical concern that Eleanor's brother and nephews would not disgrace themselves or shame the Montforts as their 'hosts' with shabby or soiled attire.[60]

The care and attention to detail suggested by Eleanor's accounts not only stand as testimony to the countess's competence as the lady of a great household, but might also have helped to make the captives' confinement a little less irksome. Such consideration possibly paid off, in political terms, when the tables were subsequently turned on Eleanor after Evesham. On 6 September 1265, Eleanor's son, Simon junior, persuaded Richard of Cornwall, prior to his release from Kenilworth, to promise that he would be a loyal friend to Eleanor, her children and their households.[61] Although Richard as Simon's hostage probably had little choice in the matter, one wonders whether his undertaking was influenced by the arrival of Wilecok, the countess's messenger, who had been sent directly by Eleanor to him four days earlier.[62] Similarly, Eleanor's earlier courtesy towards the Lord Edward might well have smoothed the path of her later negotiations with him. On 17 April 1265, her accounts refer to letters sent by her infant daughter, another Eleanor, to the Lord Edward, hinting at a rather touching and, perhaps deceptive, picture of familial harmony in view of the political climate.[63] It was, of course, with Edward that Eleanor ultimately negotiated the surrender of Dover Castle and her safe passage overseas in the autumn, having first received assurances for the safety of those in her service whom she left behind.[64] On 26 October 1265, two days before her departure to France, Edward wrote to Walter Giffard, the royal chancellor, providing him with the names of those who had been received into his favour, 'at the instance of his very dear aunt'.[65] In spite of the bitterness after Evesham, Eleanor and the Lord Edward proved capable of maintaining family appearances. What is more,

Edward apparently kept his word to Eleanor with regard to the wellbeing of her followers who remained in England. On 9 November 1265, for example, the sheriffs of Kent, Lincolnshire, Surrey, Sussex and Northamptonshire were all ordered to restore the lands of the former rebel, Sir John de la Haye, 'who was with the countess in the munition of Dover Castle'.[66]

ELEANOR AND THE WAR

During the spring of 1265, however, this still lay far in the future. The dramatic events that unfolded after the Lord Edward's escape from Hereford on 28 May can be traced within Eleanor's accounts, as can her role in the war against the resurgent royalists.[67] Their contents hint at the scale of the political crisis which engulfed her family, culminating in Evesham, widowhood and her eventual exile to France. The strength of her relationship with, and her importance to, her husband were strongly conveyed by the speed with which Earl Simon dispatched the news of Edward's flight to her at Odiham; his messengers reached her by 1 June when the countess and Simon junior left this castle in great haste, travelling by night and covering approximately forty-two miles in just one day until they reached the greater protection afforded by Portchester Castle.[68] They remained at Portchester, where Eleanor received another messenger from Earl Simon, until 11 June.[69] Here their ranks were swelled by Simon junior's men-at-arms and various supporters (the number of horses in Eleanor's stable rose dramatically from twenty-eight on 30 May[70] to eighty-four on 12 June[71]) before continuing on to the greater safety of Dover Castle, which they reached on 15 June.[72] The urgency of Eleanor's journey was demonstrated once again when her household managed to cover thirty miles a day.[73] When the countess and her son reached Dover, their combined retinue was so large that it initially proved impossible to accommodate all their followers within the castle. While Eleanor, Simon junior and their knights dined at the castle, their esquires and other followers ate in the town.[74] Simon junior's departure for London on 16/17 June, taking with him one hundred horses, considerably eased this cramped situation (and the number of horses in Eleanor's stable shrank to twenty-six).[75]

During June and July, while Earl Simon attempted to counter the Lord Edward's forces in the Welsh Marches, Eleanor presided over the castle and garrison of Dover, in the company of the acting constable, Sir John de la Haye, a man with a long history of service to Earl Simon.[76] Eleanor looked to improve the defence of the castle, purchasing arms and accommodating, at the end of July, Master William the Engineer.[77] As a domestic establishment in a time of war, the countess's household continued to function reasonably smoothly. Eleanor's accounts in the months leading up to August betray few signs of serious disruption to the functioning of Eleanor's administration, even in the fast-changing political climate of 1265. At mealtimes, the countess usually dined in the hall, at the high table, in the presence of her family and her guests, so that all who served her might thus be reminded of her authority over them.[78]

The countess's officials continued, as we might imagine they had done for many years before, to account each day for the grain, wine and other foodstuffs and victuals consumed by Eleanor, her household and her visitors. Considerate of the fact that she was a guest in her son Henry's castle at Dover and also perhaps in preparation for a siege, Eleanor kept careful records of provisions, including red wine, taken by her household from his stores.[79] At the same time, the compilers of her wardrobe accounts kept meticulous records of payments for messengers and tradesmen employed on the countess's business, as well as for various items that were purchased for the countess's own use, and that of her children, servants and supporters. In order to feed the large entourage that accompanied Eleanor to Dover in the summer of 1265, the countess's officials purchased oats, corn and wine from the nearby port of Sandwich, thirteen and a half miles away, and fish from the port of Hythe, fourteen and a half miles from Dover. They obtained further provisions from Eleanor's Kentish manor of Brabourne, situated approximately seventeen to eighteen miles from Dover.[80] On 8 July 1265, for example, the manorial reeve accounted with Eleanor for sheep with which he had supplied her household from this estate.[81] Boats were also hired to transport essential items such as peat, firewood, salt and corn to Dover.[82]

Although the identity of Eleanor's household steward remains clouded in obscurity, the surviving records preserve the names of other officials in her service. On 9 May, it was Richard of Havering, Earl Simon's steward, who made payments at Oxford on the countess's behalf for her daughter's breviary and to a chaplain for prayers on Simon junior's behalf.[83] Sir William de Wortham was another senior officer, to judge from Eleanor's frequent correspondence with him and the payments that he authorized on her behalf, recorded in her accounts.[84] Wortham, a landholder with estates in Bedfordshire, Norfolk and Suffolk, possessed long-standing connections with the Montforts and in the 1250s had also been associated with Grosseteste, their former friend.[85] His sister Hawise served as one of the Countess of Leicester's damsels in 1265 and was trusted to make payments on behalf of her mistress.[86] Sir Fulk Constable, a Yorkshire landholder who was later captured by the royalists at Kenilworth, William the clerk of Leicester and John the Scot, the countess's almoner, had all presided over the countess's offerings during Lent.[87] Fulk and John were of sufficient seniority within the countess's staff to have grooms, whose expenses in late April were also met from Eleanor's purse.[88]

Other officials, servants and agents frequently figure in Eleanor's accounts, men like Hicqe the Tailor, who often journeyed between London, Odiham, Kenilworth and Portchester on the countess's business.[89] The services of men like William the Carter, who transported food and goods from one place to another, were invaluable,[90] as were those of Petronilla, who served as the household's laundress.[91] Eleanor's regular stream of correspondence with her husband, kin, friends, acquaintances and petitioners necessitated a group of reliable messengers: Bolett,[92] Gobithest,[93] Diqon,[94] Picard,[95] Slingawai[96] and Wilecok[97] were among those who travelled constantly on their mistress's behalf. Eleanor's accounts refer to other men such as Colin the Farrier, who received a stipend from the countess,[98] S. the Cook,[99] Garbag, who served in Eleanor's kitchen at Dover,[100] Andrew the Butler and Colin the Marshal,[101] as well as various unnamed grooms who performed a variety of tasks for her.

Although, in common with other comital households, most of Eleanor's staff were men, she retained a small but significant group of women within it, as she had done in her youth.[102] In addition to Petronilla the laundress, nurses who were employed to care for Eleanor's young daughter and William de Briouze junior feature in the roll.[103] The two Eleanors, mother and daughter, enjoyed the company of a select body of damsels who saw to their personal needs and provided companionship.[104] Alongside Hawise de Wortham, a damsel by the name of Christiana de Craiwell served Eleanor and made purchases for her mistress at Dover.[105] The countess paid Christiana's expenses for undertaking a pilgrimage from Odiham to Chichester, although it remains frustratingly unclear whether this spiritual journey was at Christiana's or, in fact, Eleanor's behest.[106] The same Christiana received new shoes from the countess when the household was in residence at Dover.[107] Eleanor's responsibility for the health and welfare of her damsels is conveyed by an expense of 2s. 8d. incurred when the countess summoned a barber from Reading to bleed a damsel, who had apparently been taken ill at Odiham.[108]

The spiritual needs of Eleanor and her household were met through the services of the countess's chaplain, his assistants and John the Scot, her almoner.[109] A 'G. the chaplain' numbered among those for whom horses were borrowed during Eleanor's June flight to Dover.[110] John the Scot presided over the countess's offerings, ensuring that Eleanor as a noblewomen fulfilled her charitable responsibilities to the poor.[111] In addition to the offerings of 7s. 4d. made at Lent (22 February to 5 April in 1265),[112] he oversaw the distribution of

19s. 1d. for the period between 5 April and 8 June.[113] A more modest sum of 7s. 5d. was spent during the twenty-one days from 15 June to 5 July, and a further 7s. 5d. in the ensuing period up to 30 July.[114] During the months covered by the roll, John was provided with an average of 4d. per day for the poor, a pretty generous amount if it is borne in mind that the offerings of a churchman, Bogo de Clare (d. 1294), a notorious pluralist who was the brother of Gilbert de Clare, Earl of Gloucester, typically amounted to just 1d. on great feast days.[115] C. M. Woolgar has calculated that Eleanor maintained between fourteen to fifteen poor per day in her household in early May 1265, but it is clear, that, at other times, Eleanor provided bread for more than twenty-five paupers.[116] On 28 June, the vigil of Saints Peter and Paul, for example, Eleanor fed forty-five paupers, while on 11 July 1265, the vigil of St Benedict of Nursia, the countess fed twenty-five paupers in one day.[117] On 14 April 1265, nine days after Easter, Eleanor fed an unprecedented eight hundred poor.[118] The importance of religious observances for Eleanor's household were also reflected in its strict observance of abstinence during Lent, when meat and poultry were omitted from the daily fare, as they also were on Fridays and Saturdays, and sometimes on Wednesdays, throughout the year.[119]

Individual clergymen who visited the countess, like Richard the chaplain of Kemsing, one of Eleanor's Kentish manors, also catered for the countess's religious interests. Richard was in attendance upon his mistress at Odiham from Saturday 25 April to Saturday 9 May; upon his departure Eleanor sent him away with a gift of wine.[120] It is probable that he was the 'Richard the chaplain' who was in the service of the countess when she took up residence at Dover Castle; he was among those men who dined with her there in June.[121] Other men in religious orders who figure in Eleanor's accounts include Brother Gregory of Coventry, Brother Walter of Coventry, Brother G. Boyon, who oversaw the production of a breviary for Eleanor's daughter,[122] and Brother J. Angeli, who received personal gifts from the countess.[123] William the clerk, who was presumably in minor orders, had visited London on Eleanor's behalf at Pentecost.[124]

DOVER CASTLE

Eleanor did not wait passively for the coming storm during the summer of 1265. In an astute political manoeuvre, she turned her flight across south-eastern England and her residence at Dover Castle into an exercise in public relations for her husband's regime, especially among the Montfortian sympathizers of the Cinque Ports. Just before she arrived in Dover, for example, she entertained the burgesses of Winchelsea.[125] Once at Dover, she entertained the burgesses of Sandwich in mid June,[126] and the burgesses of both Winchelsea and Sandwich again in July.[127]

En route from Portchester to Dover, Eleanor was accompanied by Montfortian supporters, such as Sir William de Munchensy, who was later captured by the royalists at Kenilworth,[128] Sir Ingelram de Balliol, who had spent time as a prisoner of the royalists in 1264,[129] and Sir Robert Corbet, a landholder with properties in Sussex, Hampshire and Northamptonshire.[130] Although Ingelram and Robert parted company with Eleanor once she reached Wilmington Priory in Sussex, other men appeared in their places. At Dover, Sir John de Mucegros, who had served as constable of Salisbury Castle between December 1264 and 31 May 1265, dined with the countess, a little while after her arrival, in the company of Simon junior and others.[131] Once lodged at Dover, Eleanor was joined, at various points between June and August 1265, by men such as Sir Robert de Brus,[132] Sir J. of Snave, a Kentish landholder,[133] Sir Ralph Haket,[134] Sir Fulk Constable, who was with her earlier in the year,[135] Sir J. de Burton,[136] Sir Peter de Burton and his wife,[137] Master J. of London,[138] John of Dover and his wife,[139] Thomas of Sandwich, a clerk whose loyalty to the Montforts was later pardoned by the Lord Edward,[140] Sir Matthew of Hastings[141] and Master Nicholas de Hecham.[142]

In the increasingly troubled and uncertain political situation, Eleanor remained keenly appreciative of her supporters, and took care to bestow small tokens of her esteem on them. She celebrated, for example, perhaps a birthday of the son of Sir John de la Haye by purchasing gold brooches for her daughter Eleanor and her son Amaury to give to the child.[143] John was a stalwart supporter of the Montforts who, before he joined the countess at Dover, had served the Earl of Leicester at the siege of Rochester and been appointed constable of Winchelsea and Rye in 1264.[144] On 6 July, his wife received for her table half a 'beast of the chase' that had been killed during a successful hunting expedition,[145] followed later in the month by another two and a half such beasts.[146] Another 'beast of the chase' was bestowed by Eleanor upon the prior of the hospital of Dover,[147] who subsequently assisted Eleanor in the days after Evesham.[148] Sir Ralph d'Arcy and his wife, both of whom were frequent visitors to Dover, received other marks of favour from Countess Eleanor.[149] On 28 June, for example, the countess sent Ralph's wife, Philippa, a gift of wine.[150] The countess also sent wine to the wife of Thomas Saleqin on 1 July[151] and gave her part of a beast caught during a hunting expedition later that month.[152] Thomas and his wife dined with the countess at Dover Castle on 20 July[153] and Thomas dined there again on 26 July.[154] Eleanor's gift-giving and hospitality had a clear political edge. Significantly, it was also the Countess of Leicester who provided shelter and wine for messengers who arrived at Dover from the king of France that summer.[155]

In providing hospitality for her guests and in promoting her husband's regime, Eleanor and her officials made careful use of conspicuous consumption as a means of impressing upon those who visited her household the extent of her family's wealth, power and prestige. The fare served at the Countess of Leicester's table was, as Lars Kjær has recently pointed out, particularly fine when she entertained guests. Visitors to her household were often fed with venison.[156] The night before the countess arrived in Dover, the burgesses of Winchelsea were treated to a feast that included oxen, mutton, capons and geese.[157] When the countess paid host to the burgesses of Sandwich four days later (Wednesday 18 June 1265), they shared a meal with her that included plaice, bream, soles and a variety of other fish as well.[158] On Sunday 12 July 1265, another splendid feast was held at Dover Castle, at which Eleanor showed her appreciation to the burgesses of both Sandwich and Winchelsea for their support, and which was also attended by Sir Ralph d'Arcy's wife, Sir Peter de Burton and his wife and Master J. of London. On this occasion, Eleanor's guests were served with half an ox, two sheep and one pig, washed down with red and white wine, and the usual ale, a staple of the medieval diet.[159]

The splendid setting of the great stone keep at Dover Castle, remodelled less than a century earlier so that Henry II might impress continental visitors en route to Thomas Becket's shrine in Canterbury, provided a visually impressive backdrop to such festivities; the castle continues to dominate the local skyline from both sea and land today. Eleanor's brother, Henry III, invested heavily in improving the castle, spending £7,500, the largest amount spent on one castle during his reign.[160] It was under Henry III that Dover's outer curtain walls were built out as far as the edge of the cliffs, and the impressive Constable's Gate, with its six towers, was constructed on the western side. On the eastern side of the castle complex, another entrance, Fitzwilliam Gate, was added, while a steep bank was built to the south of the Roman lighthouse and the castle church. A range of new domestic buildings were also added to the site, buildings whose facilities Eleanor and her household are likely to have utilized, including a new kitchen, a new hall (Arthur's Hall), chambers and a chapel.[161] Recent renovations to the interior of Henry II's keep at Dover Castle give modern visitors to the castle a sense of the wealth and splendour in which Eleanor's grandfather had entertained guests there.

The Countess of Leicester's clothes and those of other members of her family added to the visual spectacle at Dover. Eleanor's accounts suggest that the countess continued to enjoy fine clothes and appreciated their value in enhancing impressions of dignity and status. While at Odiham during Pentecost, Eleanor had purchased a cloth of 'sanguine' scarlet from the Italian merchant, Luke de Lucca, a man previously patronized by Henry III, for the princely sum of £8 6s. 8d.[162] At Easter, the countess had acquired a hood of black muslin or fine linen for 13s.[163] Eleanor's daughter, the younger Eleanor, enjoyed similarly splendid attire to that of her mother. At Easter, the countess purchased a fur of miniver for her young daughter.[164] We can imagine the younger Eleanor's delight, on another occasion, upon discovering that her mother had purchased twenty-five gilded stars with which to decorate her hood.[165] In late July 1265, 12d. was spent on a dozen pairs of new gloves for the countess and her daughter.[166] Earlier in the year, the younger Eleanor had also been the recipient of two pairs of boots, purchased for 2s. 4d. from one Henry Leff.[167] An impression of the rich robes worn by the countess's clerical son, Amaury, is conveyed by his mother's decision to purchase a silk girdle for his use at a cost of 3s.[168] Yet it was not just the countess and her immediate kin who dressed to impress within the Montfort household: the men and women of their domestic staff also enhanced their mistress's and master's reputations through their clothing. Eleanor's accounts reveal that she purchased twenty-four and a half ells of perse, a dark-blue woollen cloth, for servants, such as Wileqin the groom of Richard de Montfort, Guillot the clerk of the chapel, and Roger and Peter, grooms of the chamber.[169] Various named individuals within Eleanor's accounts received new pairs of shoes from time to time.[170] Yet Eleanor's personal extravagance was not unlimited. In a prudent measure, which betrays a surprising sense of thrift, Eleanor dispatched Hicqe the tailor to London for three nights to have her woollen clothes re-shorn, a process that thereby allowed a new surface to become visible, reinvigorating shabby clothes.[171]

EVESHAM

As the war closed in upon her husband and sons during the summer months of 1265, Eleanor remained in close contact with them all. The countess was in receipt of letters from the Marches, where her husband pursued the war against the royalists.[172] Similarly, Simon junior and his mother exchanged news with one another throughout late June and the following month of July.[173] Eleanor's awareness of the precariousness of her family's fortunes at this time is suggested by a curious entry on her household roll, which records the movement of livestock *by night* on or about 1 August from Brabourne, presumably to augment Dover Castle's supplies.[174]

The battle of Evesham on 4 August 1265 was a personal disaster for Eleanor. It followed hot on the heels of a series of significant gains by the forces of the Lord Edward in the weeks that followed his escape from Montfortian custody. Having destroyed the bridges across the River Severn and captured Worcester and Gloucester, the Lord Edward and his supporters succeeded in trapping Earl Simon to the west of the Severn. Unable to cross the Bristol Channel and in order to counter this threat, Eleanor's husband instructed their son, Simon junior, to leave the siege of Pevensey and make for Kenilworth Castle, in the hope that this might divert the Edwardian forces. This had worked in so far as Simon junior arrived at Kenilworth on 31 July, and the Lord Edward set out to deal with him on 1 August, finally allowing Earl Simon to leave his base at Hereford and cross the Severn on 2 August. Surprised by the Lord Edward at Kenilworth, Simon junior's forces sustained a heavy defeat. This deprived Earl Simon, who hoped to join forces with his son, of essential reinforcements. When the Lord Edward caught up with Earl Simon at Evesham on 4 August, a bitter and brutal battle ensued. Having discussed tactics with his supporters, when he rested at Mosham, the Lord Edward apparently selected a death squad, a group of twelve knights, whose task it was to single out and kill Earl Simon. During the battle at Evesham, Earl Simon, along with Henry, Eleanor's eldest son and almost forty Montfortian knights were killed in cold blood.[175] In this bloody battle, Eleanor, Countess of Leicester, lost her husband of thirty-seven years and her eldest son as well as some of the family's closest political allies and supporters: Hugh Despenser and Peter de Montfort numbered among the dead.[176] Another son, Guy, was taken prisoner.[177] To add insult to injury, Earl Simon's dead body was mutilated and subjected to a series of indignities.[178]

A family disaster of such magnitude inevitably left its mark on Eleanor's accounts. The countess and her establishment immediately modified their dress in mourning; Eleanor's clerks noted the purchase in London of thirty-four ells of russet, a cloth that Eleanor had worn during her first widowhood.[179] On Tuesday 11 August 1265, the countess ceased dining within the great hall;[180] she withdrew to her chamber, only returning to eat with her household on Friday 21 August.[181] The severity of Eleanor's personal grief was conveyed in the chronicle of Thomas Wykes, who commented upon her inconsolable misery. Eleanor abstained from eating meat and fish, and adopted the widow's habit for her clothing.[182] It was also expressed through religious commemoration. Eleanor's household roll records two payments of alms for her dead husband's soul: 12s. 9d. in August and 7s. on 3 September 1265.[183] When Charles Bémont wrote his biography of Earl Simon, he commented, in a footnote, 'Was this all?'[184] Certainly, in view of Eleanor's earlier close relationship with her husband, the apparent parsimony of the countess' offerings is surprising. Had the strain of the political divisions between her natal and marital kin placed an intolerable strain on the Montforts' personal relationship after all? Or was Eleanor at this stage simply too preoccupied with the uncertainty of her own and her offspring's fates? The latter seems the more reasonable explanation. Earl Simon's commemoration and religious remembrance would simply have to wait.

The earl's death placed Eleanor firmly in the spotlight. It was a reflection of the manifold responsibilities she had assumed during her marriage and of the strategic importance of Dover Castle that Eleanor continued to form a focal point for Montfortian resistance in the south east during August and September 1265. This point was not lost on her opponents. Her accounts reveal that she was in communication with Henry III and his eldest son soon after Evesham. Just seven days after the battle, Eleanor's ally, the Prior of Dover, was dispatched by the countess to the king, although the purpose of his visit went unrecorded.[185] Between 15 and 20 August, the countess received a messenger from the Lord Edward.[186]

Eleanor, however, remained firmly entrenched within Dover Castle. Preparations for the castle's defence are suggested by the payment of two masons and two servants for making a furnace during the latter part of August.[187] She also helped her sons to discharge their obligations to their soldiers. On 15 August, Eleanor's youngest son, Richard, received twenty-nine shillings from his mother so that he might pay the twenty-nine archers who had served the Montfortians at Pevensey.[188] In the altered political climate, with the royalists closing in, Eleanor and the garrison at Dover now found it increasingly difficult to provision the household. Entries on Eleanor's household roll for 23, 24, 25 and 26 August, for example, refer to oxen consumed there that had been obtained 'by booty', presumably from raids on the neighbouring countryside, rather than by purchase or from the countess's own Kentish manors.[189] Eleanor's determination to hold out at Dover stands in stark contrast to that of another baronial widow, Hugh Despenser's former wife, who had surrendered the Tower of London to the royalists on learning of her husband's death at Evesham.[190]

As a mother, though, Eleanor's first priority was the safety of her surviving children in the months after Evesham. Her accounts document communications with Simon junior in mid-August.[191] They also refer to a boat and around 100 mariners charged with bringing her younger son Richard from Winchelsea to Dover on 12 August.[192] When Richard joined the countess's household, he too adopted black clothing associated with mourning. Eleanor's accounts reveal that his mother purchased ten ells of black serge for this son's robes and saddle-cloths.[193] In a similar fashion, they illuminate the preparations for his departure to Bigorre in September. Having furnished her son with two new pairs of boots, Eleanor paid for Richard's passage to Gravelines.[194] Fearing Eleanor's own flight to France, Henry III issued instructions to the barons and bailiffs of Dover on 28 September that the countess was to be prevented from leaving the kingdom without royal permission.[195] A letter of 10 October 1265, addressed by the king to his brother-in-law, Louis IX, recorded Henry III's indignation on discovering that Eleanor had, in fact, safely dispatched two of her younger sons – Richard and Amaury – overseas, along with 11,000 marks in cash, which had formerly belonged to Simon de Montfort, 'our enemy'.[196] Eleanor had deftly outwitted her older brother. Yet Eleanor's hold on Dover Castle was by no means impregnable. One chronicler recorded an attempt by royalist captives within the castle to bribe their guards and overwhelm the garrison from within.[197] It was apparently this that encouraged the Lord Edward to begin his siege of the castle and which culminated in Eleanor's negotiated surrender and her departure with her daughter for France on 28 October 1265.[198]

9

After Evesham

Now has king Henry land and lordship
And is king of his land, and of all that belongs to it:
He goes off with victory to hold a parliament
Straight to Northampton, sir Edward assents

In that parliament was exiled
The countess of Leicester, her sons have abjured:
Earls and barons are disinherited,
Some are to the wood, some imprisoned.[1]

As Eleanor crossed the Channel to France on 28 October 1265, in the company of her daughter, she might have taken time to reflect upon the trials and tribulations that now beset her surviving sons and their supporters. On 26 October, the day that the Lord Edward wrote to Giffard, Henry III had formally invested his younger son, Edmund, with the earldom of Leicester and bestowed upon him all the English lands formerly held by Eleanor's dead husband, an act that disinherited Simon junior.[2] Simon junior, for his part, left Kenilworth Castle after Evesham[3] and joined forces with other Montfortian sympathizers in the Isle of Axholme until a royalist army surrounded the rebels. Realizing that they were trapped, Simon junior and his supporters 'sought peace from the king' at Christmas.[4] In January 1266, at Northampton, Simon agreed to abjure the realm and cause no further trouble for the king. In return for this undertaking, it was agreed that he might draw a yearly pension from the honour of Leicester. Still, though, the distrust between the two sides was too great. When an opportunity presented itself in London for Simon junior to escape from the Lord Edward's guards, he seized it, whereupon he headed for the Sussex coast and for Winchelsea, whose burgesses his mother had entertained less than a year before. It was from Winchelsea, on or about 10 February 1266, that Simon junior secured a safe passage from England to France.[5] His escape was followed, during the spring of 1266, by that of Eleanor's younger son, Guy, who had been captured at Evesham and held first at Windsor Castle and then Dover.[6] As the

Dunstable annalist observed, both sons initially joined 'their mother'.[7] In the aftermath of the annihilation of her family's English political fortunes, Eleanor and her surviving children were finally safe in exile by the summer of 1266. How did they and their mother fare during the final decade of the countess's life?

ELEANOR IN EXILE

In the late autumn and early winter of 1265, Eleanor was very much thrown back on her own resources and her family's French lands and connections. Eleanor's immediate concern on arriving in France in 1265 was to find a safe haven for herself, her daughter and her sons, and a means of securing their futures. Eleanor might, initially, have had fears about the warmth of her reception from Louis IX and Queen Margaret, in view of their close kinship with, and earlier support for, Eleanor of Provence, during the English queen's recent exile. The French king and his wife appear, though, to have shared a surprising deal of sympathy with Countess Eleanor's plight and quickly stepped in to mediate on the Countess of Leicester's behalf in her dealings with the English crown. As early as 2 October 1265, Henry III wrote to Louis, informing him that he was dispatching envoys to the French court to engage in discussions there about the affairs of the Countess of Leicester and her sons.[8] On 16 November 1265, Henry III granted Countess Eleanor, Sir Ralph d'Arcy and Thomas of Sandwich, her erstwhile companions at Dover Castle, protection for one year. Perhaps the king hoped to encourage his sister to attend the English royal court in order to stage a public ceremony of reconciliation, possibly in the hope that her presence might persuade the remaining rebels to come to heal.[9] Eleanor's importance, even after her flight to France, as a figurehead for those Montfortians who continued to resist surrender is suggested in an account of the siege of Kenilworth by a later St Albans chronicler, William Rishanger. The rebels who withstood a siege at Kenilworth Castle in 1266 initially refused to surrender because, so Rishanger observed, they claimed to hold the castle for the Countess of Leicester.[10] It is far from clear whether Eleanor aided or abetted Simon junior's attempts at rallying forces to launch an invasion of England from the French coast during the summer and early autumn of 1266. What is clear is that the level of threat that Simon junior posed in September 1266 was considered sufficiently serious by the crown for the Pope to order members of the senior clergy throughout France to excommunicate all who participated in such enterprises. The French king, Louis IX, was urged by Pope Clement IV to prevent his subjects from assisting Eleanor and her son in recovering their lands; Louis IX was encouraged, instead, to direct his efforts to assisting Henry III in recovering his position.[11] In fact, Louis had already written to his brother-in-law in the summer of 1266, informing Henry that he had taken action to prevent his enemies from crossing to England. In the same letter, the French king strongly urged Henry to make peace with Eleanor and her sons.[12]

Once again, Louis IX was cast as a mediator between Henry III and the remaining Montforts. By means of a royal letter, issued on 25 September 1266, Henry III formally announced his decision to defer to the award of King Louis on the matter of all damages and injuries that he and his children had sustained at the hands of Simon junior, Earl Simon and 'Eleanor, sometime countess of Leicester'.[13] The circumstances that had prompted this letter were made explicit in another missive, issued on the same day, this time addressed to Louis, which recalled the earlier arrival in England of Louis's representatives, who had expressly been sent to negotiate with the king 'on the matter of the countess and Simon de Montfort, son of the sometime earl of Leicester'.[14] All this activity ultimately explains why, under the terms of the Dictum of Kenilworth proclaimed on 31 October 1266, Henry III offered the remaining rebels the chance to keep their lives, limbs and property at the price of forfeiting between two and seven years' income, but specifically excluded 'Earl Simon de Montfort and his sons, for the lord King has left this matter in the hands of the king of France'.[15]

The process of arbitration was neither smooth nor fast. In February 1267, Henry III again repeated his intention to submit to Louis's award, provided that a decision was reached by Easter.[16] It was only with the arrival in England of John of Acre, the butler of France, and other French envoys in the spring of that year that it looked as though any significant headway might be made: on 24 May 1267, Henry III, with the backing of his council, informed Louis of his offer to restore the dead earl's lands to Simon junior, and extend and value them in co-operation with Simon junior's own representatives. Unfortunately for Simon junior, this offer came with an unpalatable sting in the tail: he was to promise to sell his lands to the king or the king's children whenever he was required to do so, for a value approved by the king of France, but which took into account the damages sustained by Henry III through the 'sedition' of Earl Simon and Simon junior.[17] As F. M. Powicke observed, 'Henry still intended to keep Simon out of the country and to return to the plan of a money compensation, whose payment would depend on Simon's good behaviour.'[18] The deal failed to satisfy Simon junior, and the French king's attempts at reconciliation dragged on, but made limited progress.[19] By late 1268, Simon had joined his brother, Guy, in the service of Louis IX's brother, Charles of Anjou, during the latter's conquest of Italy.[20]

The letter of 24 May 1267 also disclosed important information about the state of negotiations over Countess Eleanor's dower. In it, Henry III, repeated his support for an arrangement between the Countess of Leicester and the tenants of the lands in which she claimed her dower that had already been reached at 'another time' in the presence of Eleanor of Provence. Under the terms of this agreement, it was set down that the countess, via her proctor, would receive £500 a year in lieu of dower. If, however, this agreement now proved unsatisfactory to the countess, the king laid down that her proctors might sue for the recovery of her rights before the royal justices.[21] It is striking that Countess Eleanor had turned to her sister-in-law, with whom she had previously enjoyed strong ties of friendship, rather than her brother, in order to pursue her dower. This offers another example of female networking within the royal family and is, perhaps, suggestive of shared sympathies between the two women, in spite of the antagonism between the king and the surviving Montforts. Perhaps Countess Eleanor found it easier to deal with the queen on personal grounds. After all, Eleanor of Provence was absent from England, herself an exile in France, for the duration of the troubles of 1264–5,[22] and as such was not tainted by close association with the bloody end of Earl Simon at Evesham or with the indignities to which his corpse was subjected after the battle.

Eleanor's actions in the late 1260s might well have been fuelled by her deep sense of personal grief. Widowed for a second time, Eleanor sought solace, as she had previously done at other troubled moments of her life, in her piety and spirituality. Yet, in doing so, Eleanor was still also able to make an overt political gesture that demonstrated the scale of the bitterness that she felt towards her eldest brother, Henry III, and her disillusionment with her family's treatment at his hands. Soon after leaving England late in 1265, Countess Eleanor entered a female religious community where she spent the remainder of her days. The community that Eleanor chose was not that of the great abbey of Fontevrault, the final resting place of her royal Angevin forebears, and of her mother, Isabella of Angoulême. Eleanor chose, instead, in an expression of loyalty and devotion to her recently deceased husband, to enter the Dominican nunnery of Montargis, a community of women religious founded by Earl Simon's sister, Amicia (d. 1252), the widow of Gaucher of Joigny.[23] Eleanor and Earl Simon's support for the Mendicant Orders has already been discussed in this study and it might simply have been the case that Eleanor preferred the spirituality of the Dominican nuns to that of the more antiquated double communities of the Order of Fontevrault.[24] Yet it is striking that a woman who had in the past traded upon her kinship with the English king, a woman who styled herself on her counterseal as 'sister of the king of England', chose in her second period of widowhood to align herself firmly with the Montforts, her kin by marriage. This move revealed the extent of her alienation from the English crown.

The constitutions of the community of Montargis, drawn up in or around 1250, and those for all Dominican nuns, drawn up in 1259, offer glimpses of the rhythms of life that Countess Eleanor might have encountered within the convent.[25] As a sister of Montargis, Eleanor would have been expected to embrace strict enclosure and a regime of religious observances, centred primarily upon singing the psalms, prayer and contemplation as a means of bringing her soul closer to God.[26] It is, therefore, likely that much of Eleanor's time at Montargis was spent in silence, a state of existence that was highly valued by Dominicans as a way of aiding their spiritual endeavours. The constitutions of 1259 forbade nuns from speaking in the oratory, cloister, refectory or dormitory, and laid down stiff penalties for those who broke this rule.[27] Value was, however, attached to the reading of devotional texts, something that a literate woman like Eleanor might well have welcomed as a source of spiritual succour and enlightenment.[28] In fact, in March 1270, Prioress Guie of Montargis borrowed a copy of one of Earl Simon's former books, *A Summary of Vices and Virtues* by the Dominican Guillaume Peyraut, from Eleanor's son Amaury, a loan that was perhaps informed by the countess's knowledge of her dead husband's library.[29] Silence at Montargis was broken at regulated points throughout the day when the community came together to celebrate the canonical hours – matins, lauds, prime, terce, sext, none, vespers and compline – that demarcated the religious day.[30] In fact, the constitutions laid down that Dominican novices ought 'diligently' to 'study psalmody and Divine Office' upon entering her house.[31]

The religious life that Eleanor encountered at Montargis did not necessarily require her to turn her back upon her family and kin. Eleanor was still able to receive guests at this family foundation. The French king, queen, local bishop and patrons of the house, both male and female, were, for example, all allowed access to the conventual cloister.[32] From Montargis, Eleanor was able to look to the interests of her children in the decade after Evesham.

LANDS AND LITIGATION

Eleanor's spiritual alignment with her Montfort in-laws did not deter Eleanor from pressing her blood relations in the maternal line – the Lusignans – for the recovery of her share of her mother's inheritance in Angoulême in the French courts. The loss of income from Eleanor's English lands and her residence in France made the matter of securing a firm financial base and future for her exiled children all the more compelling. Here, Eleanor met with a degree of success. In 1267, Eleanor secured a judgment in her favour in the parlement of Paris that upheld her rights in her mother's lands against those of Count Hugh (XII) of La Marche and Geoffrey de Lusignan. When the Count of La Marche failed to act upon this settlement with suitable speed, Eleanor secured another verdict in her favour in 1269. Under the terms of this second award, it was agreed that the count would assign the Countess of Leicester £400 a year in land and would undertake to pay her an additional £800 to cover the arrears that had built up during the last two years.[33]

Eleanor also continued to pursue her English lands and rights, as she had done for most of her life. In Louis IX, Eleanor found a useful and powerful political ally who interceded with the Pope on the countess's behalf when she took her grievances against Henry III to the Roman curia.[34] Early in 1268, for example, Louis secured the assurances of the Pope that he would be just to the Countess of Leicester and her sons.[35] It is hard to imagine that Eleanor was not party to the mission by her clerical son, Amaury, to the Roman curia, where, in the spring of 1267, he successfully petitioned Pope Clement to preserve his English ecclesiastical offices, notably the treasurership and prebend of York, which his dead father had been instrumental in securing for him.[36] It was also at Amaury's request that the papal legate to England, Ottobuono, was ordered to investigate Amaury's claims that, although Earl Simon as a good Christian had sought and obtained absolution for his sins before Evesham and had shown repentance, his body had not received a church burial, a situation that imperiled the fate of Simon's immortal soul.[37] Here, Amaury was dealing with a highly sensitive issue that was extremely close to his mother's heart. As the chief executor of Simon's will, as well as his grieving widow, it was Eleanor's duty to ensure, in spite of the extraordinary circumstances of his death, that Simon's body was given an appropriate Christian burial. It also testifies to Amaury's personal talents as a negotiator that he was able to persuade a pope, who in the recent past had vehemently opposed the Montfortian cause, to listen to and act upon his petition. Eleanor's close relationship with Amaury was witnessed by her decision to appoint him as the chief executor of her will on her death in 1275.[38]

Eleanor's contacts with her other sons – Richard, Guy and Simon – are more difficult to trace. A brief glimpse of a family reunion that took place in December 1266 is provided by a letter jointly addressed by Eleanor, Simon, Guy and Eleanor the younger to Louis IX, King of France, to which the countess's seal and those of her children were attached. The letter, which touched upon an annual rent of £500 *par.* (Parisian money) paid by Louis to Earl Simon, also referred to Amaury and Richard.[39] Shortly after leaving England, Richard appears to have found service with Theobald II of Navarre, and fought in the latter's Gascon campaign against Henry III in 1266 before disappearing from the records.[40] Guy, for his part, took part in Charles of Anjou's successful Italian and Sicilian conquests of 1268. Guy enjoyed the company of his French cousin, Philip de Montfort, a descendant of his great uncle, another Guy, and was rewarded by Charles with estates and offices in the south of Europe. After helping to secure victory at Alba in August 1268, Guy the younger received fiefs in the kingdom of Naples, namely Arienzo, Nola, Castel Cicala, Monteforte, Forino and Atripalda, and, following service to Philip de Montfort in central Italy, he was appointed vicar-general of Tuscany and vicar of Florence in 1270.[41] On 10 August 1270, Guy cemented his position by marrying Margherita Aldobrandesca, the heiress of the Count Palatine Ildebrandino of Pitigliano.[42] Simon junior, a later arrival in Italy, similarly profited from the generosity of Charles of Anjou and was granted the county of Avellino.[43] Amaury, who also travelled to Italy in 1268 and subsequently studied for three years at the University of Padua, might well have acted as a point of contact between his brothers and their mother in France.[44]

THE MURDER OF HENRY OF ALMAIN

The horrors of Evesham came back, however, to haunt the Countess of Leicester and her family in 1271. On Friday 13 March 1271, Henry of Almain, who had been dispatched to Italy by the Lord Edward, then en route to the Near East on crusade, to act as a peace-broker between the Montfort sons and the English crown, was murdered. While Henry was hearing mass in the church of San Silvestro in Viterbo, he was brutally attacked by Guy.[45] This act, which deeply shocked the courts of Europe, resulted in the flight of the murderer and his accomplice, Simon junior. Both men suffered the immediate confiscation of their estates and offices.[46] It should be seen primarily as an opportunistic act of revenge for the deaths of Guy and Simon junior's father and brother at Evesham, and perhaps also for Henry's earlier desertion by turning his back on the Montfortian cause in 1263. Another significant factor that riled Earl Simon's sons further was Henry's recent marriage to a Gascon heiress, Constance, the daughter of Gaston de Béarn, a marriage that threatened the Montforts' interests in their father's former county of Bigorre.[47]

The murder at Viterbo cast a dark shadow over all Countess Eleanor's surviving sons. The Lord Edward strongly suspected Amaury of involvement, although a spell of illness in Padua, which was subsequently confirmed by the bishop, chapter and university there, apparently proved that Amaury was not witness to, or obviously complicit in, the deed.[48] What is clear, however, is that the Lord Edward did not extend his suspicion to his aunt, Eleanor, at Montargis. Furthermore, when Simon and Guy fled in the aftermath of the murder, they remained in Italy, rather than seeking direct and open aid from their mother or their Montfort kinsmen in France. Simon died a short time later, in a castle near Siena,[49] while Guy evaded capture with the assistance of his father-in-law. After his excommunication by the Pope in April 1273, Guy surrendered and was imprisoned, albeit in the custody of his former lord, Charles of Anjou.[50]

THE ACCESSION OF EDWARD I

With the death of Henry III on 16 November 1272, the Lord Edward, who was then still absent on crusade, succeeded to the English throne as Edward I. Edward's accession smoothed the way, with a bit of help from the new French king, Philip III, for a period of reconciliation between Eleanor and the English court. When, on his way back from the East, Edward visited Melun on the outskirts of Paris in the summer of 1273, it is likely that he met with his aunt for the first time in almost eight years. At the time of his accession and, no doubt, with a view to conducting a successful exercise in public relations that was designed to heal past divisions, he offered Eleanor an olive branch. On 10 August 1273, Edward wrote to the royal chancellor, Walter of Merton, in England, announcing that, 'at the instance of the most serene prince and our dearest kinsman, Philip, by the grace of God, illustrious king of France', he had withdrawn all his indignation and all the rancour within his soul towards Eleanor, Countess of Leicester. Eleanor, the letter recorded, was now admitted 'to our grace and firm peace', provided that she continued to behave 'well and faithfully to us'.[51] During the visit, Edward felt sufficiently well disposed towards his aunt to loan her £200, a debt that she subsequently repaid in full to the keeper of the royal wardrobe in the autumn of 1274.[52]

The advent of more friendly relations paved the way for Eleanor to pursue, once more, the matter of her Marshal dower. Payments for her dower had ceased at Easter in 1265 and had not resumed since.[53] After Evesham, Eleanor lost possession of her English estates. The local jurors whose testimonies were recorded on the Kent hundred rolls in 1274–5, for example, recorded how 'William de Valence, [Eleanor's half-brother who was married to one of the Marshal co-heirs] after the battle of Evesham entered that manor [of Sutton, Kent] and claimed it by hereditary right of his wife'.[54] William de Valence also held Kemsing, together with another manor, Brabourne, from which Eleanor had transported supplies to Dover Castle in 1265. The jurors who reported on Brabourne, though, were more reticent about their new lord. Here, the jurors recalled that 'King John held Brabourne manor through escheat and now Lord William de Valence holds that manor by what warrant they do not know'.[55] Perhaps, in this expression of uncertainty about William's right to the manor, the jurors retained vestiges of loyalty to their former countess.

In recovering her lost rights, the connections that Eleanor had fostered with the French royal court again proved to be invaluable. On 10 October 1273, Philip III wrote to Edward I, expressing concern for the safety of his father's soul in the afterlife, on the grounds that the 15,000 marks which had been deposited in the New Temple at Paris during Louis IX's lifetime as security for the settlement of Eleanor's dower had been removed by the English king after Evesham.[56] Spurred into action, Edward I issued an order, just two and a half weeks later, for the Marshal heirs to answer at the English royal Exchequer for their outstanding debts to the Countess of Leicester.[57] In addition to this, Edward I took steps to ensure that Eleanor's English properties from her first marriage were restored to her.[58]

Eleanor, dowager Countess of Leicester and dowager Countess of Pembroke, died at Montargis in France on 13 April 1275 (the eve of Easter).[59] Shortly before her death, she was visited by Margaret of Provence, now the dowager Queen of France, who subsequently wrote to Edward I, relaying the final wishes of the English king's aunt. In a final act of intercession on Eleanor's behalf, the French queen urged Edward to observe the terms of Eleanor's testament and to show pity to her son Amaury by returning him to the king's grace.[60] Eleanor's death was not, however, entirely that of a defeated exile. From the convent of Montargis, she had remained active in pursuit of her family's interests right up until her death. On 9 January 1275, just three months before her death, Countess Eleanor had appointed Master Nicholas of Waltham, a canon of Lincoln, as her attorney for one year to pursue and protect her rights in the English royal courts.[61] Countess Eleanor also lived just long enough to see the marriage, by proxy, of her only surviving daughter and namesake, Eleanor, to her dead husband's former ally, Llywelyn ap Gruffudd, Prince of Wales, a match that her husband, Earl Simon, had arranged many years earlier.[62]

In death, Countess Eleanor's heart reposed in the Abbey Royal of St-Antoine-des-Champs, a Cistercian nunnery on the outskirts of Paris.[63] Although Eleanor's will is now lost, other records reveal that she bequeathed £220 16s. *par.* (Parisian money) to the nuns of this house for an earlier debt, a sum Eleanor's executors, including her son, Amaury, finally attempted to recover in 1286 with Edward I's aid from the Marshal co-heirs.[64] Even in death, the legacy of Eleanor's battle for her Irish Marshal dower, a battle that had dominated so much of her adult life, lived on.

Notes

Notes on Preface

1   F. M. Powicke (1947), *King Henry III and the Lord Edward*. Oxford: Clarendon Press, 2 vols, i, pp. 203–4.

2   For a brief but scholarly modern biography, see E. Hallam (2004), 'Eleanor, Countess of Pembroke and Leicester (1215?–1275),' *ODNB*, available online at http://www.oxforddnb.com/view/article/46703, accessed on 31 May 2011.

3   M. W. Labarge (1965, repr. 2003), *Mistress, Maids and Men: Baronial Life in the Thirteenth Century*. Phoenix: London, p. 45.

4   K. Asaji (2010), 'Household Accounts of the Countess of Leicester, 1265', in idem, *The Angevin Empire and the Community of the Realm in England*. Kansai: Kansai University Press, pp. 162–88, at p. 163.

5   Ibid., p. 184.

6   L. Kjær (2011), 'Food, Drink and Ritualised Communication in the Household of Eleanor de Montfort, February to August 1265', *Journal of Medieval History*, 37, 75–89. I am grateful to Lars for sending me a copy of his article.

Notes on Chapter 1

1   *Wendover*, iii, p. 113.

2   Prinet expressed doubt about the identity of this tomb's incumbent. The heart of another lady from the Montfort family, whose name was not recorded, was buried in the cloister there in 1294. Prinet also considered it odd that the tomb apparently displayed the arms of Eleanor's sons, rather than her ancestors: M. Prinet (1917), 'Deux monuments funéraires de l'abbaye de Saint-Antoine des Champs', *Bulletin de la Société de l'histoire de Paris et de l'Ile-de-France*, 80–83; C. Bémont (1930), *Simon de Montfort* (2nd edn), trans. E. F. Jacob. Oxford: Clarendon Press, p. 259 n. 1.

3   One aunt was also the grandmother of King Louis IX of France: *Wendover*, iii, p. 113; L. J. Wilkinson (2009), 'The Imperial Marriage of Isabella of England, Henry III's Sister', in E. Oakley-Brown and L. J. Wilkinson (eds), *The Rituals and Rhetoric of Queenship, Medieval to Early Modern*. Dublin: Four Courts Press, pp. 20–36, at pp. 26–7. Eleanor's maternal uncle, Peter de Courtenay, was the Latin emperor of Constantinople: N. Vincent (1999), 'Isabella of Angoulême: John's Jezebel', in S. D. Church (ed.), *King John: New*

Interpretations. Woodbridge: Boydell Press, pp. 165–219, at pp. 177–8, 180–1 tables 2–3. For an excellent biographical study of Eleanor's cousin, Berenguela of Castile, see: M. Shadis (2009), *Berenguela of Castile (1180–1246) and Political Women in the High Middle Ages*. New York: Palgrave MacMillan.

4   Majorie Chibnall, for example, observed much the same about Eleanor's great grand-mother, the Empress Matilda: M. Chibnall (1991), *The Empress Matilda*. Oxford: Blackwell, pp. 9–10.

5   Isabella, Eleanor's older sister, appears to have been born in 1214. See p. 5. On chroni-clers as preservers of 'dynastic' and 'institutional' histories, see C. Given-Wilson (2003), *Chronicles: The Writing of History in Medieval England*. London: Hambledon, ch. 4.

6   Eleanor's surviving siblings were: Henry, the future King of England, Richard, the future Earl of Cornwall, and her sisters Joan and Isabella. See D. A. Carpenter (1990), *The Minority of Henry III*. London: Methuen; N. Denholm-Young (1947), *Richard of Cornwall*. Oxford: Basil Blackwell; J. Nelson (2007), 'Scottish Queenship in the Thirteenth Century', in B. Weiler et al. (eds), *Thirteenth Century England XI: Proceedings of the Gregynog Conference 2005*. Woodbridge: Boydell Press, pp. 61–81, at pp. 68–70; Wilkinson, 'The Imperial Marriage of Isabella of England', pp. 20–36. On high rates of infant mortality, even among the wealthy, see N. Orme (1984), *From Childhood to Chivalry: The Education of the English Kings and Aristocracy, 1066–1530*. London: Methuen and Co., p. 3; D. Youngs (2006), *The Life Cycle in Western Europe, c. 1300–c. 1500*. Manchester: Manchester University Press, pp. 24–5.

7   On this see J. C. Holt (1992), *The Northerners* (revised edn). Oxford: Clarendon Press, p. 144.

8   On John's reign, see J. C. Holt (1992), *Magna Carta* (2nd edn). Cambridge: Cambridge University Press; Holt, *The Northerners*; W. L. Warren (1961), *King John*. London: Eyre Methuen.

9   For the best English biography of Isabella, see Vincent, 'Isabella of Angoulême'.

10   Alice (d. after 1215) married: (1) Andrew of La Ferté-Gaucher in Champagne (d. c. 1177); (2) William of Joigny (marriage annulled in c. 1184); and (3) Adomar, Count of Angoulême (d. 1202): ibid., pp. 175–82. For her Courtenay ancestry, see *Chronica Albrici monachi trium fontium*, ed. P. Scheffer-Boichorst (1874), Monumenta Germaniae Historica, SS 23, p. 874.

11   Vincent, 'Isabella of Angoulême', pp. 170–2.

12   Ibid., pp. 172–3.

13   Ibid., pp. 184–93. See also L. L. Huneycutt (2002), '"Alianora Regina Anglorum": Eleanor of Aquitaine and her Anglo-Norman Predecessors as Queens of England', in B. Wheeler and J. C. Parsons (eds) *Eleanor of Aquitaine: Lord and Lady*. Basingstoke: Palgrave Macmillan, pp. 115–32.

14   Isabella's experiences in this respect stand in stark contrast to those of her future daughter-in-law and eventual successor as queen in England, Eleanor of Provence. See, for example, M. Howell (1998), *Eleanor of Provence: Queenship in Thirteenth-Century England*. Oxford: Blackwell, esp. chs 3 and 6.

15   Vincent, 'Isabella of Angoulême', pp. 184–93. On Queen's Gold and its administration

under Henry II, see *The Dialogue concerning the Exchequer*, book II, ch. XXVI, in E. F. Henderson (ed.) (1896), *Select Historical Documents of the Middle Ages*. London: George Bell and Sons, available online at http://avalon.law.yale.edu/medieval/excheq.asp#b2p26, accessed on 1 December 2009.

16 Vincent, 'Isabella of Angoulême', pp. 193, 196–7. For Isabella of Gloucester, see R. B. Patterson (2004/5), 'Isabella, *suo jure* Countess of Gloucester (c.1160–1217)', *ODNB*, available online at http://www.oxforddnb.com/view/article/46705, accessed on 7 December 2009.

17 Vincent, 'Isabella of Angoulême', pp. 193–5; N. Vincent (1996), *Peter des Roches: An Alien in English Politics, 1205–1238*. Cambridge: Cambridge University Press, p. 70. For the bishop discharging the queen's expenses, see *The Pipe Roll of the Bishopric of Winchester, 1210–11*, ed. N. R. Holt (1964). Manchester: Manchester University Press, pp. 34 (Downton, Wilts), 37 (x2, Downton, Wilts).

18 *RLP*, i.i, p. 117; *RLCl*, i, p. 169b; Vincent, 'Isabella of Angoulême', p. 195.

19 Warren, *King John*, pp. 219–21.

20 Vincent, 'Isabella of Angoulême', pp. 195–6. See also *RLP*, i.i, pp. 143b (1215), 192b (1216). For the sojourn at Exeter, mentioned in a later letter close, see *RLCl*, i, p. 433.

21 *RLCl*, i, p. 177. See also ibid., i, p. 154b; *RLP*, i.i, p. 105b. For Berkhampsted as dower, see *RLC*, i, p. 293.

22 *RLP*, i.i, p. 124b; *RLCl*, i, p. 180b.

23 *RLCl*, i, p. 189b; *RLP*, i.i, p. 136 (x2).

24 *RLP*, i.i, p. 136 (x2). For Isabella at Marlborough, see also *RLCl*, i, p. 213b.

25 Corfe was then in the custody of des Roches's associate, Peter de Maulay: *Histoire des ducs de Normandie et des rois d'Angleterre*, ed. F. Michel (1840). Paris: Jules Renouard, p. 152; Vincent, *Peter des Roches*, p. 71. Richard, the younger son, was also in de Maulay's charge: *Histoire des ducs*, p. 180.

26 For a useful essay on medieval ideas about gender, see J. Murray (1995), 'Thinking about Gender: The Diversity of Medieval Perspectives', in J. Carpenter and S. MacLean (eds), *Power of the Weak: Studies on Medieval Women*. Urbana, IL: University of Illinois Press, pp. 1–26.

27 This was in spite of King John's disregard for the rights of his nephew, Arthur of Brittany, the son of John's older brother, Geoffrey (d. 1186), in the matter of his own accession to the throne: M. Jones (2004), 'Geoffrey, Duke of Brittany (1158–1186)', *ODNB*, available online at http://www.oxforddnb.com/view/article/10533, accessed on 4 December 2009. The crown apparently retained the right to bypass the rules of inheritance and succession in this period. See, for example, J. C. Holt (1997), 'The "casus regis": The Law and Politics of Succession in the Plantagenet Dominions, 1185–1247,' in idem, *Colonial England, 1066–1215*. London: Hambledon Press, pp. 307–26.

28 D. Alexandre-Bidon and D. Lett (1999), *Children in the Middle Ages, Fifth to Fifteenth Centuries*, trans. J. Gladding. Notre Dame, IN: University of Notre Dame Press, pp. 64–5; J. C. Parsons (1993), 'Mothers, Daughters, Marriage, Power: Some Plantagenet Evidence, 1150–1500,' in idem (ed.), *Medieval Queenship*. Stroud: Sutton, pp. 63–78, at pp. 68–9.

29 For the birth of Henry III, see, for example, 'Annales de Wintonia', in *Ann. mon.*, ii, p. 80;

'Annales de Waverleia', in *Ann. mon.*, ii, p. 259. For the birth of Richard of Cornwall, see, for example, 'Annales de Margan', in *Ann. mon.*, i, p. 29; 'Annales de Waverleia', p. 264. For the birth of Joan, see, for example, 'Annales de Theokesberia', in *Ann. mon.*, i, p. 59; 'Annales prioratus de Wigornia', in *Ann. mon.*, iv, p. 399.

30 *Wendover*, iii, p. 108.

31 In or around 1224, Henry III referred to Eleanor as his 'younger sister': *Royal Letters*, i, pp. 244–6 no. CCXI, esp. p. 246. See also M. A. E. Green (1857), *Lives of the Princesses of England from the Norman Conquest, Volume II.* London: Longman, Brown, Green, Longman and Roberts, pp. 1, 3–4, n. 5; J. R. Maddicott (1994), *Simon de Montfort.* Cambridge: Cambridge University Press, p. 38 n. 1.

32 Medical writers recommended the use of a wet-nurse: W. F. MacLehose (1996), 'Nurturing Danger: High Medieval Medicine and the Problem(s) of the Child', in J. C. Parsons and B. Wheeler (eds), *Medieval Mothering.* London: Garland, pp. 3–24, at pp. 12–13.

33 *RLCl*, i, p. 225. For another gift of robes to Isabella and her damsels in December 1215, see *RLCl*, i, p. 242.

34 N. Orme (2001), *Medieval Children.* New Haven: Yale University Press, pp. 19–21.

35 *Chronica majora*, iii, pp. 566–7.

36 Vincent, *Peter des Roches*, p. 71. See also *Pipe Roll, Winchester, 1210–11*, p. 65.

37 P. Stafford (1997), *Queen Emma and Queen Edith: Queenship and Women's Power in Eleventh-Century England.* Oxford: Blackwell, pp. 128–31; L. L. Huneycutt (2003), *Matilda of Scotland: A Study in Medieval Queenship.* Woodbridge: Boydell Press, pp. 37, 41, 69.

38 'Annales de Wintonia', pp. 82–3.

39 *Earldom of Gloucester Charters: The Charters and Scribes of the Earls and Countesses of Gloucester to A.D. 1217*, ed. R. B. Patterson (1973). Oxford: Clarendon Press, p. 7.

40 *RLCl*, i, pp. 275, 285 (June and August). In February 1216, Terric was awarded custody of the abbey of St Augustine, Bristol: *RLP*, i.i, p. 166. See also *RLCl*, i, p. 251; *RLP*, i.i, pp. 174b.

41 Warren, *King John*, p. 254.

42 See also p. 28 below.

43 *RLC*, i, p. 293. For these and other properties which Isabella held in dower, see also ibid., pp. 294, 302, 302b (French dower), 304b, 315, 328b, 349b, 389b.

44 Carpenter, *The Minority*, pp. 13–19.

45 Ibid., p. 14 and n. 6; Warren, *King John*, p. 255.

46 Vincent, 'Isabella of Angoulême', p. 198.

47 Carpenter, *The Minority*, pp. 44–9.

48 *Wendover*, i, pp. 295, 314, esp. 317.

49 See, for example, Alexandre-Bidon and Lett, *Children in the Middle Ages*, p. 61; Parsons, 'Mothers, Daughters', pp. 68–75. Royal and aristocratic children were usually placed in the care of nurses, some of whom were presumably wet nurses, shortly after birth. References to payments made to the nurses of John and Isabella's children litter the pipe rolls. See, for example, *Pipe Roll 16 John*, pp. 127 (Christiana, nurse of Joan), 35, 54 (Elena, nurse of the king's son), 1, 79 (Eva, nurse of Richard the king's son), 39 (Hodierna, nurse of Richard), 1 (Matildis, nurse of Richard).

50 *RLP*, i.i, p. 117.

51 Denholm-Young, *Richard of Cornwall*, p. 3; *Histoire des ducs*, p. 180; Vincent, *Peter des Roches*, p. 71.

52 On education, see Orme, *From Childhood to Chivalry*, p. 45.

53 Isabella's role in her sons' early upbringings might help to explain why, much later in life, Henry III extended so warm a welcome to the children of his mother's second marriage. See H. W. Ridgeway (1989), 'Foreign Favourites and Henry III's Problems of Patronage, 1247–1258', *EHR*, 104, 590–610; Howell, *Eleanor of Provence*, pp. 54–5.

54 Vincent, 'Isabella of Angoulême', p. 208.

55 Vincent, *Peter des Roches*, pp. 153–4.

56 *PR, 1216–25*, p. 234. It was agreed that Isabella would marry Alexander if Joan failed to return from the south of France in time: ibid., p. 235; Carpenter, *The Minority*, p. 196.

57 Vincent, *Peter des Roches*, p. 153.

58 I am grateful to Dr Jennifer Ward for this suggestion.

59 On this, see Carpenter, *The Minority*, pp. 249–52.

60 See *Wendover*, iii, pp. 77; Vincent, *Peter des Roches*, pp. 414–15.

61 Similar arrangements are found with the higher nobility. See, for example, J. C. Parsons (1998), ' "Que nos in infancia lactauit": The Impact of Childhood Care-givers on Plantagenet Family Relationships in the Thirteenth and Early Fourteenth Centuries', in C. M. Rousseau and J. T. Rosenthal (eds), *Women, Marriage and Family in Medieval Christendom: Essays in Memory of Michael M. Sheehan*. C. S. B., Kalamazoo, MI: Western Michigan University, pp. 289–324, at pp. 293–4.

62 I was alerted to the existence of the following entries by Vincent, *Peter des Roches*, p. 153 n. 93. I am grateful to the staff of the Hampshire Record Office (Archives and Local Studies) for their assistance in accessing the unpublished pipe rolls of the bishopric of Winchester.

63 HRO, 11M59/B1/6, mm. 12, 12d.

64 HRO, 11M59/B1/7, mm. 10d, 11. See also HRO, 11M59/B1/9, m. 5.

65 Orme, *From Childhood to Chivalry*, p. 19 n. 93; Vincent, *Peter des Roches*, p. 155; N. Vincent (2004), 'Aubigny, Philip d' (d. 1236)', *ODNB*, available online at http://www.oxforddnb.com/view/article/47227, accessed on 22 September 2010; Alexandre-Bidon and Lett, *Children in the Middle Ages*, pp. 43–5.

66 For a letter from Peter de Maulay to Hubert de Burgh, justiciar, that recommends to him 'Roger of Acaster, master of Richard, brother of the lord king', see *Royal Letters*, i, pp. 179–80 no. CLVI. See also Carpenter, *The Minority*, pp. 241–2; Orme, *From Childhood to Chivalry*, p. 24.

67 Carpenter, *The Minority*, p. 241; Vincent, *Peter des Roches*, p. 154.

68 French was the language spoken in court circles: M. T. Clanchy (1993), *From Memory to Written Record, England 1066–1307* (2nd edn). Oxford: Blackwell, p. 161.

69 Ibid., p. 161; Howell, *Eleanor of Provence*, p. 60.

70 Howell, *Eleanor of Provence*, pp. 83, 87–92. On the patronage of literary works in the vernacular by royal women, see P. Ranft (2002), *Women in Western Intellectual Culture, 600–1500*. Basingstoke: Palgrave Macmillan, p. 89. On Henry III's devotion to Edward the

Confessor and his encouragement of his wife's devotion to this saint, see D. A. Carpenter (2007), 'King Henry III and Saint Edward the Confessor: The Origins of the Cult', *EHR*, 122 (498), 865–91.

71   See, for example, J. C. Ward (2002), *Women in Medieval Europe, 1200–1500*. Harlow: Pearson Education, pp. 16–19; K. M. Phillips (2003), *Medieval Maidens: Young Women and Gender in England, 1270–1540*. Manchester: Manchester University Press, ch. 2.

72   Parsons, 'Mothers, Daughters', pp. 71–5; L. L. Huneycutt (1996), 'Public Lives, Private Ties: Royal Mothers in England and Scotland, 1070–1204', in Parsons and Wheeler (eds), *Medieval Mothering*, pp. 295–311.

73   *The Writings of Agnes of Harcourt: The Life of Isabelle of France and the Letter on Louis IX and Longchamp*, ed. S. L. Field (2003). Notre Dame, IN: University of Notre Dame Press, pp. 52–9. Like Blanche, Eleanor was a granddaughter of Eleanor of Aquitaine.

74   Ibid., pp. 52–5.

75   Ibid., pp. 54–5.

76   Ibid., pp. 54–5, 58–61. In these respects, Isabella's upbringing accorded well with the advice contained in the work of Vincent of Beauvais, whose treatise *De eruditione filiorum nobilium* was commissioned by Isabella's sister-in-law, Margaret of Provence, in c. 1247–9. Vincent, who was heavily influenced by the writings of Jerome, recommended that noble girls should be educated in reading and writing to help inculcate Christian devotion, values and virtues, and in textile work and how to be a good wife: *Vincent of Beauvais, De eruditione filiorum nobilium*, ed. A. Steiner (1938). Menasha, WI: Medieval Academy of America, pp. 172–219, chs xlii–li.

77   *Writings of Agnes of Harcourt*, pp. 60–61.

78   Ward, *Women in Medieval Europe*, pp. 17–18.

79   *Wendover*, iii, p. 108; Wilkinson, 'Isabella of England', p. 28.

80   *Chronica majora*, iii, p. 471.

81   Margaret's grandfather was probably Manasser Biset, Henry II's steward: Parsons, ' "Que nos in infancia lactauit" ', p. 307.

82   *Chronica majora*, iii, pp. 497–8; *Historia anglorum*, ii, p. 468; Wilkinson, 'The Imperial Marriage', p. 28; Howell, *Eleanor of Provence*, pp. 22–3.

83   *Chronica majora*, v, p. 235.

84   Ibid. Cecily died in 1251 and was buried before the altar of St Andrew in St Albans Abbey. For William de Gorham and his son, see *Collectanea Topographica et Genealogica, Vol. VIII*, eds F. Madden, B. Bandinel and J. G. Nichols (1843). London: Society of Antiquaries, p. 93. For the grief of Cecily's brother, Nicholas, at her demise, see *Chronica majora*, v, p. 236.

85   *Chronica majora*, v, p. 235.

86   Ibid.

87   J. Röhrkasten (2004), *The Mendicant Houses of Medieval London, 1221–1539*. Münster: Lit Verlag Münster, part I, chs 1–3; A. G. Little (1892), *The Grey Friars in Oxford*. Oxford: The Oxford Historical Society, part I, chs 1–2. See also the various essays in N. Rogers (ed.), *The Friars in Medieval Britain: Proceedings of the 2007 Harlaxton Symposium*. Donington: Shaun Tyas.

88 On female patronage of the Franciscans, see: L. L. Gees (2002), *Women, Art and Patronage from Henry III to Edward III: 1216–1377*. Woodbridge: Boydell Press, pp. 123–4.

89 For Marsh's letters to Eleanor, see *The Letters of Adam Marsh*, ed. C. H. Lawrence (2006, 2010). Oxford: Clarendon Press, 2 vols, ii, pp. 377–91 nos 155–62.

90 Ibid., ii, pp. 378–83 no. 157, 386–7 no. 160.

91 Ibid., ii, pp. 378–83 no. 157, esp. pp. 378–9.

92 Ibid., ii, pp. 378–83 no. 157, esp. pp. 380–1.

93 Ibid.

94 Ibid., ii, pp. 386–7 no. 160.

95 Ibid.

96 See, for example, ibid., ii, pp. 376–7 no. 155, 382–5 no. 158, 388–9 no. 161, 388–91 no. 162.

97 Ibid., ii, pp. 388–9 no. 161.

98 On female book ownership and on aristocratic mothers who taught their daughters to read, see S. G. Bell (1988), 'Medieval Women Book Owners: Arbiters of Lay Piety and Ambassadors of Culture', in M. Erler and M. Kowaleski (eds), *Women and Power in the Middle Ages*. Athens, GA: University of Georgia Press, pp. 149–87.

99 *Manners*, p. 9.

100 Ibid., p. 24.

101 C. de Hamel (1986), *A History of Illuminated Manuscripts*. London: Guild, pp. 192–6.

102 Vincent, *Peter des Roches*, p. 280.

103 *Letters of Medieval Women* (2002), ed. A. Crawford. Stroud: Sutton, p. 51.

104 Ibid., pp. 52–3; *Royal Letters*, i, pp. 219–20 no. CXCV; Nelson, 'Scottish Queenship', pp. 68–70.

105 *Historia anglorum*, ii, p. 405; Nelson, 'Scottish Queenship', pp. 69–70.

106 'The Chronicle of Melrose', in *The Church Historians of England, Vol. IV, Pt I*, ed. J. Stevenson (1856). London: Seeleys, p. 181; Nelson, 'Scottish Queenship', p. 70.

107 'The Chronicle of Melrose', in *Church Historians*, p. 181.

108 Maddicott, *Simon de Montfort*, p. 39.

Notes on Chapter 2

1 *Royal Letters*, i, pp. 244–6 no. CCXI, at p. 245. See also *Diplomatic Documents*, i, no. 140.

2 D. Crouch (2002), *William Marshal: Knighthood, War and Chivalry, 1147–1219* (2nd edn). London: Pearson Education, pp. 12–24.

3 For Isabella see M. T. Flanagan (2004), 'Clare, Isabel de, *suo jure* Countess of Pembroke (1171x6–1220)', *ODNB*, available online at http://www.oxforddnb.com/view/article/47208, accessed on 14 March 2010.

4 Warren, *King John*, p. 255; Carpenter, *The Minority*, p. 14; Crouch, *William Marshal*, p. 124.

5 Carpenter, *The Minority*, pp. 35–44.

6 Crouch, *William Marshal*, pp. 139–41.

7   Ibid., p. 139.

8   *Chronica majora*, ii, pp. 604–5. See also M. Strickland (2005), 'Enforcers of Magna Carta (*act.* 1215–16)', *ODNB*, available online at http://www.oxforddnb.com/view/theme/93691, accessed on 16 March 2010. Although William junior's decision to support the opposing side to his father might seem, at first glance, like the actions of a dissatisfied and resentful son, his actions might well have been part of a family strategy to preserve the Marshal family's estates no matter which side secured victory: S. Painter (1982 reprint), *William Marshal: Knight-Errant, Baron and Regent of England*. Toronto: University of Toronto Press, pp. 185–6; Crouch, *William Marshal*, pp. 121–2. William junior and his father were in contact with one another during the war. See, for example, *RLP*, i.i, p. 175; 'Annales prioratus de Wigornia', p. 406.

9   Carpenter, *The Minority*, p. 39. William junior's return to the king's grace was apparently prompted, on the one hand, by competition with Adam de Beaumont, another of Louis's supporters, over the office of marshal and, on the other, by Louis's decision to award Robert, Count of Dreux, custody of Marlborough Castle, a stronghold once held by William junior's grandfather, John. Robert was the Duke of Brittany's brother. For Louis's anger at William junior's decision to desert him, see: *De antiquis legibus liber. Cronica maiorum et vicecomitum Londoniarum*, ed. T. Stapleton (1846). London: Camden Society, p. 205. William junior's actions receive fuller discussion in Carpenter, *The Minority*, pp. 29–30; Crouch, *William Marshal*, p. 123.

10   See K. J. Stringer (1985), *Earl David of Huntingdon: A Study in Anglo-Scottish History*. Edinburgh: Edinburgh University Press, pp. 52–3.

11   Ibid., p. 53; Carpenter, *The Minority*, p. 148. For the complaints of Earl David's widow against William Marshal junior and his efforts to refute these, see *Royal Letters*, i, pp. 47–8 nos XL–XLI.

12   For background, see *Royal Letters*, i, pp. 141–4 nos CXXIII–CXXIV. For William's letter to Hubert de Burgh, informing him of Llywelyn's actions in Pembrokeshire and the peace terms which the Welsh prince forced upon William junior's knights and other men there, see ibid., i, pp. 144–5 no. CXXV. See also R. F. Walker (1972), 'Hubert de Burgh and Wales', *EHR*, 87, 465–94, at p. 472.

13   *RLCl*, i, p. 429b; *Royal Letters*, i, p. 150 no. CXXIX.

14   *Royal Letters*, i, p. 150 no. CXXIX.

15   Alexander II had secured the custody of the honour of Huntingdon during the minority of Earl David's heir: Stringer, *Earl David*, p. 53; G. W. S. Barrow (1989 reprint), *Kingship and Unity: Scotland 1000–1306*. Edinburgh: Edinburgh University Press, p. 150.

16   M. Brown (2004), *The Wars of Scotland, 1214–1371*. Edinburgh: Edinburgh University Press, p. 24; Carpenter, *The Minority*, p. 196.

17   *RLCl*, i, p. 429; Carpenter, *The Minority*, p. 219. The young Marshal managed to delay finally handing over the castle until late November 1220: *PR, 1216–25*, p. 272; Carpenter, *The Minority*, p. 220.

18   Ibid., p. 196.

19   *Royal Letters*, i, pp. 244–6 no. CCXI, esp. p. 246.

20   Carpenter, *The Minority*, p. 245.

21 *Royal Letters*, i, pp. 244–6 no. CCXI, esp. p. 244.

22 Ibid., i, pp. 244–6 no. CCXI (pp. 244–5); Powicke, *Henry III*, i. pp. 157–8; Carpenter, *The Minority*, pp. 244–5.

23 *Royal Letters*, i, pp. 244–6 no. CCXI, esp. p. 245.

24 Henry's eldest daughter, Marie, married Otto in May 1214. For the marriage and the battle, see: *Chronique des ducs de Brabant, Tome II*, ed. E. de Dynter (1854). Bruxelles: L'Académie Royale de Belgique, pp. 349–50. See also G. Smets (1908), *Henri I, duc de Brabant, 1190–1235*. Bruxelles: Lamertin.

25 *Genealogia ducum Brabantiae heredum Franciae*, ed. I. Heller (1853), Monumenta Germaniae Historica, SS 25, p. 390 (ch. 7). According to the Dunstable annalist, the duke had returned his wife to her father when he entered into a confederacy with King John and the counts of Flanders and Boulogne: 'Annales prioratus de Dunstaplia', in *Ann. mon.*, iii, pp. 39–40 (recorded under 1212, rather than 1213).

26 His eldest daughter, Marie, now the widow of Emperor Otto IV, had recently married in July 1220 as her second husband William (I), Count of Holland. Another daughter, Margaret, was the wife of Gerhard (III), Count of Guelders. Her sister, Adelaide, was the widow of Arnoul (III), Count of Loos and Graf of Rieneck, and another sister, Mathilde, the wife of Floris, the son and heir of Count William (I), of Holland by William's first wife, Adelaide of Guelders: Smets, *Henri I, duc de Brabant*, p. 165; *Genealogia Ducum Brabantiæ Heredum Franciæ*, p. 390 (ch. 7); *Oude Kronik van Brabant* (1855), Codex Diplomaticus Neerlandicus, Utrecht, Second Series, deerde deel, part i, p. 62.

27 For Arnoul's death in 1221, see *Biographie nationale, volume 1* (1866). Bruxelles: L'Academie Royale des Sciences, des Lettres et des Beaux-Arts de Belgique, p. 451.

28 For the financial predicament of the crown, see Carpenter, *The Minority*, p. 248.

29 That the Marshal had, indeed, considered taking other brides is confirmed by a papal mandate issued on 16 June 1222: 'Regesta 11: 1220–1222' in *Calendar of Papal Registers relating to Great Britain and Ireland, Volume 1, 1198–1304*, ed. W. H. Bliss (1893). London: HMSO, p. 88, available online at http://www.british-history.ac.uk/report.aspx?compid=96004, accessed on 14 March 2010.

30 *Royal Letters*, i, pp. 244–6 no. CCXI, esp. p. 244; Carpenter, *The Minority*, p. 245.

31 Carpenter, *The Minority*, p. 245.

32 *Royal Letters*, i, pp. 244–6 no. CCXI, esp. p. 244; Carpenter, *The Minority*, p. 247.

33 Carpenter, *The Minority*, pp. 247–8.

34 'Annales prioratus de Dunstaplia', p. 68; Carpenter, *The Minority*, p. 247.

35 *Royal Letters*, i, pp. 244–6 no. CCXI, esp. p. 245.

36 'Regesta 11: 1220–1222', in *Calendar of Papal Registers, Volume 1: 1198–1304*, p. 88. The process of securing the consent of a number of leading figures, including the king's uncle, the Earl of Salisbury, might well have been facilitated by a series of generous royal grants from the summer of 1220 onwards: Carpenter, *The Minority*, p. 246.

37 *Royal Letters*, i, pp. 244–6 no. CCXI, esp. p. 245; Powicke, *Henry III*, i, p. 158.

38 Carpenter, *The Minority*, pp. 271–2; *Royal Letters*, i, pp. 244–6 no. CCXI, esp. p. 245.

39 *Royal Letters*, i, pp. 244–6 no. CCXI, esp. p. 245; Powicke, *Henry III*, p. 157.

40 Holt, *Magna Carta*, p. 453 (appendix 6).

41   At the time of this marriage, de Burgh had not yet attained the rank of earl; he was granted the earldom of Kent in 1227: F. J. West (2004), 'Burgh, Hubert de, Earl of Kent (c.1170–1243)', *ODNB*, available online at http://www.oxforddnb.com/view/article/3991, accessed on 15 April 2010; W. W. Scott (2004), 'Margaret, Countess of Kent (1187x95–1259)', *ODNB*, available online at http://www.oxforddnb.com/view/article/49377, accessed on 15 April 2010.

42   Upon his return to England in 1226, Salisbury complained directly to the king that the justiciar had sent 'a man of low birth … to contract an adulterous marriage with her [his wife] by force': *Wendover*, ii, pp. 294–5, 297–8.

43   *Royal Letters*, i, pp. 244–6, no. CCXI, esp. p. 246.

44   *Wendover*, ii, p. 270; 'Annales de Dunstaplia', pp. 82–3; Walker, 'Hubert de Burgh and Wales', 474.

45   *PR, 1216–25*, pp. 413–14; Walker, 'Hubert de Burgh and Wales', 475.

46   *Royal Letters*, i, pp. 244–6 no. CCXI, esp. p. 246. Philip's daughter, Marie, had married Philip, Marquis of Namur, and his sister, Alice, had married the Count of Ponthieu: *Catalogue des actes de Philippe-Auguste*, ed. L. Delisle (1856). Paris: Auguste Durand, p. 230 nos 1001, 1002 (marriage of Marie); D. Power (2004), *The Norman Frontier in the Twelfth and Early Thirteenth Centuries*. Cambridge: Cambridge University Press, p. 168 n. 127 (marriage of Alice).

47   *Royal Letters*, i, pp. 244–6 no. CCXI, esp. p. 246. In 1223, Agnes of Beaujeu, the eldest daughter of Guichard of Beaujeu by Sibyl of Hainaut, the sister of Isabella (the first wife of Philip Augustus), and therefore a cousin of Louis VIII, married Count Thibaut (IV) of Champagne: T. Evergates (1999), 'Aristocratic Women in the County of Champagne', in idem (ed.), *Aristocratic Women in Medieval France*. Philadelphia, PA: University of Pennsylvania Press, pp. 74–110, at p. 80; C. B. Bouchard (1987), *Sword, Miter and Cloister: Nobility and the Church in Burgundy, 980–1198*. Ithaca, NY: Cornell University Press, p. 294 (Appendix A: Family Trees).

48   *Royal Letters*, i, pp. 244–6 no. CCXI, esp. p. 246.

49   *L'histoire de Guillaume le Maréchal*, ed. P. Meyer (1891–1901). Paris: La sociéte de l'histoire de France, 3 vols, iii, pp. ii-xix; Crouch, *William Marshal*, pp. 1–2. For the most recent edition of this text, see *History of William Marshal*, ed. A. J. Holden (2002–6), trans. S. Gregory, with historical notes by D. Crouch. London: Anglo-Norman Text Society, 3 vols.

50   On the date of composition of the text, see *History of William Marshal*, iii, pp. 23–6; D. Crouch (2006), 'Writing a Biography in the Thirteenth Century: The Construction and Composition of the "History of William Marshal"', in D. Bates, J. Crick and S. Hamilton (eds), *Writing Medieval Biography, 750–1250*. Woodbridge: Boydell, pp. 221–35, at p. 223. For discussion of the 'chivalry' of William senior, see Crouch, *William Marshal*, ch. 7. See also L. Ashe (2008), 'William Marshal, Lancelot and Arthur: Chivalry and Kingship', in C. P. Lewis (ed.), *Anglo-Norman Studies XXX: Proceedings of the Battle Conference 2007*. Woodbridge: Boydell, pp. 19–40.

51   *History of William Marshal*, iii, p. 4.

52   Ibid., iii, p. 40.

53 Ibid., iii, p. 24.

54 Ibid.; Crouch, 'Writing a Biography', pp. 223, 225.

55 See p. 26.

56 *History of William Marshal*, ii, pp. 244–5, ll. 14873–82.

57 See pp. 34–5.

58 There might just possibly have been another copy in the possession of the Beauchamp earls of Warwick: *History of William Marshal*, iii, pp. 10–11; Crouch, *William Marshal*, pp. 2–3.

59 'Regesta 11: 1220–1222', in *Calendar of Papal Registers, Volume 1: 1198–1304*, p. 88.

60 Carpenter, *The Minority*, ch. 8.

61 Ibid., pp. 306–7, 316–17, 345–6.

62 Ibid., p. 343.

63 *PR, 1216–1225*, p. 426.

64 *The Historical Works of Gervase of Canterbury*, ed. W. Stubbs (1879–80). London: Longman, Rolls Series, ii, p. 113 ('Gesta Regum Continuata'). See also: 'Annales prioratus de Wigornia', pp. 415–6 (under 1224); 'Annales de Oseneia', in *Ann. Mon.*, iv, p. 64 (under 1224); 'Annales prioratus de Dunstaplia', p. 91 (under 1225); 'Annales de Waverleia', p. 299 (under 1224).

65 For the betrothal, see *Rotuli chartarum in turri Londinensi asservati, vol. I, pars 1, 1199–1216*, ed. T. D. Hardy (1837). London: Record Commission, pp. 112b–113. See also R. F. Walker (2004), 'William Marshal (II), Fifth Earl of Pembroke (c. 1190–1231), Magnate', *ODNB*, available online at http://www.oxforddnb.com/view/article/18127, accessed on 22 April 2010.

66 *Royal Letters*, i, pp. 244–6 no. CCXI, esp. p. 246.

67 'Annales prioratus de Dunstaplia', p. 91.

68 *PR, 1216–1225*, p. 437 (appointment as justiciar). The Marshal held the office of justiciar in Ireland until 22 June 1226: *Cal. Docs. Ireland*, i, p. xxxvi, p. 209 no. 1380; *GEC*, x, p. 366.

69 Parsons, 'Mothers, Daughters', pp. 66, 68.

70 M. Howell (2002), 'Royal Women of England and France in the Mid-Thirteenth Century: A Gendered Perspective', in B. K. U. Weiler and I. W. Rowlands (eds), *England and Europe in the Reign of Henry III (1216–1272)*. Aldershot: Ashgate, pp. 163–82, at p. 166.

71 K. Norgate (2004, rev. T. Reuter), 'Matilda, Duchess of Saxony (1156–1189)', *ODNB*, available online at http://www.oxforddnb.com/view/article/18339, accessed on 22 April 2010.

72 Shadis, *Berenguela of Castile (1180–1246)*, pp. 24–5.

73 D. S. H. Abulafia (2004), 'Joanna, Countess of Toulouse (1165–1199)', *ODNB*, available online at http://www.oxforddnb.com/view/article/14818, accessed on 22 April 2010. William was born in 1154: G. A. Loud (1999), 'William the Bad or William the Unlucky? Kingship in Sicily, 1154–1166', *Haskins Society Journal*, 8, 99–113.

74 On this, see Howell, 'Royal Women of England', p. 166.

75 *Charters of the Redvers Family and the Earldom of Devon, 1090–1217*, ed. R. Bearman (1994). Exeter: Devon and Cornwall Record Society, new series, vol. 37, pp. 16, 172 no. 30.

76 Vincent, 'Isabella of Angoulême', pp. 175–8, 180 (table 2). In 1238, Robert, son of Robert de Courtenay, is styled the 'king's kinsman': *CLR, 1226–40*, p. 323.

77 Vincent, 'Isabella of Angoulême', pp. 217–18 no. 2. In January 1217, Robert also handed over control of Exeter Castle to Isabella as her dower: *PR, 1216–1225*, p. 23.

78 *CChR, 1226–1257*, p. 102 (Luton is misidentified as Linton).

79 Pembroke's father had obtained possession of half the count's estates after Perche was slain at the battle of Lincoln in 1217: Painter, *William Marshal*, pp. 271–2; Carpenter, *The Minority*, pp. 244, 287; Crouch, *William Marshal*, pp. 137–8. Prior to this, William junior himself had been granted eight of these manors in hereditary right in 1203 on the occasion of his betrothal to his first wife, the daughter of the count of Aumale: *Rotuli chartarum*, i.i, pp. 112b–13.

80 Parsons, 'Mothers, Daughters', p. 67.

81 *Wendover*, i, pp. 295, 314, esp. 317. Vincent points out, though, that there is some uncertainty surrounding Isabella's age in 1200 – she might well have been as young as nine: Vincent, 'Isabella of Angoulême', pp. 174–5.

82 *Historia anglorum*, ii, pp. 385–6, 422; Parsons, 'Mothers, Daughters', p. 67.

83 *Historia anglorum*, iii, pp. 117–18, 322, 347; *Chronica majora*, v, pp. 267–72, 501–2, 505–6; Parsons, 'Mothers, Daughters', p. 67; Nelson, 'Scottish Queenship', p. 74.

84 *The Trotula*, ed. M. H. Green (2001). Philadelphia, PA: University of Pennsylvania Press, pp. 20, 66(4).

85 Ibid., p. 79(90).

86 See pp. 11–12.

87 *Foedera*, i pt i, p. 182; *CPR, 1225–32*, pp. 80–1; Green, *Lives*, ii, pp. 52–3.

88 *Wendover*, iii, p. 4.

89 *Royal Letters*, i, pp. 364–5 no. CCCII, esp. p. 364; Green, *Lives*, ii, p. 55 (Green confuses Nicholas with Hugh de Nevill).

90 *Royal Letters*, i, pp. 364–5 no. CCCII, esp. p. 364.

91 Ibid.

92 It is possible that Eleanor was in the early stages of an unsuccessful pregnancy and that her seasickness and the king's concern for her reflected her condition. I owe this suggestion to Dr Michael Ray.

93 *Royal Letters.*, i, pp. 364–5 no. CCCII (p. 365).

94 Ibid., i, pp. 370–1 no. CCCVII (p. 370).

95 For arrangements made by the king in late September 1230, ahead of his departure from Brittany, for Pembroke to remain overseas in his service, see *CPR, 1225–32*, pp. 400, 401. See also *Wendover*, iii, p. 7; 'Annales de Theokesberia', p. 76.

96 L. J. Wilkinson (2007), *Women in Thirteenth-Century Lincolnshire*. Woodbridge: Boydell Press, pp. 2–6.

97 For discussion, see, for example, R. E. Archer (1992), ' "How Ladies … Who Live on their Manors Ought to Manage their Households and Estates": Women as Landholders and Administrators in the Later Middle Ages', in P. J. P. Goldberg (ed.), *Woman is a Worthy Wight: Women in English Society, c. 1200–1500*. Stroud: Alan Sutton, pp. 149–81.

98 See, for example, S. Farmer (1986), 'Persuasive Voices: Clerical Images of Medieval

Wives', *Speculum*, lxi, 517–43; S. M. Johns (2003), *Noblewomen, Aristocracy and Power in the Twelfth-Century Anglo-Norman Realm*. Manchester: Manchester University Press, pp. 69–70; Wilkinson, *Women in Thirteenth-Century Lincolnshire*, p. 78.

99 *GEC*, x, p. 367.

100 *Reading Abbey Cartularies*, ed. B. R. Kemp (1986–7). London: Royal Historical Society, Camden Fourth Series, 2 vols, ii, nos 1056 (a grant by Isabella, Countess of Pembroke, with William junior's assent), 1057 (a grant by William junior).

101 *Monasticon anglicanum*, v, pp. 267–9; *GEC*, x, p. 367.

102 *CChR*, i, p. 41; *GEC*, x, p. 367.

103 *Early Charters of the Cathedral Church of St Paul, London*, ed. M. Gibb (1939). London: Royal Historical Society, nos 221–2.

104 *CChR*, i, pp. 167–9; *GEC*, x, p. 367.

105 *Monsticon anglicanum*, vi pt 1, p. 454 n. e. William senior and William junior also witnessed charters issued by tenants to the priory of Bradenstoke, Wilts: *The Cartulary of Bradenstoke Priory*, ed. V. C. M. London (1979). Devizes: Wiltshire Record Society, vol. 35, pp. 153–5 nos. 518–9, 524; *Monasticon anglicanum*, vi pt 1, pp. 338–9.

106 *Monasticon anglicanum*, vi pt 2, pp. 1134–5.

107 See, for example, *Register of the Abbey of St Thomas, Dublin*, ed. J. T. Gilbert (1899). London: Longman, Rolls Series, pp. 118–19 no. cxxxvii; *GEC*, x, p. 367, n. h.

108 See, for example, *The Cartulary of Bradenstoke Priory*, p. 92 no. 264.

109 *Reading Abbey Cartularies*, ii, no. 1056. For charters of William junior which confirmed his father's grants to Tintern Abbey and Duisk which referred to Isabella in his *pro anima* requests, see *Monasticon anglicanum*, v, pp. 267–9; ibid. vi pt 2, p. 1135.

110 *Monasticon anglicanum*, vi pt 2, p. 843.

111 Ibid.

112 E. Mullally (1996), 'The Portrayal of Women in the *Histoire de Guillaume le Maréchal*', *Peritia*, 10, 351–62, at pp. 357–8.

113 Ibid., 358–9.

114 *History of William Marshal*, ii, pp. 176–9, ll. 13532–43. See also Mullally, 'The Portrayal of Women', 359; Crouch, *William Marshal*, pp. 102–8.

115 Isabella had travelled overseas when heavily pregnant in 1190: Crouch, *William Marshal*, p. 107. It is, though, perhaps worth noting that by 1207, Isabella was significantly older and might well have regarded pregnancy as a greater physical burden.

116 *History of William Marshal*, ii, pp. 204–7, ll. 14067–100; Mullally, 'The Portrayal of Women', 359. See also *History of William Marshal*, ii, pp. 170–71, ll. 13378–94.

117 *History of William Marshal*, ii, pp. 168–9, ll. 13344–6.

118 Ibid., ii, pp. 168–9, ll. 13339, 13352.

119 Ibid., ii, pp. 244–5, l. 14860, pp. 246–7, ll. 14919–22.

120 Ibid., ii, pp. 248–9, esp. ll. 14935, 14939.

121 Ibid., ii, pp. 248–9, ll. 14948–55.

122 Ibid., ii, pp. 246–9, esp. ll. 14925–8, 14932, 14936, 14940–56.

123 Ibid., ii, pp. 248–53, ll. 14965–15027, esp. ll. 14981–7.

124 On 11 July 1230, while still in France, Henry III informed John of Monmouth, an English

Marcher baron, crown agent and keeper of the forests of Buckholt, Clarendon, New and Panchet, that he had given twenty deer in his bailiwick 'to the use of our sister, the wife of our beloved and faithful Earl William Marshal': *CR, 1227–31*, p. 418. On John, see A. F. Pollard (2004), 'Monmouth, John of (c.1182–1248)', rev. R. R. Davies, *ODNB*, available online at http://www.oxforddnb.com/view/article/18959, accessed on 2 November 2010.

125 *CR, 1227–31*, p. 448.

126 'Annales de Theokesberia', p. 77.

127 *The Royal Charter Witness Lists of Henry III (1226–1272)*, ed. M. Morris (2001). Kew: List and Index Society 291–2, 2 vols, i, p. 100.

128 'Annales de Theokesberia', p. 78.

129 *CPR, 1225–32*, p. 412; M. Altschul (1965), *A Baronial Family in Medieval England: The Clares, 1217–1314*. Baltimore: John Hopkins Press, p. 60.

130 For a brief summary, see Vincent, 'Richard, First Earl of Cornwall'. See also Vincent, *Peter des Roches*, p. 266.

131 For a brief summary, see Walker, 'Marshal, William (II), Fifth Earl of Pembroke'.

132 Vincent, 'Richard, First Earl of Cornwall'.

133 'Annales de Theokesberia', p. 78.

134 Ibid.; 'Annales de Waverleia', p. 309. See also 'Annales de Margan', p. 38; 'Annales de Wintonia', p. 85; 'Annales prioratus de Dunstaplia', p. 126; 'Annales Londonienses', in *Chronicles of the Reigns of Edward I, and Edward II, Volume I*, ed. W. Stubbs (1882). London: Longman, Rolls Series, p. 30.

Notes on Chapter 3

1 *Chronica majora*, iii, p. 201.

2 *CPR, 1225–32*, p. 435.

3 An entry on the fine rolls dated 12 April 1231 recorded that the king, 'lamenting' William junior's death, had committed his estates in Ireland to the keeping of Waleran the Teuton: *CFR, 1230–31*, nos 138–9. See also ibid., no. 174.

4 *CPR, 1225–32*, pp. 435–6.

5 *Wendover*, iii, p. 13. See also *Historia anglorum*, ii, p. 334.

6 *Chronica majora*, v, p. 235.

7 Paris referred to Eleanor as Cecily's 'disciple'. Paris confused Eleanor's identity with that of her sister Joan, describing her as Joan, Countess of Pembroke: *ibid.*, v, p. 235. On russet, see Labarge, *Mistress, Maids and Men*, p. 133.

8 *Wendover*, iii, pp. 50–1, 78; *Historia anglorum*, ii, pp. 355–6, 367; C. H. Lawrence (2004), 'Edmund of Abingdon [St Edmund of Abingdon, Edmund Rich] (c.1174–1240)', *ODNB*, available online at http://www.oxforddnb.com/view/article/8503, accessed on 30 November 2010.

9 See p. 28.

10 Wilkinson, *Women in Thirteenth-Century Lincolnshire*, pp. 53–4.

11 Ibid., p. 54.

12 J. S. Loengard (1993), "Rationabilis dos": Magna Carta and the Widow's "Fair Share" in the Earlier Thirteenth Century', in S. S. Walker (ed.), *Wife and Widow in Medieval England*. Michigan: University of Michigan Press, pp. 59–80, at p. 60.

13 The widow was also to enjoy estover of common: Holt, *Magna Carta*, pp. 503–4.

14 *CR, 1227–31*, p. 493.

15 Ibid., p. 492.

16 Ibid., p. 498. Henry's concern for his youngest sister also found a more personal expression a day later on May Day 1231, when he made Eleanor a gift of six deer from Feckenham Forest (Worcestershire), presumably for her to enjoy at Inkberrow: ibid.

17 Ibid., p. 502. For a gift that Henry made to her two days later of three tuns 'from the king's better wines', see ibid., p. 504.

18 On 22 June, Henry III also ordered his English sheriffs to ensure that Eleanor was granted seisin of the ten and a half manors that had been settled on her for life in 1229: ibid., p. 518. Six days later, Thomas of Moulton and Hugh of Bath received orders that, once an extent had been made of William junior's lands and tenements, they were to assign Eleanor 'her reasonable dower according to the custom of the kingdom': ibid., p. 520.

19 Ibid., pp. 527, 528.

20 There was considerable unrest among the Marshal tenants who opposed Richard Marshal's exclusion from his Welsh and Irish lordships. Richard Marshal's return to the king's court in late June 1231 was also followed by the return to England from crusade of de Burgh's rival, Peter des Roches: Vincent, *Peter des Roches*, pp. 272–3; Walker, 'Hubert de Burgh and Wales', 485–7.

21 This was with the exception of those lands in Newbury and Shrivenham that would remain in the possession of the Countess of Pembroke 'for all her life by the king's charter': *CR, 1227–31*, p. 541.

22 Ibid., p. 555. In the following spring, when the royal court was at Marlborough, Eleanor complained to Henry that her late husband's debtors were attempting to recover their money from her lands in Wiltshire, whereupon the king ordered the local sheriff to see that the debts were recovered from Richard Marshal's properties instead: *CR, 1231–4*, p. 42.

23 For example, on 28 May 1231, the local sheriff was instructed to see that the oxen and ploughs remained on the manor of Weston (Hertfordshire) to cultivate the lands until the king should order otherwise: *CR, 1227–31*, p. 509. Similar arrangements were made for the ploughs on the countess's manors of Sutton, Kemsing and Brabourne in Kent, and Luton and Toddington in Bedfordshire in July 1231: *CFR, 1230–31*, nos 220, 221. See Figure 3 above for a map of Eleanor's principal English dower manors.

24 V. Hoyle (2008), 'The Bonds that Bind: Money Lending between Anglo-Jewish and Christian Women in the Plea Rolls of the Exchequer of the Jews, 1218–80', *Journal of Medieval History*, 34, 119–29, at p. 124.

25 *CR, 1231–4*, p. 5.

26 Ibid., p. 49.

27 *CPR, 1225–32*, p. 454.

28   Vincent, *Peter des Roches*, p. 295.

29   *CR, 1231–4*, pp. 144–5. An entry on the fine rolls in the preceding autumn noted the presence of John Marshal, an executor of William junior, in Ireland; John had set out to receive Eleanor's dower there (*CFR, 1230–1*, no. 311). This entry is indicative of the lengthy process and delays involved in securing her Irish dower.

30   The Archbishop of Dublin was sent another letter along similar lines: ibid., pp. 144–5.

31   D. A. Carpenter (1980), 'The Fall of Hubert de Burgh', *Journal of British Studies*, 19, 1–17; B. Weiler (2007), *Kingship, Rebellion and Political Culture: England and Germany, c. 1215–c.1250*. Basingstoke: Palgrave Macmillan, pp. 13–14.

32   Vincent, *Peter des Roches*, pp. 303–20.

33   *Wendover*, iii, p. 34.

34   Richard witnessed no fewer than twenty-eight royal charters between July 1232 and April 1233: Vincent, *Peter des Roches*, pp. 310–11.

35   *CR, 1231–4*, pp. 233, 310. See also TNA: PRO KB 26/159, mm. 2d–3d for a later legal dispute that recalled the terms of Richard's settlement with Eleanor, and which dated it to 29 July 1232 (16 Henry III).

36   For the troubles that a later absentee landlady and widow encountered in Ireland, see C. O'Cléirigh (1996), 'The Absentee Landlady and the Sturdy Robbers: Agnes de Valence', in C. E. Meek and M. K. Simms (eds), *The Fragility of her Sex? Medieval Irish Women in their European Context*. Dublin: Four Courts Press, pp. 101–18.

37   See pp. 78–9.

38   KB 26/159, m. 3d.

39   *CR, 1231–4*, p. 310.

40   Vincent, *Peter des Roches*, pp. 318, 327–31, 334–9; Weiler, *Kingship*, pp. 14–15.

41   Vincent, *Peter des Roches*, pp. 339, 372, 375.

42   Ibid., pp. 387-9.

43   *CR, 1231–4*, p. 310.

44   Ibid., p. 233.

45   Green, *Lives*, ii, p. 60.

46   Ibid.

47   See p. 79.

48   Mabel was to enjoy the forge just as she was accustomed to have it in the reign of King John and his predecessors: *CPR, 1227–31*, p. 451.

49   J. Birrell (2006), 'Procuring, Preparing, and Serving Venison in Late Medieval England', in C. M. Woolgar, D. Serjeantson and T. Waldron (eds), *Food in Medieval England*. Oxford: Oxford University Press, pp. 176–88, at pp. 178–80. J. Birrell has calculated that between William Marshal junior's death in 1231 and 1235, for example, Henry III provided Eleanor with no fewer than 181 deer in total – or between 30 and 46 deer a year – from the royal forests, but conflates entries relating to Eleanor and her cousin Eleanor of Brittany: ibid., pp. 186.

50   *CR, 1227–31*, p. 528 (five deer); *CR, 1231–34*, pp. 9 (five deer), 79 (six deer), 92 (two deer), 167 (ten deer), 217 (three deer), 218 (five deer), 224 (five deer), 226 (five deer), 253 (ten deer).

51 Vincent, *Peter des Roches*, pp. 399–428.

52 Ibid., pp. 401–13.

53 Ibid., pp. 427–8.

54 Ibid., pp. 429, 434–6, 438–40. For the new archbishop, see C. H. Lawrence (1960), *Edmund of Abingdon: A Study in Hagiography and History*. Oxford: Clarendon Press; *The Life of St Edmund of Abingdon by Matthew Paris*, ed. C. H. Lawrence (1999). London: Sandpiper Books; Lawrence, 'Edmund of Abingdon [St Edmund of Abingdon, Edmund Rich] (c.1174–1240)'.

55 *Life of St Edmund*, pp. 52–6; Vincent, *Peter des Roches*, pp. 440–5.

56 *Life of St Edmund*, p. 53.

57 Gilbert was knighted by the king on 11 June 1234 and formally recognised as Earl of Pembroke and Earl Marshal: 'Annales prioratus de Dunstaplia', p. 137; D'A. J. D. Boulton (1995), 'Classic Knighthood as Nobiliary Dignity: The Knighting of Counts and Kings' Sons in England, 1066–1272', in S. Church and R. Harvey (eds), *Medieval Knighthood, V*. Woodbridge: Boydell Press, pp. 41–100, at p. 90; Weiler, *Kingship*, pp. 139–41.

58 Björn Weiler's comparative study of the Marshal rebellion and the rebellion of Henry (VII) in Germany, for example, observes that 'very little' can be said about the role of women in politics, but overlooks Eleanor's involvement in the events of 1233–4: Weiler, *Kingship*, pp. 151–2.

59 Green, *Lives*, ii, p. 57.

60 *The Life of St Edmund*, pp. 132–3. On Isabella and Matthew, see R. Vaughan (1958), *Matthew Paris*. Cambridge: Cambridge University Press, pp. 13, 170, 173, 181.

61 See p. 28.

62 See p. 45.

63 Magna Carta laid down that widows should not be forced to remarry: Holt, *Magna Carta*, p. 504. It is, however, likely that had Eleanor not taken a vow of chastity, considerable pressure might have been brought to bear in persuading her to give her free consent to marriage. On the crown's 'control' over widows during the reign of King Henry III, see S. L. Waugh (1988), *The Lordship of England: Royal Wardships and Marriages in English Society and Politics, 1217–1327*. Princeton, NJ: Princeton University Press, pp. 68–70, 86–7, esp. 87.

64 Abulafia (2004), 'Joanna, Countess of Toulouse', *ODNB*, available online at http://www.oxforddnb.com/view/article/14818, accessed on 30 November 2010.

65 Nelson, 'Scottish Queenship', pp. 69–70.

66 Wilkinson, 'Isabella of England', p. 22.

67 *Wendover*, iii, p. 77; Vincent, *Peter des Roches*, pp. 414–15. On Eleanor of Brittany, see G. Seabourne (2007), 'Eleanor of Brittany and her Treatment by King John and Henry III', *Nottingham Medieval Studies*, 51, 73–110.

68 *CR, 1231–4*, p. 369.

69 Ibid., p. 371. In March 1234, however, Eleanor was still waiting to receive £50 from the issues of the manor for her sustenance from Peter de Rivallis: ibid., p. 393.

70 *CPR, 1232–47*, pp. 46, 56.

Notes on Chapter 4

1   *CRR, 1233–7*, no. 1088.
2   Eleanor also sought the recovery of 100 marks from Richard Marshal's sale of the custody of the land and heir of Paulinus de Teyden', together with other rights and smaller properties from Pembroke's English estates: ibid.
3   Gilbert also recognized Eleanor's right to 100 marks as her share from the sale of the wardship. In return for this concession, Eleanor resigned all her claims to dower in the remainder of William junior's former lands in England: ibid. The king ordered the executors of Earl William to satisfy Eleanor for the £550 in arrears that had built up for her Irish dower from the earl's chattels and goods, although it was Richard Marshal who had allowed the arrears to accumulate. If this money still went unpaid, then Gilbert was to satisfy the king's sister for this sum: ibid. Curiously, Eleanor had enjoyed possession of Weston during Richard Marshal's lifetime: See p. 39.
4   *CPR, 1232–47*, pp. 65–6.
5   The grant of Magor included common of pasture in the forest of Netherwent and the right to all pleas on the manor, including crown pleas. Eleanor, for her part, promised to resign her rights in the remainder of her dead husband's lands in Netherwent and Tidenham: *CRR, 1233–7*, no. 1154. Gilbert also granted Eleanor a further ten librates of land in Badgeworth if the land there was valued at more than the forty librates previously granted to Eleanor. See also KB 26/159, m. 3d.
6   *CR, 1231–4*, pp. 526–7.
7   *CRR, 1233–7*, no. 1279.
8   *CPR, 1232–47*, p. 125.
9   In the meantime, the earl was to receive just enough money to cover the expenses of administering and maintaining each manor in cultivation: ibid.
10   The assignment was witnessed by some of the greatest men of the realm, including the bishops of Chichester, Exeter and Carlisle, and the earls of Lincoln, Cornwall, Norfolk and Kent, as well as leading figures in the king's administration (e.g. Ralph fitz Nicholas and Godfrey of Crowcombe, both of whom were royal household stewards): ibid., pp. 125–6. Gilbert also entered into a second undertaking, whereby he assigned the issues of the manor of Bosham to Eleanor until she had recovered £350 in outstanding arrears from Richard Marshal's time as earl. This second agreement laid down that, should Eleanor die before full payment had been made, the remainder of the sum would be paid to her legatees or assigns: ibid., p. 126.
11   That the countess possessed her own, distinctive seal serves as a reminder of the independent legal authority that she now enjoyed in widowhood. The witnesses of Eleanor's bond were: the Earl of Norfolk, Ralph fitz Nicholas, Walter Marshal (Eleanor's younger brother-in-law, who also witnessed Gilbert's deeds), Geoffrey of Langley, William Bluet (previously identified as one of the countess's knights) and Walter de Hide: ibid., p. 126.
12   Ibid. (where Marjorie is confused with her sister, Margaret).
13   Eleanor was pardoned from paying a further 200 marks that she owed to the king as a prest: *CR, 1234–7*, pp. 150–1.

14 *CPR, 1232–47*, p. 65.

15 Eleanor's vow of perpetual widowhood presumably explains why Eleanor did not appear among those noble widows who felt compelled to fine with the crown to stay single, even in the years after Magna Carta's provisions on the issue were first published. See, for example, D. A. Carpenter (March 2008), 'Hubert de Burgh, Matilda de Mowbray, and Magna Carta's Protection of Widows', Fine of the Month (March 2008), available online at http://www.finerollshenry3.org.uk/content/month/fm-03-2008.html, accessed on 13 December 2010.

16 See Figure 3. TNA, PRO: C 47/9/20, mm. 3–5. The roll details the partition of Eleanor's Marshal dower properties between the Marshal co-heirs (see pp. 78–9). Strictly speaking, some of Eleanor's manors had formed part of the grant made to William junior and her in 1229. See p. 28. For further discussion, see also Maddicott, *Simon de Montfort*, p. 50.

17 For aristocratic widows as estate managers, see, for example, Archer, '"How Ladies … Who Live on their Manors"', pp. 149–81; E. Cavell (2007), 'Aristocratic Widows and the Medieval Welsh Frontier: The Shropshire Evidence', *Transactions of the Royal Historical Society*, 17, 57–82, at p. 69.

18 For the officials who staffed the estate and household administrations of thirteenth-century English nobles, see N. Denholm-Young (1937), *Seignorial Administration in England*. Oxford: Oxford University Press, esp. chs 1 and 2; L. J. Wilkinson (2003), 'The *Rules* of Robert Grosseteste Reconsidered: The Lady as Estate and Household Manager', in C. Beattie, A. Maslakovic and S. Rees Jones (eds), *The Medieval Household in Christian Europe, c. 850–c. 1550: Managing Power, Wealth and the Body*. Turnhout, Belgium: Brepols, pp. 293–306.

19 Wilkinson, 'The *Rules* of Robert Grosseteste Reconsidered', pp. 293–306.

20 See, for example, J. C. Ward (1992), *English Noblewomen in the Later Middle Ages*. Harlow: Longman, chs 3 and 6.

21 *CR, 1227–31*, p. 555. See also *CR, 1231–4*, p. 3 for an example of Eleanor soliciting her brother's help to recover rights of estover.

22 *CR, 1231–4*, p. 174.

23 Ibid., pp. 256, 264.

24 Ibid., p. 275.

25 Ibid., p. 509.

26 *CRR, 1233–7*, no. 1145.

27 *CR, 1231–4*, p. 466. The countess's enjoyment of her brother's favour was demonstrated when the king accompanied this pardon with a personal gift of venison to his sister: ibid.

28 *CR, 1234–7*, p. 257.

29 *CR, 1231–4*, p. 527.

30 Vincent, *Peter des Roches*, pp. 396–8. This is, however, at odds with Wendover's description of Richard's friendly reception by the Marshal tenants in Ireland and Wales: *Wendover*, iii, p. 14.

31 Labarge, *Mistress, Maids and Men*, p. 49.

32 William Bluet also witnessed Eleanor's bond: *CPR, 1232–47*, pp. 125–6. In July 1237, the

same knights witnessed Gilbert Marshal's confirmation of a gift of land made by Eleanor to Andrew de la Brech: *CChR, 1226–57*, p. 230.

33   *Monasticon anglicanum*, v, pp. 267–9.

34   Crouch, *William Marshal*, pp. 149–50, 220–21; *Book of Fees*, ii (1242–3), p. 724; *The Cartulary of Cirencester Abbey, Gloucestershire, Volume III*, ed. C. D. Ross and M. Devine (1977). Oxford: Oxford University Press, p. 760; C. S. Taylor (1889), *An Analysis of the Domesday Survey of Gloucestershire*. Bristol and Gloucestershire Archaeology Society, pp. 167–9; E. Brooks (1950), *Knights' Fees in Counties Wexford, Carlow and Kilkenny*. Ireland: Manuscripts Commission, p. 26. The Bluet family patronised Lacock Abbey, Wiltshire. See, for example, *Lacock Abbey Charters*, ed. K. H. Rogers (1979). Devizes: Wiltshire Record Society, vol. 34, p. 25 nos 49–51, p. 44 no. 157, p. 47 no. 169.

35   The countess secured, for example, royal grants of protection for men like Bartholomew de Crek: *CPR, 1232–47*, p. 2.

36   *CR, 1234–7*, p. 425.

37   *CR, 1231–4*, p. 152.

38   *CRR, 1233–7*, no. 498.

39   Ibid., no. 669.

40   In order to placate Eleanor and, perhaps, in recognition of her forceful personality, Henry ordered the sheriffs to compensate Eleanor with other lands in their place: *CR, 1231–4*, pp. 231–2.

41   See pp. 39, 40.

42   *CR, 1231–4*, p. 210.

43   Ibid., p. 243.

44   Ibid., p. 23.

45   For the way in which a later noblewoman pursued similar strategies in Stuart England, see J. L. Malay (2009), 'Anne Clifford: Appropriating the Rhetoric of Queens to Become the Lady of the North', in Oakley-Brown and Wilkinson (eds), *The Rituals and Rhetoric of Queenship*, pp. 157–70, at pp. 160–2.

46   *CR, 1234–7*, p. 131.

47   See Figure 3 above. As part of the process whereby Eleanor took possession of Odiham, the king's oxen on the manor were valued and purchased from the crown, together with the last year's corn and hay, so that she might acquire and maintain her new property with a minimum of disruption: *CPR, 1232–47*, pp. 161, 166. Just a few days after this gift, the king also assigned Eleanor the park there, together with the vert and the venison: *CR, 1234–7*, p. 387.

48   P. MacGregor (1983), *Odiham Castle, 1200–1500*. Gloucester: Alan Sutton, ch. 2.

49   Ibid., pp. 48–9.

50   Ibid., pp. 49–50.

51   Green, *Lives*, ii, p. 63; *CFR, 1243–4*, no. 64 (a later entry on the fine rolls whereby Henry pardoned this debt), available online at http://frh3.org.uk/content/calendar/roll_041.html, accessed on 1 January 2011.

52   In common with other noble households in the first half of the thirteenth century, that over which Eleanor presided was a peripatetic institution: C. M. Woolgar (1999), *The*

Great Household in Late Medieval England. New Haven: Yale University Press, pp. 46–7; Wilkinson, 'The *Rules* of Robert Grosseteste Reconsidered', pp. 293–306.

53   *CR, 1234–7*, p. 96.

54   See 'The *Rules* of Robert Grosseteste' (1971), in D. Oschinsky (ed.), *Walter of Henley and Other Treatises on Estate Management and Accounting*. Oxford: Clarendon Press, pp. 390–3, 396–9, esp. nos iv, x, xii.

55   Birrell, 'Procuring, Preparing and Serving Venison', p. 180.

56   Eleanor received ten bucks (*damos*) on 14 April from Rockingham: *CR, 1231–4*, p. 207. On 10 May 1233, she was given three roe-bucks (*capreolos*) from Chute and five bucks (*damos*) from Savernake (ibid., p. 217), followed by five bucks (*damos*) from Chute on 29 May 1233 (ibid., p. 224), five bucks (*damos*) from Savernake on 6 June (*ibid.*, p. 226), ten bucks (*damos*) from Rockingham on 25 August 1233 (ibid., p. 253), and two stags (*cervos*) from Chute on 20 September 1233 (ibid., p. 269).

57   Eleanor received ten does (*damas*) from Chute in late January (*CR, 1231–4*, p. 371), and five bucks (*damos*) from Feckenham at the beginning of June (ibid., p. 466). A further gift of five bucks (*damos*) in Savernake on 12 July 1234 was followed a month later by another gift of ten bucks (*damos*) and two stags (*cervos*) in Chute (ibid., pp. 473, 497).

58   On 16 May 1235, Eleanor received six deer (*damos*) from Savernake: *CR, 1231–4*, p. 92. On 30 May, Eleanor received fifteen deer (*damos*) from Rockingham and five from Dean: *CR, 1234–7*, p. 95. On 9 August 1235, Henry III gave her a stag (*cervum*) in Chute: *CR, 1234–7*, p. 128.

59   In June 1236, the king's forester was instructed to deliver fifteen deer (*damos*) to Eleanor from Wychwood, Whittlewood and Bernwood: *CR, 1234–7*, p. 278. This gift was followed by another three deer (*damos*) from the forest of Dean, and another three from the forest of Braden on 23 July 1236, together with four stags (*cervos*) on 24 July: *CR, 1234–7*, pp. 291, 292. On 17 August 1236, the constable of St Briavels Castle was instructed to allow Eleanor to have two stags (*cervos*) in St Briavels Forest: ibid., p. 303.

60   In February 1237, Henry gave Eleanor a further fifteen deer (five *damos* and ten *damas*) from Savernake for the express purpose of allowing his sister to stock her own park at Badgeworth: *CR, 1234–7*, p. 414. In August 1237, Eleanor received eight deer (*damos*) from Bernwood and eight (*damos*) from Clarendon: ibid., p. 485.

61   Ibid., p. 386.

62   As the clerk who compiled Henry III's wardrobe accounts noted, more than £250 was spent on wax for lighting the royal chapel and the chambers of the English king and queen, Joan, Queen of Scots, during her visit, and Eleanor, Countess of Pembroke: TNA: PRO, E 372/81, rot. 1, m. 2. A splendid edition of Henry III's wardrobe accounts is being prepared by Dr Ben Wild for publication by the Pipe Roll Society.

63   *Wendover*, iii, p. 19.

64   The annalist had presumably received his information from Robert: 'Annales de Theokesberia', p. 84.

65   The Christmas court was held at Worcester, again in the presence of des Roches: *Wendover*, iii, p. 47; *CR, 1231–4*, p. 167.

66   *Wendover*, iii, p. 70.

67   Ibid., iii, p. 101.

68   *Chronica majora*, iii, pp. 334, 380.

69   Ibid., iii, pp. 336.

70   Ibid., iii, pp. 336–9; M. W. Labarge (1962), *Simon de Montfort*. London: Eyre and Spottiswoode, p. 44.

71   *Chronica majora*, iii, p. 338.

72   Ibid., iii, pp. 336–7.

73   Wilkinson, 'The Imperial Marriage of Isabella of England', pp. 29–31.

74   See pp. 13–14.

75   See, for example, Woolgar, *The Great Household*, pp. 12–14. On Henry III's lavish almsgiving, see S. Dixon-Smith (1999), 'The Image and Reality of Alms-Giving in the Great Halls of Henry III', *The Journal of the British Archaeological Association*, 152, 76–96.

76   See pp. 118–19. See also R. E. Archer (2003), 'Piety in Question: Noblewomen and Religion in the Later Middle Ages', in D. Wood (ed.), *Women and Religion in Medieval England*. Oxford: Oxbow, pp. 118–40, at p. 129.

77   Woolgar, *The Great Household*, p. 90. This, again, appears to have been the case in 1265. See p. 119.

78   Woolgar, *The Great Household*, pp. 90–1.

79   Ibid., pp. 84–9.

80   'Chronicle of Melrose', p. 181.

81   Nelson, 'Scottish Queenship in the Thirteenth Century', p. 69.

82   See, for example, P. Ricketts (2003), 'Widows, Religious Patronage and Family Identity: Some Cases from Twelfth-Century Yorkshire', *Haskins Society Journal*, 14, 117–36, at pp. 124–7.

83   M. Vale (2001), *The Princely Court: Medieval Courts and Culture in North-West Europe*. Oxford: Oxford University Press, p. 236.

84   Wilkinson, 'The Imperial Marriage of Isabella of England', p. 36. I have not, as yet, uncovered any specific grants to religious houses made by Eleanor in her dead husband's memory. On the royal feeding of poor for the souls of Henry III's kin, see Dixon-Smith, 'The Image and Reality of Almsgiving', 89–90.

85   Aristocratic women skilled in needlework were also found in early modern England: B. Harris (2002), *English Aristocratic Women, 1450–1550: Marriage and Family, Property and Careers*. Oxford: Oxford University Press, p. 230.

86   *Writings of Agnes of Harcourt*, pp. 62–5.

87   TNA: PRO C 47/3/4/1.

88   Vale, *The Princely Court*, pp. 172–3.

89   B. B. Rezak (1988), 'Women, Seals, and Power in Medieval France, 1150–1350', in M. Erler and M. Kowaleski (eds), *Women and Power in the Middle Ages*. Athens, GA: University of Georgia Press, pp. 61–82, at pp. 76–7.

90   See, for example, Ward, *English Noblewomen*, pp. 96–7.

91   *CPR, 1232–47*, p. 208.

92   Ibid., p. 214.

93 Barbara Harris's work on aristocratic women at the Yorkist and Tudor royal courts has offered interesting points of comparison here, albeit in a rather different political and religious context: Harris, *English Aristocratic Women*, pp. 224–7.

Notes on Chapter 5

1 *Chronica majora*, iii, pp. 470–1.

2 Ibid.; Maddicott, *Simon de Montfort*, p. 21.

3 Maddicott, *Simon de Montfort*, pp. xxiv–xxv (figure 1).

4 Ibid., pp. 1–21.

5 Ibid., pp. 8–13.

6 Ibid., pp. 8–16.

7 Ibid., p. 19.

8 It is also worth noting that Simon was described as the Earl of Leicester in Paris's narrative, even though he had not yet received a formal grant of the earldom itself: *Chronica majora*, iii, p. 338.

9 Maddicott, *Simon de Montfort*, p. 17.

10 Ibid., p. 18. Joan was the daughter of Baldwin (IX), Count of Flanders. Her first husband was the son of King Sancho I of Portugal: C. Petit-Dutaillis (repr. 1966), *The Feudal Monarchy in France and England from the Tenth to the Thirteenth Century*. New York: Harper and Row, pp. 223–4; J. Bradbury (2004), *The Routledge Companion to Medieval Warfare*. London: Routledge, p. 36.

11 As one chronicler observed 'God provided the sister of the king of England for him': *Chronica Albrici monachi trium fontium*, pp. 940–1.

12 Richard of Cornwall's marriage to Isabella Marshal had yet to produce a living heir, in spite of Isabella's progeny by her first husband: N. Vincent (2004), 'Richard, First Earl of Cornwall and King of Germany (1209–1272)', *ODNB*, available online at http://www.oxforddnb.com/view/article/23501, accessed on 1 January 2011.

13 *Chronica majora*, iii, p. 471.

14 Ibid.

15 The entries relating to Eleanor and Simon were recorded next to one another on the same membrane of the close roll: *CR, 1234–7*, p. 292.

16 *Chronica majora*, v, p. 235; Howell, 'Royal Women of England and France', pp. 163–81, at p. 169.

17 Howell, 'Royal Women of England and France', p. 169.

18 Maddicott, *Simon de Montfort*, pp. 8–9, 16.

19 The queen's uncle, William of Savoy, accompanied his niece to England and remained there, serving as a royal counsellor, until his departure in May 1238: Howell, *Eleanor of Provence*, pp. 24–6.

20 Archer, '"How Ladies … Who Live on their Manors"', p. 170.

21 Wilkinson, 'The Imperial Marriage of Isabella of England', pp. 20–36.

22 Vincent, 'Isabella of Angoulême', pp. 206–16.

23 *Chronica majora*, iii, pp. 470–1, 475.

24 Ibid., iii, pp. 475–6; Maddicott, *Simon de Montfort*, p. 21.

25 See, for example, Howell, *Eleanor of Provence*, pp. 85–6.

26 'Annales prioratus de Wigornia', p. 430.

27 'Annales de Waverleia', p. 318. See also 'Annales de Theokesberia', p. 106, which dates the marriage to 14 January. This annalist's confusion presumable resulted from the secrecy surrounding the union.

28 *Chronica majora*, iii, p. 471; v, p. 235.

29 See, for example, *Chronica majora*, ii, p. 563.

30 See, for example, *CPR, 1232–47*, p. 208.

31 *Historia anglorum*, ii, p. 403.

32 The Tewkesbury annalist, for example, recorded how 'The sister of the king of England, formerly the wife of the younger Marshal, married Simon de Montfort, whereupon the Earl of Cornwall was excited to anger': 'Annales de Theokesberia', p. 106. See also *Chronica majora*, iii, pp. 475–6.

33 For other grievances, including hostility to aliens and to papal appointees within the church: *Chronica majora*, iii, pp. 475–8.

34 See, for example: 'Annales Londonienses', p. 35. For the Clare marriage, see also *CPR, 1232–47*, p. 208.

35 *CPR, 1232–47*, p. 209.

36 Maddicott, *Simon de Montfort*, p. 22.

37 *CLR, 1226–40*, p. 311. For other loans to Simon and Eleanor, see ibid., p. 312.

38 *Chronica majora*, iii, pp. 479–80.

39 *CPR, 1232–47*, p. 214.

40 *Chronica majora*, iii, p. 518.

41 Ibid., iii, pp. 474, 480.

42 Ibid., iii, p. 480.

43 The debt predated Eleanor's marriage to Simon: *CR, 1237–42*, pp. 44, 45.

44 Ibid, pp. 52, 64, 83, 96, 103; *CLR, 1226–40*, p. 337.

45 *CLR, 1226–40*, p. 329.

46 *CR, 1237–42*, pp. 60–1.

47 *CPR, 1232–47*, p. 231.

48 *Chronica majora*, iii, p. 487.

49 'Regesta 19: 1238–1240', in *Calendar of Papal Registers, Volume 1: 1198–1304*, pp. 169–88, available online at http://www.british-history.ac.uk/report.aspx?compid=96012, accessed on 27 July 2010.

50 *Chronica majora*, iii, p. 567.

51 Ibid., iii, p. 487.

52 Ibid.

53 Ibid. For a recent study of Peter, see P. W. Rosemann (2004), *Peter Lombard*. Oxford: Oxford University Press.

54 Paris's sympathetic treatment of Simon is discussed in Vaughan, *Matthew Paris*, p. 149.

55 *Chronica majora*, iii, p. 498. Although the witness lists of charters issued in October

1238 are damaged, those for November 1238 confirm Simon's absence from court: *Royal Charter Witness Lists*, i, pp. 167–8.

56 *Chronica majora*, iii, p. 518.

57 For this alternative date, see R. Stacey (1987), *Politics, Policy and Finance under Henry III, 1216–1245*. Oxford: Clarendon Press, p. 124 n. 168. For the almoner's roll see TNA, PRO C 47/3/44.

58 For Henry's presence at Joan's deathbed, see 'Chronicle of Melrose', p. 181. See also *Chronica majora*, iii, p. 479.

59 Stacey, *Politics, Policy and Finance*, p. 124 n. 168. See also C. Bémont (1884), *Simon de Montfort, Comte de Leicester*. Paris: Alphonse Picard, Libraire, p. 9.

60 The bishop subsequently became ill and died: *Chronica majora*, iii, p. 518.

61 Ibid.

62 *CLR, 1226–40*, p. 356. For baudekyn, see L. Monnas (2008), *Merchants, Princes and Painters: Silk Fabrics in Italian and Northern Paintings, 1300–1500*. New Haven: Yale University Press, pp. 298–9, 301. For Isabella's robes, see TNA: PRO C 47/3/3; Green, *Lives*, ii, p. 14.

63 *CLR, 1226–40*, p. 356.

64 Ibid.

65 Simon witnessed a royal grant to Hugh Paynel on this date: *Royal Charter Witness Lists*, i, p. 168.

66 *CLR, 1226–40*, p. 360.

67 *Chronica majora*, iii, p. 524; Maddicott, *Simon de Montfort*, p. 23.

68 The bishops of London and Carlisle, Richard, Earl of Cornwall, and Humphrey de Bohun, Earl of Hereford and Essex, were also among those who fulfilled this role: *Chronica majora*, iii, pp. 539–40; Howell, *Eleanor of Provence*, pp. 27–8.

69 *Chronica majora*, iii, p. 540.

70 Howell, *Eleanor of Provence*, pp. 24–5, 29–30.

71 Robert Stacey calculated that between February and May 1238, Henry directed 'almost half the recorded total of the king's receipts' from a subsidy of a thirtieth on movables that he had been granted in 1237 towards his brother's planned expedition. This expenditure was on top of the loans and fees which the king made or paid to those in his service overseas: Stacey, *Politics, Policy and Finance*, pp. 126–7.

72 The original debt was owed by Montfort to Peter of Dreux, Count of Brittany, but was transferred by Peter to Thomas of Savoy: Maddicott, *Simon de Montfort*, pp. 24–5; *CR, 1237–42*, pp. 234–5; *CLR, 1226–40*, p. 472; Howell, *Eleanor of Provence*, p. 28; Bémont, *Simon de Montfort*, pp. 333–4 no. xxxiv.

73 *Chronica majora*, iii, pp. 566–7; Howell, *Eleanor of Provence*, p. 28; Maddicott, *Simon de Montfort*, p. 25.

74 *Chronica majora*, iii. p. 566; Howell, *Eleanor of Provence*, p. 28; Maddicott, *Simon de Montfort*, p. 25.

75 *Chronica majora*, iii, p. 566.

76 Ibid.

77 Ibid., iii, p. 567.

78 Bémont, *Simon de Montfort*, pp. 333–4 no. xxxiv. A point made in Labarge, *Simon de Montfort*, p. 54.

79 *Chronica majora*, iii, p. 567. As Earl Simon later recalled, he escaped imprisonment thanks to Richard of Cornwall's intervention. See also Bémont, *Simon de Montfort*, p. 334 no. xxxiv; Maddicott, *Simon de Montfort*, p. 25.

80 This line of argument is strongly promoted by Maddicott: *Simon de Montfort*, pp. 25–6.

81 TNA, PRO E 372/83, rot. 7; *CLR, 1226–40*, p. 410. See also Stacey, *Politics, Policy and Finance*, pp. 126–7.

82 Henry III paid 500 marks of Earl Simon's debt to Thomas and, according to Montfort's own account, raised the remainder from Simon's English estates: Bémont, *Simon de Montfort*, p. 334 no xxxiv; Labarge, *Simon de Montfort*, pp. 54–5.

Notes on Chapter 6

1 *The Letters of Adam Marsh*, ii, pp. 390–1 no. 162.

2 *Chronica majora*, iv, p. 7.

3 Labarge, *Simon de Montfort*, p. 55.

4 *Chronica majora*, iv, p. 7; 'Annales prioratus de Dunstaplia', p. 152.

5 Paris lists those who travelled with Earl Richard and Earl Simon separately: *Chronica majora*, iv, p. 44 n. 6 (marginal note).

6 'Annales prioratus de Dunstaplia', p. 152.

7 *Chronica majora*, iv, p. 44 n. 6.

8 Ibid., iv, p. 44 n. 6; Labarge, *Simon de Montfort*, p. 57. I have not managed to trace further details of Eleanor's stay at Brindisi in the works of chroniclers within the Holy Roman Empire.

9 Bémont, *Simon de Montfort*, p. 334 no. xxxiv; Maddicott, *Simon de Montfort*, pp. 30–1.

10 Maddicott, *Simon de Montfort*, pp. 31–2.

11 Richard of Cornwall's first wife, Isabella, died in childbirth in 1240: *Chronica majora*, iv, p. 2. For Beatrice's visit, see ibid., iv, pp. 261, 263, 283–4.

12 For Beatrice's assistance to the Montforts, see Bémont, *Simon de Montfort*, p. 335 no. xxxiv.

13 *CFR, 1243–4*, no. 64, available online at http://www.frh3.org.uk/content/calendar/roll_041.html, accessed on 2 August 2010. On 12 February 1244, the king issued the Earl and Countess of Leicester with a formal pardon that itemised the debts which Simon and Eleanor had each incurred to the crown: *CR, 1242–7*, p. 159.

14 No dowry had accompanied her marriage to Simon in January 1238: Bémont, *Simon de Montfort*, p. 335 no. xxxiv; Labarge, *Simon de Montfort*, p. 69.

15 Bémont, *Simon de Montfort*, p. 335 no. xxxiv.

16 *Chronica majora*, iv, p. 135.

17 Ibid., iv, pp. 157–8.

18 *CPR, 1232–47*, p. 415.

19 Ibid., p. 416.

20 Maddicott, *Simon de Montfort*, p. 52. Walter made payments to Eleanor and Simon. In March 1245, a letter patent referred to 300 marks Walter Marshal had placed in the custody of the treasurer of the Temple in London for the Montforts' use to cover the money that he owed for Michaelmas term last: *CPR, 1232-47*, p. 449. Walter paid another 300 marks to cover the money he owed to the earl and countess after Easter: ibid., p. 453. In July 1245, Henry III acknowledged receipt of £200 from Walter, which Walter owed Eleanor a month after Easter: ibid., p. 456.

21 *CLR, 1240–45*, p. 231.

22 *CChR, 1226–57*, p. 278.

23 See, for example, *Bracton: de legibus et consuetudinibus Angliae*, ed. G. Woodbine and trans. S. E. Thorne (1968–77). Cambridge, MA: Belknap Press of Harvard University, 3 vols, ii, p. 77.

24 *CPR, 1232-47*, p. 419. See also p. 67.

25 *CR, 1242-7*, p. 195.

26 *CPR, 1232-47*, p. 433.

27 Maddicott, *Simon de Montfort*, pp. 33–7.

28 His presence was noted in the Chester annals: 'The Chronicle: 1235–61', *Annales Cestrienses: Chronicle of the Abbey of S. Werburg, at Chester*, ed. R. C. Christie (1887). Publications of the Record Society of Lancashire and Cheshire, vol. 14, pp. 60–79, available online at http://www.british-history.ac.uk/report.aspx?compid=67181, accessed on 14 October 2009.

29 These manors had been granted to Mabel, Eleanor's damsel, for her marriage: *CR, 1242-7*, p. 264. See also p. 60.

30 *CLR, 1240–45*, p. 281.

31 *CR, 1242-7*, p. 452. On the next day Henry exempted Eleanor from paying £30 for the fee farm of her Wiltshire manor of Wexcombe for the remainder of her life: *CPR, 1232-47*, p. 485. In July 1246, Henry III loaned Eleanor a tun of wine from the king's stores at Brill: *CR, 1242-7*, p. 441.

32 *CR, 1242-7*, pp. 518, 521.

33 *CR, 1247–51*, p. 22. Eleanor can also be found ensuring that her household was stocked with wine: *CR, 1247–51*, pp. 3–4.

34 He also wrote off three years' worth of arrears that had been allowed to accumulate: ibid., p. 22; *CPR, 1247–58*, p. 5.

35 Andrew secured a further exemption in 1253. The first exemption also covered exemption from suit of the king's hundred of Kintbury Eagle in Berkshire; the second covered exemption from all suits belonging to the king's courts: *CPR, 1247–58*, pp. 34, 179.

36 Ibid., pp. 293 (pardon for John son of Thomas Hykedun at the instance of William de Valence and Eleanor the king's sister, 30 May 1254), 398 (pardon for Eudo fitz Robert of Metheringham at the instance of Eleanor, 18 February 1255), 457 (pardon for Alexander fitz Giles of Lincoln at the instance of Eleanor, 10 January 1256).

37 Bémont, *Simon de Montfort*, pp. 264–5 no. ii; Maddicott, *Simon de Montfort*, pp. 107–14.

38 *Chronica majora*, v, p. 293; Maddicott, *Simon de Montfort*, pp. 109–10.

39 Maddicott, *Simon de Montfort*, p. 110.

40   The earl had, after all, prolonged his stay in Gascony at the end of the 1242–3 expedition: ibid., p. 32.

41   See pp. 80–2.

42   *Chronica majora*, iv, p. 491; Wilkinson, *Women in Thirteenth-Century Lincolnshire*, pp. 49, 53.

43   Wilkinson, *Women in Thirteenth-Century Lincolnshire*, pp. 52 fig. 3, 53. See also Figure 2.

44   Since Anselm's death came so soon after that of his older brother, before he had an opportunity to pay his relief and perform homage to the king for the earldom of Pembroke, Matilda de Bohun's dower rights were more modest than those of Margaret de Lacy, whose claim to lands rivalled the amount claimed by Eleanor. Matilda, for her part, received the old and new vill in county Kilkenny: Wilkinson, *Women in Thirteenth-Century Lincolnshire*, p. 54.

45   Ibid.

46   KB 26/159, mm. 2d-3d, esp. m. 3d. See also Maddicott, *Simon de Montfort*, pp. 52, 131.

47   KB 26/159, m. 3d; Maddicott, *Simon de Montfort*, p. 131.

48   A point made by Maddicott: *Simon de Montfort*, p. 130. See also Figure 2.

49   *CLR, 1245–51*, pp. 46, 85.

50   Ibid., pp. 118, 142, 178–9, 214–15, 226, 285, 312, 349; *CLR, 1251–60*, pp. 4, 44, 112, 154, 167. See also *CPR, 1247–58*, p. 257.

51   A letter patent, issued on 14 June 1248, referred to £40 which the Earl of Gloucester and Hertford had paid to the treasurer of the New Temple for his share of the arrears for 1247–8: *CPR, 1247–58*, p. 19.

52   *CR, 1247–51*, pp. 134–5; Maddicott, *Simon de Montfort*, p. 130. On Henry's policy of benevolence towards the magnates, see D. A. Carpenter (1996), 'King, Magnates and Society: The Personal Rule of Henry III, 1234–58', in idem, *The Reign of Henry III*. London: Hambledon Press, pp. 75–106.

53   For discussion, see Maddicott, *Simon de Montfort*, pp. 131–3. Already, in May 1250, the king had felt compelled to enter into an undertaking that he would answer for the £400 a year due for Eleanor's Irish dower for the term of Eleanor's life, should Simon predecease her: *CPR, 1247–51*, p. 67.

54   *CLR, 1251–60*, p. 180. Maddicott noted that the memoranda roll suggests that, in fact, nothing was paid after Easter 1254: *Simon de Montfort*, p. 132.

55   *CLR, 1251–60*, p. 285; Maddicott, *Simon de Montfort*, p. 132.

56   If the arrears collected were insufficient to clear the debt, then the king promised to find the remainder of the sum from the money collected by the justices in eyre when they visited Northumberland and five other counties: *CPR, 1247–58*, pp. 493–4. See also Maddicott, *Simon de Montfort*, p. 132.

57   *CR, 1254–6*, pp. 340, 438; *CPR, 1247–58*, p. 493. Margaret might well have hoped that this would smooth the path of her grandson's marriage to Margaret Longespée. Simon de Montfort was among those who negotiated the match and the king lent his approval to the union: Wilkinson, *Women in Thirteenth-Century Lincolnshire*, pp. 55–6. Henry III might, though, have compensated Margaret de Lacy for her heavy outlay. In December 1256, the king authorized a writ of allocate, authorizing payment

to Margaret de Lacy of the 1,600 marks that she paid to Simon and Eleanor: *CLR, 1251–60*, p. 347.

58 TNA: PRO E 159/30, mm. 4d, 15. It is not, in fact, entirely clear whether this was actually the case, or whether the crown was having difficulty in simply keeping track of the arrears owing to Eleanor. In May 1257, a further payment of £400 was authorized by Henry, this time to cover one missed payment at Michaelmas 1256, and the remainder now due at Easter 1257: *CLR, 1251–60*, pp. 372–3. Yet in 1258, Earl Simon received £600, according to the issue rolls, for the period from Easter 1255 to Easter 1256: Maddicott, *Simon de Montfort*, p. 132.

59 For Simon's initial success in Gascony, see *Chronica majora*, v, pp. 48–9. For a summary of his lieutenancy, see Maddicott, *Simon de Montfort*, pp. 106–14.

60 *Chronica majora*, v, p. 294.

61 Ibid., v, p. 48.

62 See, for example, *CPR, 1247–51*, p. 34; *CLR, 1245–51*, pp. 214–15.

63 *The Letters of Adam Marsh*, i, pp. 56–63 no. 25, esp. pp. 56–9.

64 *Chronica majora*, v, p. 77; Labarge, *Simon de Montfort*, p. 112.

65 *The Letters of Adam Marsh*, i, pp. 96–101 no. 34, esp. pp. 96–9.

66 E. Boutaric, *Saint Louis et Alfonse de Poitiers*. Paris: Henri Plon, p. 73; Labarge, *Simon de Montfort*, p. 114.

67 *Chronica majora*, v, p. 117. For Simon in Gascony in 1250, see ibid., pp. 103–4. Simon had attended the Paris parlement in March 1250 on Henry III's behalf: Maddicott, *Simon de Montfort*, p. 112.

68 *CR, 1247–51*, p. 302; Labarge, *Simon de Montfort*, pp. 114, 116. A letter written by Marsh to Eleanor in May/June 1250, however, requested news from the countess 'when you next send a courier to England': *The Letters of Adam Marsh*, ii, pp. 376–7 no. 155.

69 *Chronica majora*, v, p. 208. See also ibid., v, p. 222.

70 Maddicott, *Simon de Montfort*, pp. 113–14.

71 *Chronica majora*, v, p. 263; Labarge, *Simon de Montfort*, pp. 117–18.

72 *Letters of Adam Marsh*, ii, pp. 326–9 no. 134, esp. pp. 326–7.

73 Discussed in Maddicott, *Simon de Montfort*, pp. 114–15.

74 Ibid., p. 115; *Chronica majora*, v, pp. 277, 284, 287–96, 313–16, 334–5, 337–8. A letter dated 7 March 1252, which was sent by Marsh to Grosseteste, offers tantalizing glimpses of Simon and Eleanor's movements at this time, as the tide of Gascon grievances rose against the earl. Marsh, who acted as a tireless go-between for the Montforts and the crown, described how, at the queen's request, he had set out for Reading on 25 February 1252, 'where discussions were held concerning the business of the lord king and his heirs'. 'On the following Friday', the friar visited the Montforts' residence at Odiham, 'on the same business'. There Marsh remained until the following Monday, when he returned to Reading. He then travelled on to the Berkshire priory of Bromhall on Thursday in the third week of Lent 'to meet the earl *and* countess of Leicester': *The Letters of Adam Marsh*, i, pp. 126–9 no. 47, esp. pp. 128–9.

75 Ibid., i, pp. 78–91 no. 30, esp. pp. 78–9.

76 Ibid.

77 Peter was not a relation of Simon, but was the nephew of his close friend, Walter de Cantilupe, Bishop of Worcester: D. A. Carpenter (2008), 'Peter de Montfort', in *ODNB*, available online at http://www.oxforddnb.com/view/article/37845, accessed on 09 August 2010.

78 *Letters of Adam Marsh*, i, pp. 78–91 no. 30, esp. pp. 80–1.

79 Ibid.

80 Ibid., i, pp. 78–91 no. 30, esp. pp. 88–91.

81 BnFr MS Clairambault 1188, f. 16v. Eleanor's seal is reproduced in Maddicott, *Simon de Montfort*, p. 45 plate 3.

82 *The Letters of Adam Marsh*, ii, pp. 378–9 no. 157, 382–3 no. 158, 388–9 no. 161, 388–9 no. 162.

83 Ibid., ii, pp. 384–7 no. 159, esp. pp. 384–5.

84 Ibid., i, pp. 158–61 no. 60, esp. 158–9.

85 Ibid.

86 Ibid., ii, pp. 341–51 no. 141, esp. 348–9, 376–7 no. 155. See also ibid., ii, pp.357–9 no. 144, esp. 358–9 for Geoffrey's delay in joining the earl and countess in Gascony in 1250, and pp. 382–3 no. 158 for the difficulties that Marsh encountered in finding a suitable priest to enter the Montforts' household.

87 Ibid., ii, pp. 562–3 no. 241.

88 Ibid., ii, pp. 326–9 no. 134.

89 Ibid., ii, pp. 341–51 no. 141, esp. pp. 350–1.

90 C. H. Lawrence (1994), *The Friars: The Impact of the Early Mendicant Movement on Western Society*. Longman: Harlow, p. 168.

91 Ibid., pp. 169–70.

92 On this, see Maddicott, *Simon de Montfort*, pp. 92–3.

93 *Monasticon anglicanum*, vi, pt iii, p. 1486.

94 C. Douais (1885), *Les Frères prêcheurs en Gascogne au XIIIme et au XIVme siècle*. Paris: Société historique de Gascogne, 2 vols, i, p. 265; Maddicott, *Simon de Montfort*, p. 44.

95 *CR, 1254–6*, p. 244.

96 *The Letters of Adam Marsh*, ii, pp. 370–3 no. 151.

97 Ibid., ii, pp. 326–9 no. 134, esp. pp. 326–7.

98 John founded Beaulieu Abbey in Hampshire, which later served as the burial place of Richard of Cornwall's wife, Isabella Marshal. Richard also founded Hailes Abbey in 1246, which served as his burial place and that of Sanchia of Provence, his son Henry of Almain and another son who died in infancy. See *The Beaulieu Cartulary*, ed. S. F. Hockey (1974). Southampton: Southampton Record Series, vol. 17; D. Westerhoff (2008), *Death and the Noble Body in Medieval England*. Woodbridge: Boydell Press, pp. 58–9.

99 'Annales de Waverleia', p. 336. Waverley was situated just ten miles from Odiham Castle: Labarge, *Simon de Montfort*, p. 79.

100 'Annales de Waverleia', p. 336; Maddicott, *Simon de Montfort*, p. 42.

101 'Annales de Waverleia', p. 336.

102 'Early Charters and Patrons of Leicester Abbey, Appendix: The Charters of Leicester Abbey, 1139–1265 ', ed. D. Crouch (2006), in J. Story, J. Bourne and R. Buckley

(eds), *Leicester Abbey: Medieval History, Archaeology and Manuscript Studies*. Leicester: Leicestershire Archaeological Society, pp. 225–87, at pp. 269–70. No mention was made of Eleanor in another charter issued by the earl in c. 1239: ibid., pp. 267–8.

103 BnFr MS Clairambault 1021; Maddicott, *Simon de Montfort*, p. 104. According to the Dunstable annalist, Earl Simon secured similar rights from Dunstable Priory in 1263, but Eleanor's involvement, on this occasion, was not recorded: 'Annales prioratus de Dunstaplia', p. 226.

104 BnFr MS Clairambault 1021.

105 BL MS Cotton Otho D. III (St Albans cartulary), f. 111r.

106 Maddicott, *Simon de Montfort*, p. 55.

107 *CR, 1247–51*, pp. 22, 74, 302; *CR, 1251–3*, p. 356; *CR, 1254–6*, pp. 87, 329, 330.

108 The Montforts' voluntary exile prompted Henry to grant Odiham to Engelard de Cigogné. After Cigogné's death in 1243, Odiham was restored to them: MacGregor, *Odiham Castle*, p. 52; *CFR, 1243–4*, no. 451, available online at http://www.finerollshenry3.org.uk/content/calendar/roll_041.html, accessed on 06 April 2011.

109 *CR, 1242–7*, p. 424.

110 Ibid., p. 458.

111 See p. 55.

112 *CPR, 1232–47*, p. 419.

113 R. Allen-Brown (1955), 'Royal Castle-Building in England, 1154-1216', *EHR*, 276, pp. 353–98, at pp. 368, 394.

114 A. Pettifer (1995), *English Castles: A Guide by Counties*. Woodbridge: Boydell Press, pp. 256–8.

115 *CLR, 1226–40*, p. 220.

116 *CLR, 1240–45*, pp. 32–3.

117 Ibid., p. 71. For renovations to the castle, see also *The Great Roll of the Pipe for the Twenty-Sixth Year of the Reign of King Henry III, A.D. 1241-1242*, ed. H. L. Cannon (1918). New Haven: Yale University Press, p. 177; Bémont, *Simon de Montfort* (2nd edn), p. 32.

118 *CPR, 1247–58*, p. 5.

119 Ibid., p. 250.

120 SCLA, DR10/1356.

121 *The Letters of Adam Marsh*, ii, pp. 378–83 no. 157, esp. pp. 378–9.

122 *Chronica majora*, v, p. 1; Maddicott, *Simon de Montfort*, pp. 106–7.

123 *Chronica majora*, v, pp. 98–9.

124 Harris, *English Aristocratic Women*, p. 99.

125 See, for example, Howell, *Eleanor of Provence*, pp. 255–6; Parsons, 'Mothers, Daughters', pp. 73–5; J. C. Parsons (1996), 'The Pregnant Queen as Counsellor and the Medieval Construction of Motherhood', in Parsons and Wheeler (eds), *Medieval Mothering*, pp. 39–61.

126 *Chronica majora*, iii, p. 518; Stacey, *Politics, Policy and Finance*, p. 124 n. 168.

127 Paris noted that Eleanor was 'then pregnant': *Chronica majora*, iii, p. 567.

128 *Chronica majora*, iv, p. 44 n. 6 (marginal note); Maddicott, *Simon de Montfort*, p. 43.

129 For discussion on this, see Maddicott, *Simon de Montfort*, p. 43.

130 Ibid., pp. 43–4.

131 See p. 84.

132 Breastfeeding helps to suppress a new mother's fertility.

133 For an image of a noblewoman testing the breast of a wet nurse, see BL MS Sloan 2435, f. 28v (Aldobrandino of Siena, *Li Livres dou Santé*, France, late thirteenth century). See also W. F. MacLehose (2010), 'Health and Science', in L. J. Wilkinson (ed.), *A Cultural History of Childhood and Family*, Oxford: Berg, pp. 161–78, at pp. 168–70, esp. fig. 9.1.

134 'Annales prioratus de Dunstaplia', p. 152.

135 L. J. Wilkinson (2010), 'Education', in idem (ed.), *A Cultural History of Childhood and Family*, pp. 91–108, at p. 98.

136 *The Letters of Adam Marsh*, i, pp. 57–63 no. 25, esp. pp. 57–8, pp. 145–9 no. 52, esp. pp. 146–7.

137 Ibid., i, pp. 56–9 no. 25, esp. pp. 58–9.

138 *Chronica majora*, v, p. 416. See also Maddicott, *Simon de Montfort*, p. 122.

139 *Letters of Adam Marsh*, ii, pp. 385–7 no. 159, 386–7 no. 160.

140 Ibid., ii, pp. 388–91 no. 162, esp. pp. 390–1.

141 Ibid., ii, p. 334–7 no. 138, esp. pp. 336–7.

142 Ibid., ii, pp. 338–9 no. 139.

143 Ibid., ii, pp. 341–51 no. 141, esp. pp. 350–1.

144 Ibid., ii, pp. 326–9 no. 134, esp. pp. 326–7.

145 Ibid., ii, pp. 376–9 no. 156.

146 For Eleanor of Provence's children, see Howell, *Eleanor of Provence*, pp. 27–8, 30, 35, 44–5. Another daughter, Katherine, was born in 1253: ibid., pp. 117–18.

147 TNA: PRO E 101/308/1, m. 1. For another messenger, Robert de Gaugy, who was dispatched to Kenilworth, see ibid.

148 E 101/308/1, m. 1.

149 Ibid.

150 Ibid., m. 2.

151 Ibid.

152 Ibid.; Green, *Lives*, ii, p. 105.

153 TNA: PRO E 101/349/18, m. 1. In the autumn, the queen also paid for a russet robe of Eleanor's to be sheared and purchased a red squirrel fur for the countess's use: ibid.

154 TNA: PRO E 101/349/12, m. 1.

155 Ibid., m. 3. By this time, Richard of Havering was Earl Simon's steward and 'righthand' man: Maddicott, *Simon de Montfort*, p. 67.

156 Bémont, *Simon de Montfort*, pp. 321–4 no. xxviii bis; Maddicott, *Simon de Montfort*, p. 119. The king had granted the Lord Edward the province in April 1252: *CChR, 1226–57*, p. 386.

157 Maddicott, *Simon de Montfort*, pp. 120–1, 124.

158 *Chronica majora*, v, pp. 415–16.

159 It was also on this occasion that the king improved the terms by which the couple held the castle of Kenilworth and the manor of Odiham, so that both properties were now held for the life of the earl and/or countess: *CPR, 1247–58*, pp. 249–50. The 600 mark fee

was, essentially, an extension of, and in the fine detail of its terms an extremely generous re-working of, a fee of 500 marks that the king had granted the earl and countess in 1244: Maddicott, *Simon de Montfort*, pp. 122–3.

160 H. W. Ridgeway (1989), 'Foreign Favourites and Henry III's Problems of Patronage, 1247–58', *EHR*, 104, 590–610; Howell, *Eleanor of Provence*, ch. 3.

161 See p. 79. See also *CR, 1256–9*, pp. 28, 34.

162 *Chronica majora*, v, pp. 634, 676–7; Howell, *Eleanor of Provence*, pp. 142, 148.

163 Maddicott, *Simon de Montfort*, pp. 128–9.

164 In December 1257, the king acknowledged that he owed a total of £1,198 14s. 10½d., for all the debts Henry owed to the earl and the countess: *CPR, 1247–58*, p. 609; Maddicott, *Simon de Montfort*, pp. 133–4. Henry III had also become indebted to Earl Simon in the county of Bigorre, south of Gascony, when Esquivat de Chabnais, the grandchild of Simon's sister-in-law, Petronilla, Countess of Bigorre, transferred the debts Henry III owed to him for leasing his castles and for military service during the Gascon campaign to Simon de Montfort, to whom Esquivat was indebted from the time when Simon had been appointed guardian of the county on Petronilla's death in 1251: *CPR, 1247–58*, p. 609; Maddicott, *Simon de Montfort*, pp. 134–5.

165 *Chronica majora*, v, p. 366, 415.

166 Ibid., v, p. 415.

167 Maddicott, *Simon de Montfort*, p. 140. The earl also pursued his own business in France during the early part of 1255: ibid., p. 141.

168 Ibid., pp. 139–40.

Notes on Chapter 7

1 *DBM*, pp. 96–113 no. 5, esp. 96–9 (The Provisions of Oxford, 1258).

2 These developments are summarized in Maddicott, *Simon de Montfort*, p. 126.

3 D. A. Carpenter (1996), 'What Happened in 1258?', in idem, *The Reign of Henry III*, pp. 183–98; Maddicott, *Simon de Montfort*, p. 153.

4 Carpenter, 'What Happened in 1258?', p. 183; Maddicott, *Simon de Montfort*, pp. 153–4.

5 *CPR, 1247–58*, p. 627. See also pp. 91–2.

6 *Chronica majora*, v, p. 560; Maddicott, *Simon de Montfort*, p. 126.

7 *CR (Supplementary), 1244–66*, p. 15 no. 172.

8 Maddicott, *Simon de Montfort*, p. 155.

9 Ibid.

10 Ibid., pp. 155–7.

11 Richard of Cornwall had been elected king of the Romans (i.e. of Germany) in January 1257 after the German throne became vacant in 1256: Vincent, 'Richard, First Earl of Cornwall and King of Germany (1209–1272)', *ODNB*.

12 See, for example, I. J. Sanders (1951), 'The Texts of the Treaty of Paris', *EHR*, 66, 81–97, at 89.

13 *CPR, 1247–58*, p. 663.

14   *DBM*, pp. 194–211 no. 29, esp. pp. 194–5.

15   Ibid.

16   Bémont, *Simon de Montfort*, pp. 328–30 no. xxxi, esp. p. 328; Maddicott, *Simon de Montfort*, p. 40 (who translates this passage).

17   The earl wanted the couple's mutual friends, Richard Gravesend, Grosseteste's successor as Bishop of Lincoln, and Adam Marsh, to counsel his executors should the need arise: Bémont, *Simon de Montfort*, pp. 328–30 no. xxxi.

18   The second visit was dominated by Earl Simon's desire to pursue his own claims to the county of Bigorre, which had been granted to him in 1256, and re-granted in 1258 by Esquivat de Chabnais: Maddicott, *Simon de Montfort*, pp. 142, 155–6, 159, 172–8.

19   Simon also refused to renounce his claims to his family's ancestral French lands: *CPR 1258–66*, pp. 25, 106–7.

20   *DBM*, pp. 194–211 no. 29, esp. pp. 196–7.

21   See p. 91.

22   P. Chaplais (1952), 'The Making of the Treaty of Paris (1259) and the Royal Style', *EHR*, 67, 235–53, esp. 243–4; Labarge, *Simon de Montfort*, p. 156.

23   Chaplais, 'The Making of the Treaty of Paris', 244; Labarge, *Simon de Montfort*, p. 156.

24   *CPR, 1258–66*, p. 18.

25   *DBM*, pp. 194–211 no. 29, esp. pp. 196–7.

26   Ibid.

27   Chaplais, 'The Making of the Treaty of Paris', 244–7; Labarge, *Simon de Montfort*, p. 156.

28   *Chronica majora*, v, p. 745.

29   *CLR, 1251–60*, p. 460; *DBM*, pp. 194–211 no. 29, esp. pp. 196–9; *CChR, 1257–1300*, p. 18 (Melbourne, Kingshawe and Gunthorpe, Notts; Dilwyn, Lugwardine and Marden, Heref; Bere Regis, Dorset; Rodley and Minsterworth, Glos); *CPR, 1258–66*, p. 52–3; Maddicott, *Simon de Montfort*, p. 182, 188–9. The grant of manors was later amended so that the couple also received the Yorkshire manors of Easingwold and Huby: *CPR, 1258–66*, pp. 34–5; *CChR, 1257–1300*, p. 20; BnFr MS Clairambault 1188, ff. 13–13v. For an order to extend the Montforts' new manors, see *CPR, 1258–66*, pp. 98–9. The speed with which the couple took possession of their new properties did not endear them to the previous tenants. On 19 August 1259, Simon and Eleanor were instructed to return the corn and livestock on the manor of Bere Regis to the Abbess of Tarrant, and, on 5 September 1259, those on the manor of Kingshawe to William le Latymer: *CR, 1256–9*, pp. 426, 433.

30   *CPR, 1258–66*, pp. 24–5. Henry also undertook to protect the interests of the king of France against Eleanor: ibid., pp. 26–7. Significantly, the English king arranged for the drafting of two texts of the Treaty of Paris, both dated 20 May: one included the renunciation of Eleanor's and Richard of Cornwall's claims, while the other omitted these clauses, in recognition of Eleanor's intransigence: *Treaty Rolls*, i, pp. 37–40 no. 103; Sanders, 'The Texts of the Peace of Paris', 84–5, 89–90, 94; Chaplais, 'The Making of the Treaty of Paris', 244–5.

31   *CPR, 1258–66*, p. 25; Sanders, 'The Texts of the Peace of Paris', 89.

32   *CPR, 1258–66*, pp. 25–6.

33 See p. 79.

34 *CPR, 1258–66*, p. 26.

35 BnFr MS Clairambault 1188, ff. 10v–11v.

36 Chaplais, 'The Making of the Treaty of Paris', 245.

37 *Treaty Rolls*, i, p. 48 no. 120; BnFr MS Clairambault 1188, f. 11v; Maddicott, *Simon de Montfort*, pp. 182–3. See also *Treaty Rolls*, i, pp. 43–8 nos 113–19, pp. 48–9 no. 121, pp. 51–2 no. 128; BnFr Clairambault MS 1188, ff. 11v–12, 12–13v, 15–15v.

38 Chaplais, 'The Making of the Treaty of Paris', 246–7; Maddicott, *Simon de Montfort*, p. 185.

39 Maddicott, *Simon de Montfort*, pp. 185–6.

40 *Diplomatic Documents*, i, p. 215 no. 306; Bémont, *Simon de Montfort*, pp. 330–1 no. xxxii; *CPR, 1258–66*, pp. 106–7; Maddicott, *Simon de Montfort*, p. 187; Labarge, *Simon de Montfort*, pp. 189–90.

41 Earl Simon followed suit by resigning his claims to the territories conquered by his father during the Albigensian crusade, and those of his brother in Evreux and Normandy: *Foedera*, i, pt i, p. 392; *Layettes du trésor des chartres. Tome troisième*, ed. J. de Laborde (1875). Paris: E. Plon, part ii, pp. 497–8 nos 4565–6; Chaplais, 'The Making of the Treaty of Paris', 247; Labarge, *Simon de Montfort*, p. 160; Maddicott, *Simon de Montfort*, p. 188.

42 *CPR, 1258–66*, p. 135.

43 Once more, if Louis proved reluctant to perform this role, Henry hoped that Queen Margaret or Peter the Chamberlain might fill the French king's shoes: *CPR, 1258–66*, pp. 145–6; Labarge, *Simon de Montfort*, pp. 190–1. Documents relating to the case presented to the French by the Earl and Countess of Leicester in 1261 are printed in Bémont, *Simon de Montfort*, pp. 332–53 nos xxxiv–xxxvii.

44 *CPR, 1258–66*, p. 162.

45 Ibid., p. 169.

46 Ibid., p. 241. For letters sent by Henry III to Queen Margaret in April 1262, see *CR, 1261–4*, pp. 120–1.

47 'Visitationibus Odonis Rigaudi, archiepiscopi Rothomagensis', in Dom. M. Bouquet and L. Delisle (eds, 1840–1904), *Recueil des historiens des Gaules et de la France. Tome 21*. Paris: V. Palmé, p. 581.

48 *CR, 1256–9*, p. 415.

49 *DBM*, pp. 149–64 no. 12.

50 *CPR 1258–66*, p. 45.

51 BnFr MS Clairambault 1188, f. 13v; Maddicott, *Simon de Montfort*, p. 186; D. A. Carpenter (1996), 'The Lord Edward's Oath to Aid and Counsel Simon de Montfort, 15 October 1259', in idem, *The Reign of Henry III*, pp. 241–52, esp. p. 251.

52 *CR, 1259–61*, p. 12.

53 For detailed analysis of these events, see Labarge, *Simon de Montfort*, pp. 180–205; Maddicott, *Simon de Montfort*, pp. 192–224.

54 See Labarge, *Simon de Montfort*, pp. 206–36; Maddicott, *Simon de Montfort*, pp. 225–78.

55 *Lettres des rois, reines, et autres personages des cours de France et d'Angleterre. Tome I*, ed.

M. Champollion-Figeac (1839). Paris: Imprimerie Royale, pp. 62–4 no. li; Labarge, *Simon de Montfort*, p. 191.

56 BnFr MS Clairambault 1188, f. 16v; Labarge, *Simon de Montfort*, p. 192.

57 Labarge, *Simon de Montfort*, p. 192.

58 BnFr MS Clairambault 1188, ff. 18–18v, 18v–19, 21–21v, 23, 31; Labarge, *Simon de Montfort*, p. 193.

59 BnFr MS Clairambault MS 1188, f. 29; Labarge, *Simon de Montfort*, pp. 192–3, 264. See also p. 132.

60 Labarge, *Simon de Montfort*, p. 201.

61 *CPR, 1258–66*, p. 266.

62 Ibid., pp. 263–5; Maddicott, *Simon de Montfort*, pp. 227–8.

63 Maddicott, *Simon de Montfort*, pp. 227–8. The scale of the escalating crisis was reflected by the fact that just three days after the Montforts' safe conduct was issued, Henry withdrew to the comparative safety of the Tower of London: ibid., p. 228.

64 For Eleanor of Provence's activities at this time, see Howell, *Eleanor of Provence*, ch. 9. For Eleanor of Castile, see J. C. Parsons (1995), *Eleanor of Castile: Queen and Society in Thirteenth-Century England*. New York: St Martin's Press, p. 24.

65 'Annales Londonienses', p. 64. See also Battle abbey chronicle, an excerpt from which is printed in Bémont, *Simon de Montfort*, p. 377.

66 See 'Annales prioratus de Dunstaplia', pp. 232–3, which records the transfer of Edward, Henry and later Richard to Wallingford, but without specific reference to Eleanor, and *De antiquis legibus liber. Cronica maiorum et vicecomitum Londoniarum*, ed. T. Stapleton (1846). London: Camden Society, pp. 63, 65, which notes the imprisonment of royal captives at Dover and the Tower, and the later transfer of 'the king of Almain' to Berkhamsted Castle. See also *Flores historiarum*, ii, p. 498.

67 'Chronicon vulgo dictum chronicon Thomae Wykes', in *Ann. mon.*, iv, p. 153.

68 M. Prestwich (1988), *Edward I*. New Haven: Yale University Press, p. 47.

69 For the activities of the queen, see 'Annales prioratus de Dunstaplia', p. 233; *Cronica maiorum … Londoniarum*, p. 67; 'Chronicon Thomae Wykes', p. 154; *Flores historiarum*, ii, pp. 499–500.

70 'Annales prioratus de Dunstaplia', p. 233. See also *Flores historiarum*, ii, p. 499.

71 Powicke, *King Henry III and the Lord Edward*, ii, p. 486.

72 Maddicott, *Simon de Montfort*, p. 307.

73 No reference was made to Richard of Cornwall: *CR, 1261–4*, p. 396; Powicke, *King Henry III and the Lord Edward*, ii, p. 477 and n. 1.

74 Powicke, *King Henry III and the Lord Edward*, ii, pp. 480–1; Maddicott, *Simon de Montfort*, pp. 292, 296.

75 *The Metrical Chronicle of Robert of Gloucester*, ed. W. A. Wright (1887). London: Rolls Series, ii, pp. 751–2; Maddicott, *Simon de Montfort*, p. 307; Prestwich, *Edward I*, p. 47; Powicke, *King Henry III and the Lord Edward*, ii, p. 486. See also *Flores historiarum*, ii, p. 503.

76 *CPR, 1258–66*, pp. 388–9. The king appears to have authorized payments for Eleanor's Irish dower up until the end of 1263, according to the liberate rolls. See, for example, *CLR, 1260–7*, pp. 77 (February 1262, £200 for Michaelmas term 1261), 89 (May 1262, £200 for

Easter term 1262), 111 (October 1262, £200 for Michaelmas term 1262), 125 (November 1263, £200 for Michaelmas 1263). There is, however, no reference to a payment for Easter term 1263 in the liberate roll, probably due to its poor condition.

77 *CPR, 1258–66*, p. 392. For Richard of Havering and his son, see Maddicott, *Simon de Montfort*, pp. 67–8. See also p. 53.

78 *CPR, 1258–66*, p. 431.

79 Their middle son, Guy, for example, was awarded the keeping of Richard of Cornwall's lands in the far south west of England: ibid., p. 394; Maddicott, *Simon de Montfort*, pp. 309–10. See also p. 111.

80 Simon junior had been captured by the royalists at the battle of Northampton in 1264, but was released after Lewes: *CPR, 1258–66*, p. 318.

81 Bémont, *Simon de Montfort*, pp. 353–5 no. xxxviii; Maddicott, *Simon de Montfort*, pp. 325–6.

82 Maddicott, *Simon de Montfort*, pp. 325–6; *Manners*, pp. 9, 10, 57, 65, 66, 74.

83 See, for example, *Manners*, pp. 15–16, 31, 32, 33, 35. It was also during this month that orders were issued that Isabella's estates should be taken into the hands of the crown because she had not paid her relief. The order was subsequently cancelled: Powicke, *King Henry III and the Lord Edward*, ii, pp. 707–8, esp. p. 708 n. 2.

84 Powicke, *King Henry III and the Lord Edward*, ii, pp. 708 and n. 2.

Notes on Chapter 8

1 *CR, 1264–8*, p. 306.

2 Ibid.

3 Maddicott, *Simon de Montfort*, pp. 334–40.

4 Ibid. pp. 340–2.

5 For Christmas 1264, see *Flores historiarum*, ii, p. 504.

6 An edition of this document was published in *Manners*, pp. 1–85. I am preparing a new edition of this roll for publication by the Pipe Roll Society. For modern commentaries on various aspects of the roll, see Labarge, *Mistress, Maids and Men*; Asaji, 'Household Accounts of the Countess of Leicester, 1265', pp. 162–88; Kjær, 'Food, Drink and Ritualised Communication', 75–89.

7 *Manners*, pp. 14-15.

8 K. Mertes (1988), *The English Noble Household, 1250–1600*. Oxford: Basil Blackwell, pp. 11–12; Woolgar, *The Great Household*, pp. 46–7. The average number of people present was calculated by Woolgar: ibid., p. 12 table 1.

9 *Manners*, pp. 1–4; Labarge, *Mistress, Maids and Men*, p. 156.

10 *Manners*, pp. 42, 47–9.

11 Maddicott, *Simon de Montfort*, pp. 309, 316–30.

12 See pp. 107–8.

13 *CPR, 1258–66*, p. 319. Henry was also given Corfe Castle (Dorset): Labarge, *Simon de Montfort*, p. 237.

14   BnFr MS Clairambault 1188, ff. 24v–25; Maddicott, *Simon de Montfort*, pp. 335–6.

15   *CR, 1264–68*, p. 80. He was also the holder of all John Mansel the elder's lands: ibid. p. 238.

16   Maddicott, *Simon de Montfort*, pp. 43, 309–10, 324. See also p. 107.

17   Maddicott, *Simon de Montfort*, p. 324.

18   *Manners*, p. 8.

19   Ibid.

20   Ibid., p. 14.

21   Ibid., p. 13.

22   Ibid., p. 12.

23   Ibid., pp. 13–14.

24   Ibid., p. 13; MacGregor, *Odiham Castle*, pp. 58, 59.

25   *Manners*, pp. 17–18. For Pevensey, see, for example, 'Annales Londonienses', p. 64.

26   *Manners*, p. 24.

27   Ibid., pp. 41, 42; *Royal Letters*, ii, p. 288 no. DCXXXVII (a letter of mid June, anticipating Simon junior's relief of Gloucester).

28   This figure excludes the visitors' retinues: Labarge, *Mistress, Maids and Men*, p. 48.

29   *Manners*, pp. 8, 24.

30   Wilkinson, *Women in Thirteenth-Century Lincolnshire*, pp. 52 (figure 3), 56.

31   Ibid., pp. 18, 24.

32   Ibid., pp. 12–13; Labarge, *Mistress, Maids and Men*, pp. 49–50. Margery de Crek had secured a licence to found a nunnery at Flixton in Suffolk in or around 1258: S. Thompson (1991), *Women Religious: The Founding of English Nunneries after the Norman Conquest*. Oxford: Clarendon Press, p. 174.

33   *Manners*, p. 37.

34   Ibid., p. 37 n. 2.

35   Ibid., p. 30. For Catherine's gifts to Lacock Abbey in Wiltshire and a charter of Philip Basset where she is described as his sister, see: *Lacock Abbey Charters*, pp. 79–80 nos 308–15, 317. Philip Basset, a former royal justiciar, was among the king's supporters captured at Lewes: R. M. Hogg (2004), 'Basset, Philip (d. 1271)', *ODNB*, available online at http://www.oxforddnb.com/view/article/1643, accessed on 22 July 2011.

36   *Manners*, p. 34 and n. 8; H. W. Blaauw (1844), *The Barons' War including the Battles of Lewes and Evesham*, London: Nichols and Son, p. 283 n. 1.

37   The wife of Hugh Despenser was also the daughter of Philip Basset: *Manners*, p. 65 and n. 9.

38   Ibid., p. 24.

39   Ibid., pp. 19, 24 (messenger from prioress), 31 (messenger for carrying letters of countess and the king to the prioress), 34 (messenger from prioress). For Amesbury's royal connections, see Thompson, *Women Religious*, pp. 121–3, 218.

40   *Manners*, p. 24.

41   Ibid., p. 18. A Walter de Fauconberg married Agnes, a sister and co-heiress of Peter de Brus, eighth lord of Skelton. For Walter and the Fauconberg family, see G. Poulson (1840) *The History and Antiquities of the Seigniory of Holderness, Volume I*. Hull: Robert Brown,

p. 403; J. W. Ord (1846), *The History and Antiquities of Cleveland*. London: Simpkin, Marshall and Co., p. 250. See also pp. 90–1.

42 *Manners*, pp. 6, 11 (wine), 16 (wine), 18 (cope), 19 (wine), 29 (wine).

43 Ibid., p. 33.

44 Ibid., p. 10; Maddicott, *Simon de Montfort*, pp. 81–2.

45 *Manners*, p. 5; Maddicott, *Simon de Montfort*, pp. 42, 44. See also p. 85.

46 *Manners*, p. 6 and n. 3.

47 Ibid., p. 75.

48 *The Letters of Adam Marsh*, i, pp. 170–5 nos 71–2, 175–7 no. 74.

49 *Manners*, pp. 6, 21; Kjær, 'Food, Drink and Ritualised Communication', 79.

50 Maddicott, *Simon de Montfort*, p. 142.

51 Ibid., pp. 68–9.

52 *Manners*, p. 11; MacGregor, *Odiham Castle*, p. 57.

53 *Manners*, pp. 9, 31. For the settlement, see *CPR, 1258–66*, p. 414.

54 *Manners*, p. 14.

55 Ibid.

56 Ibid., pp. 23, 71.

57 Ibid., p. 25. Edmund also received gifts of miniver: ibid., p. 26.

58 Ibid.

59 See pp. 44, 56–7, 69, 77.

60 On the importance of dress to personal honour and rank, see 'The *Rules* of Robert Grosseteste', pp. 402–3 no. xxi.

61 Powicke, *King Henry III and the Lord Edward*, ii, pp. 505–6.

62 *Manners*, p. 67.

63 Ibid., p. 18. For the younger Eleanor, see pp. 13–14, 88.

64 Powicke, *King Henry III and the Lord Edward*, ii, p. 518.

65 Those with Eleanor at the end included: J. of Snave, Thomas of Sandwich, Richard, rector of Kemsing, William the clerk of Leicester, Ralph d'Arcy, Michael of Kemsing, William de Lacu, Walter Penchecouste, John Spinard, Damsel Hawise de Wortham, Geoffrey Norfolk, Geoffrey the Cook, John de la Haye, Robert Corbet, B. de Otringbere, John of Betteshanger, Roger de Tilemanson, Thomas de Crevequer, Simon of Bodiham, John de Ostregate, Robert of Chilham, Nicholas Karrok, Stephen de Pirie, Sampson de Soles, Damsel Christiana de Craiwell, William de St Philibert and Simon de Fernham: TNA: PRO, SC 1/8/23; *Royal Letters*, ii, pp. 294–6 no. DCXLIV; Powicke, *Henry III*, ii, p. 518 n. 2.

66 *CR, 1264–8*, pp. 217–18.

67 For the Lord Edward's escape, see *CR, 1264–8*, pp. 124–5.

68 *Manners*, p. 42.

69 Ibid., pp. 42–7.

70 Ibid., p. 41 (just before she left Odiham and just before Simon junior's arrival on 31 May).

71 Ibid., p. 47 (at Bramber Castle in Sussex).

72 Ibid., pp. 46–8; Maddicott, *Simon de Montfort*, pp. 335–6.

73 Labarge, *Mistress, Maids and Men*, p. 156.

74 *Manners*, pp. 49–50.

75 Ibid., p. 50.

76 Maddicott, *Simon de Montfort*, p. 66.

77 *Manners*, pp. 76–7. See also ibid., pp. 55, 57, 67.

78 On the importance of dining in the hall, see 'The *Rules* of Robert Grosseteste', pp. 402–3 no. xxii.

79 See, for example, *Manners*, pp. 49, 58–9.

80 See, for example, ibid., pp. 52, 53, 54, 58, 59, 60, 61, 62, 63.

81 Ibid., p. 60.

82 Ibid., pp. 59, 63. Some items, including additional ale, wine, fish and meat, were purchased in Dover itself: ibid., pp. 49, 58, 60, 61–2.

83 Ibid., p. 24.

84 See, for example, ibid., pp. 8, 9–10, 14–15, 32, 56; Labarge, *Mistress, Maids and Men*, p. 63.

85 *CPR, 1247–58*, p. 61; Labarge, *Mistress, Maids and Men*, p. 63. Wortham fought with Earl Simon and died with him at Evesham: W. H. Blaauw and C. H. Pearson (1871), *The Barons' War including the Battles of Lewes and Evesham* (2nd edn). London: Bell and Daldy, p. 318 n. 5. At the time of Evesham, he also held the wardship of Richard le Bretun's heir in Stondon, Beds: *CIM*, p. 187 no. 611.

86 *Manners*, pp. 18, 18 n. 10, 55.

87 Ibid., p. 17 and n. 3; *CIM*, pp. 286–7 no. 939, esp. p. 287 (lands in Dikering wapentake, Yorks). For William the clerk, see also *Royal Letters*, ii, pp. 294–6 no. DCXLIV, esp. p. 295.

88 *Manners*, p. 32. Fulk was later among those dispatched from Dover to London in July: ibid., p. 57.

89 Ibid., pp. 10, 26, 33, 55, 64.

90 Ibid., pp. 8, 11, 31, 40, 57, 63.

91 Ibid. p. 31.

92 Ibid., pp. 21, 24, 32, 33, 34, 56.

93 Ibid., pp. 24, 31, 65, 66.

94 Ibid., p. 24.

95 Ibid., p. 56.

96 Ibid., p. 66.

97 Ibid., p. 67.

98 Ibid., p. 57.

99 Ibid., pp. 57, 58.

100 Ibid., p. 64.

101 Ibid., pp. 58, 66.

102 See pp. 59–60.

103 *Manners*, pp. 18, 57.

104 Ibid., pp. 34, 39.

105 Ibid., p. 68. Christiana held lands in Hampshire: *Royal Letters*, ii, pp. 294–6 no. DCXLIV, esp. p. 296. See also the reference to Damsel A. de Watham: ibid., p. 26.

106 Ibid., p. 18.

107 Ibid., p. 66.

108 Ibid., p. 31.

109 Labarge, *Mistress, Maids and Men*, pp. 64–7.

110 *Manners*, p. 39.

111 For discussion, see Ward, *English Noblewomen*, pp. 146-7. See also pp. 58–9.

112 *Manners*, p. 17. See also ibid., p. 18.

113 Ibid., p. 33.

114 Ibid., pp. 56, 64. See also pp. 67, 73.

115 These are Labarge's calculations: Labarge, *Mistress, Maids and Men*, pp. 64–5.

116 Woolgar, *The Great Household*, p. 13 n. 2; Archer, 'Piety in Question', p. 129; *Manners*, pp. 16, 20, 22, 29, 36, 41, 53, 54, 62.

117 *Manners*, pp. 54, 62.

118 Ibid., p. 20; Archer, 'Piety in Question', p. 129.

119 Kjær, 'Food, Drink and Ritualised Communication', 88; Woolgar, *The Great Household*, p. 90. See also p. 58.

120 *Manners*, pp. 26–30.

121 Ibid., pp. 50, 60, 71. Eleanor dispatched letters to Richard at Portchester on or about 29 May: ibid., p. 33. See also *Royal Letters*, ii, pp. 294–6 no. DCXLIV, esp. p. 295.

122 *Manners*, pp. 9, 24.

123 Ibid., pp. 18, 29.

124 Ibid., pp. 33, 58.

125 See, for example, ibid., pp. 47-8; MacGregor, *Odiham Castle*, p. 63.

126 *Manners*, p. 50.

127 Ibid., pp. 62 (the burgesses of both places), 77–8 (the burgesses of Winchelsea).

128 Ibid., p. 46 and n. 3.

129 Ibid., pp. 46–7; Blaauw and Pearson, *The Barons' War*, p. 323 and n. 3.

130 *Manners*, pp. 46–7. See also *Royal Letters*, ii, pp. 294–6 no. DCXLIV, esp. p. 295. Blaauw and Pearson, *The Barons' War*, p. 325 confuses him with Richard Corbet.

131 *Manners*, p. 49; Blaauw and Pearson, *The Barons' War*, p. 326.

132 It is not entirely clear whether Robert was a guest or prisoner: *Manners*, p. 50; Blaauw and Pearson, *The Barons' War*, p. 327.

133 *Manners*, pp. 50, 59, 61. See also *Royal Letters*, ii, pp. 294–6 no. DCXLIV, esp. p. 295. For the manor of Snave in Kent, see W. H. Ireland (1829), *England's Topographer, or a New and Complete History of the County of Kent, Volume II*. London: G. Virtue, p. 313.

134 *Manners*, pp. 59, 76. Ralph's lands in Kent, valued at £20, were later seized for his rebellion against the crown: *CIM*, pp. 310–14 no. 1024, esp. p. 313.

135 Ibid., p. 59. See also pp. 117–18.

136 Ibid., p. 60.

137 Ibid., pp. 60, 62, 69, 70, 78. Peter probably held lands in Warwickshire: Blaauw and Pearson, *The Barons' War*, p. 376.

138 *Manners*, pp. 61, 62.

139 Ibid., pp. 69 (John with his wife), 78 (John on his own).

140 Ibid., p. 76 and n. 3. An inquisition in c. 1275 into former rebels' lands described Thomas as a member of Earl Simon's household whose lands in Kent were valued at five marks:

CIM, pp. 310–14 no. 1024, esp. p. 313. Thomas also held lands in Norfolk: *Royal Letters*, ii, pp. 294–6 no. DCXLIV, esp. p. 295.

141 Sir Matthew of Hastings was subsequently pardoned by the king in 1266: *Manners*, p. 78 and n. 1; *CIM*, pp. 310–14 no. 1024, esp. 314 (which recorded Matthew's presence at the siege of Rochester with Earl Simon).

142 *Manners*, p. 79. A Nicholas de Hecham was Dean of Lincoln in the 1280s: *Statutes of Lincoln Cathedral: The Complete Text of "Liber niger" with Mr. Bradshaw's Memorandums*, eds H. Bradshaw and C. Wordsworth (1892). Cambridge: Cambridge University Press, p. 100.

143 *Manners*, p. 65.

144 Blaauw, *The Barons' War*, pp. 290–1. For letters written by Adam Marsh to Earl Simon and Countess Eleanor that were carried by Sir John de la Haye, see *The Letters of Adam Marsh*, ii, pp. 334–7 no. 138, esp. pp. 336–7, pp. 384–7 no. 159, esp. pp. 386–7.

145 *Manners*, p. 60.

146 Ibid., p. 70.

147 Ibid.

148 See p. 124.

149 The d'Arcys visited Eleanor at Dover on no fewer than eighteen days: Kaer, 'Food, Drink and Ritualised Communication', p. 79; *Manners*, pp. 59–61, 62, 69–70, 75–6, 78. They held lands in Lincolnshire: *CIM*, p. 242 no. 792; Blaauw and Pearson, *The Barons' War*, p. 326 n. 5. They also possessed property interests in Oxfordshire: *CFR, 1261–2*, no. 1162, available online at http://www.finerollshenry3.org.uk/content/calendar/roll_059. html#d102990e44222, accessed on 02 May 2011. See also *Royal Letters*, ii, pp. 294-6 no. DCXLIV, esp. p. 295.

150 *Manners*, p. 54. Philippa also received half a 'beast of the chase' in July, along with Sir Peter de Burton: ibid., p. 70.

151 Ibid., p. 58.

152 Ibid., p. 70.

153 Ibid.

154 Ibid., p. 76. Thomas was pardoned for his rebellion against the crown in 1266: Blaauw and Pearson, *The Barons' War*, p. 327 n. 2.

155 *Manners*, pp. 51–2, 65, 72, 76. For a gift of capons, see ibid., pp. 77-8.

156 A point made in Kjær, 'Food, Drink and Ritualised Communication', 80 (who notes that pike and capons were other foodstuffs that Eleanor served her guests).

157 *Manners*, pp. 47–8; Kjær, 'Food, Drink and Ritualised Communication', 81.

158 *Manners*, p. 50.

159 Ibid., p. 62. On ale, see J. M. Bennett (1996), *Ale, Beer and Brewsters in England: Women's Work in a Changing World, 1300–1600*. Oxford: Oxford University Press.

160 N. J. G. Pounds (1990), *The Medieval Castle in England and Wales*. Cambridge: Cambridge University Press, p. 82.

161 J. Coad (2007), *Dover Castle*. London: English Heritage, pp. 44–5, offers a useful summary of this work.

162 *Manners*, p. 25. For Henry's purchases from Luke, see Labarge, *Mistress, Maids and Men*, p. 134.

163 *Manners*, p. 18.

164 Ibid., p. 18. In late May, Eleanor the younger had also received a gilded plate that had been bought in London for her use by her mother's officials: ibid., p. 32.

165 Ibid., p. 65.

166 Ibid., p. 64; Labarge, *Mistress, Maids and Men*, p. 144.

167 *Manners*, p. 26.

168 *Ibid.*, p. 33.

169 *Ibid.*, p. 85; Labarge, *Mistress, Maids and Men*, p. 132.

170 See, for example, *Manners*, p. 31 (shoes for Robert de Valle and Petronilla the laundress at Odiham).

171 Ibid., p. 10. See also ibid., p. 26; Labarge, *Mistress, Maids and Men*, pp. 135–6.

172 See, for example, ibid., p. 63.

173 *Manners*, pp. 55, 56.

174 Ibid., p. 65.

175 O. de Laborderie, J. R. Maddicott and D. A. Carpenter (2000), 'The Last Hours of Simon de Montfort: A New Account', *EHR*, 115, 378–412, at 396–406.

176 Ibid., 409, 411.

177 Ibid.

178 Maddicott, *Simon de Montfort*, pp. 342–3.

179 *Manners*, p. 72; Labarge, *Mistress, Maids and Men*, p. 133. See also p. 38.

180 *Manners*, p. 81.

181 Ibid., p. 83.

182 'Chronicon Thomae Wykes', p. 179.

183 *Manners*, pp. 67, 68.

184 Bémont, *Simon de Montfort* (2nd edn), p. 251 n. 4.

185 *Manners*, p. 66.

186 Ibid., p. 67.

187 Ibid.

188 Ibid.

189 Ibid., pp. 83–4; Blaauw and Pearson, *The Barons' War*, p. 328 n. 3.

190 Her father was the royalist Philip Basset: Labarge, *Simon de Montfort*, p. 260.

191 *Manners*, p. 66.

192 Ibid.

193 Ibid.

194 Ibid., p. 74.

195 TNA: PRO, SC 1/2/46; *Royal Letters*, ii, p. 292 no. DCXLI.

196 *CR, 1264–68*, p. 136.

197 *Historical Works of Gervase of Canterbury*, ii, p. 243; Labarge, *Simon de Montfort*, p. 262.

198 Labarge, *Simon de Montfort*, p. 262. See also 'Annales de Waverleia', p. 367; *Chronica Johannis de Oxenedes*, ed. H. Ellis (1859). London: Longman, Rolls Series, p. 230; *Chronica monasterii S. Albani, Willelmi Rishanger*, ed. H. T. Riley (1865). London: Longman, Rolls Series, p. 38.

Notes on Chapter 9

1   *The Chronicle of Pierre de Langtoft, in French Verse, from the Earliest Period to the Death of King Edward I*, ed. T. Wright (1868). London: Longman, Rolls Series, pp. 146–7.

2   *Foedera*, i, pt i, p. 465.

3   'Annales prioratus de Dunstaplia', p. 259; *The Chronicle of Bury St Edmunds, 1212–1301*, ed. A. Gransden (1964). London: Thomas Nelson and Sons, p. 33.

4   Ibid., p. 33; BnFr MS Clairambault 1188, ff. 26v, 28.

5   These events are summarized in Powicke, *King Henry III and the Lord Edward*, ii, pp. 518–19. For the submission of Simon junior and his subsequent flight, see *Chronica Johannis de Oxenedes*, p. 230; *Gervase of Canterbury*, ii, pp. 243–4; 'Annales Londonienses', pp. 71–2 (which gives the date of his flight); 'Annales prioratus de Dunstaplia', p. 259; *Chronicle of Bury St Edmunds*, p. 33. See also BnFr MS Clairambault 1188, f. 26v; *CPR, 1258–66*, pp. 608–10.

6   'Annales prioratus de Dunstaplia', p. 259; *Gervase of Canterbury*, ii, pp. 244–5; Powicke, *King Henry III and the Lord Edward*, ii, p. 519. For Guy's capture, see de Laborderie, Maddicott and Carpenter, 'The Last Hours', 409, 411.

7   'Annales prioratus de Dunstaplia', p. 259.

8   *Royal Letters*, ii, p. 293 no. DCXLII.

9   *CPR, 1258–66*, p. 506. On the rebels who held out in, for example, East Anglia, see *Chronicle of Bury St Edmunds*, pp. 33–7.

10   *Chronica ... Willelmi Rishanger*, p. 43.

11   'Regesta 32: 1265–1268', in *Calendar of Papal Registers, Volume 1: 1198–1304*, pp. 425–35, available online at http://www.british-history.ac.uk/report.aspx?compid=96027, accessed on 25 August 2010; Powicke, *King Henry III and the Lord Edward*, ii, p. 527 n 1.

12   *Royal Letters*, ii, pp. 304–5 no. DCLII.

13   *CPR, 1258–66*, p. 641.

14   Ibid., p. 678.

15   *Statutes of the Realm, Volume I* (1810). London: Record Commission, pp. 12–18; Powicke, *King Henry III and the Lord Edward*, ii, p. 535. See also Powicke, *King Henry III and the Lord Edward*, ii, pp. 533–7.

16   *CPR, 1266–72*, p. 130.

17   Ibid., pp. 140–1.

18   Powicke, *King Henry III and the Lord Edward*, ii, p. 536.

19   *CPR, 1266–72*, pp. 216–17; *CR, 1264–8*, pp. 386–8. See also *Royal Letters*, ii, pp. 314–16 no. DCLIX.

20   F. M. Powicke, 'Guy de Montfort (1265–71)', in idem, *Ways of Medieval Life and Thought*. London: Odhams Press, pp. 69–88, at p. 79.

21   *CPR, 1266–72*, pp. 140–1.

22   For Eleanor of Provence's return to England in 1265 after Countess Eleanor's departure, see 'Chronicon Thomae Wykes', p. 179; *Chronica Johannis de Oxenedes*, p. 230.

23   *Chronica ... Willelmi Rishanger*, p. 87. On Montargis, see Maddicott, *Simon de Montfort*, p. 102; Bémont, *Simon de Montfort* (2nd edn), pp. 258–9.

24 See pp. 83–4.

25 These constitutions were all drawn up under the guiding hand of Master Humbert of Romans, who had been elected Master of the Order in 1254: *Early Dominicans: Selected Writings*, ed. S. Tugwell (1982). Mahwah, NJ: Paulist Press, p. 32. The constitutions are printed in: 'Consuetudines sororum monasterii beati Dominici de Monte-Agri', in R. Creytens (ed., 1947), 'Les constitutions primitives des soeurs Dominicaines de Montargis', *Archivum Fratrum Praedicatorum*, 17, 41–84 at 67–83; 'Liber constitutionum sororum ordinis praedicatorum' (1897), in *Analecta sacri ordinis fratrum predicatorum*, 3, 337–48.

26 P. Lee (2001), *Nunneries, Learning and Spirituality in Late Medieval English Society: The Dominican Priory of Dartford*. Woodbridge: York Medieval Press, p. 149; L. P. Hindsley O.P. (1997), 'Monastic Conversion: The Case of Margaret Ebner', in J. Muldoon (ed.), *Varieties of Religious Conversion in the Middle Ages*. Gainesville, Fla: University Press of Florida, pp. 31–46, at p. 34.

27 Hindsley, 'Monastic Conversion', pp. 32–3.

28 Lee, *Nunneries, Learning and Spirituality*, pp. 153–4.

29 BnFr MS Clairambault 1188, f. 29v; Bémont, *Simon de Montfort* (2nd edn), p. 41 n. 2.

30 Hindsley, 'Monastic Conversion', p. 33–4.

31 Cited in ibid., p. 34.

32 J. A. Smith (2010), ' "Clausura districta": Conceiving Space and Community for Dominican Nuns in the Thirteenth Century', *Parergon*, 27(2), 13–36, at 30–1.

33 Aresta O. SS. ann. 1269 in 1 Reg. Parlam. Fo. 60, available online at http://ducange.enc. sorbonne.fr/APANARE, accessed on 25 August 2010. See also BnFr MS Clairambault 1188, f. 29; Labarge, *Simon de Montfort*, p. 264. See also BnFr MS Clairambault 1188, f. 31 for a document relating to an agreement Eleanor reached with her half-brother, Guy de Lusignan, dated June 1268.

34 For a letter sent early in 1267 by the Pope to Louis IX, which touched on the countess's business, see 'Regesta 34: 1265–1267', in *Calendar of Papal Registers, Volume 1: 1198–1304*, pp. 437–9, available online at http://www.british-history.ac.uk/report. aspx?compid=96029, accessed on 25 August 2010.

35 'Regesta 30: 1265–1268', in *Calendar of Papal Registers, Volume 1: 1198–1304*, pp. 419–22, available online at http://www.british-history.ac.uk/report.aspx?compid=96025, accessed on 25 August 2010; Labarge, *Simon de Montfort*, p. 267.

36 'Regesta 32: 1265–1268', in *Calendar of Papal Registers, Volume 1: 1198–1304*, pp. 425–35, available online at http://www.british-history.ac.uk/report.aspx?compid=96027, accessed on 25 August 2010.

37 Ibid.

38 Bémont, *Simon de Montfort*, pp. 369–70 no. li (a document of 1286 relating to Eleanor's will).

39 BnFr MS Clairambault 1188, f. 25v.

40 M. R. G. Arancón (1980), 'Ricardo de Montfort al servicio de Teobaldo II de Navarra (1266)', *Principe de Viana*, 41, no. 160–1, 411–18, at 412, 415–16. This son's entrée into Theobald's service was smoothed perhaps by Eleanor's decision, in collaboration with

Simon junior, to relinquish their rights to the county of Bigorre in October 1265. The letters that recorded this deal are, though, problematic. The letter from Eleanor is dated October 1265 (the month of her flight from England), as is that from Simon junior: L. Merlet (1857), 'Procès pour la possession du comté de Bigorre, 1254-1503', *Bibliothèque de l'École des Chartres*, series 4, t. 3, 305–24, at 317–18 nos viii–ix; Arancón, 'Ricardo de Montfort', 412.

41   Powicke, 'Guy de Montfort', pp. 76–7, 79.

42   Ibid., p. 80. For Guy's career in Italy, see also 'Annales prioratus de Dunstaplia', p. 259.

43   Powicke, 'Guy de Montfort', p. 79.

44   Labarge, *Simon de Montfort*, p. 269; J. R. Maddicott (2004), 'Montfort, Amaury de, Styled Eleventh Earl of Leicester (1242/3–c.1300)', *ODNB*, available online at http://www. oxforddnb.com/view/article/19045, accessed on 26 August 2010.

45   *Flores historiarum*, iii, pp. 21–2; *Foedera*, i, pt ii, pp. 501–2 (bull of excommunication for Guy, 1273); Powicke, 'Guy de Montfort', pp. 82–5; Labarge, *Simon de Montfort*, pp. 268–9.

46   Blaauw and Pearson, *The Barons' War*, pp. 342–7; Powicke, 'Guy de Montfort', p. 88; Maddicott, *Simon de Montfort*, pp. 370–1.

47   But on Bigorre, see note 18 on p. 170. On Henry's dealings with the Montfortians, see N. Vincent (2004), 'Henry of Almain (1235–1271)', *ODNB*, available online at http://www.oxforddnb.com/view/article/12958, accessed on 26 May 2011; Powicke, 'Guy de Montfort', pp. 82–5; Maddicott, *Simon de Montfort*, pp. 244–6, 370–1.

48   BnFr MS Clairambault 1188, ff. 29v–30; Bémont, *Simon de Montfort*, pp. 365–7 no. xlviii.

49   *Flores historiarum*, iii, p. 22.

50   By 1281 Guy had returned to liberty in Charles's service. For his subsequent life and history, see Powicke, 'Guy de Montfort', pp. 86–7; J. R. Maddicott (2004), 'Montfort, Guy de (c.1244–1291/2)', *ODNB*, available online at http://www.oxforddnb.com/view/article/19047, accessed on 26 August 2010.

51   Printed in Green, *Lives*, ii, appendix, p. 456 no. viii.

52   *CPR, 1272–81*, p. 59.

53   *CPR, 1266–72*, p. 549.

54   'Eyhorne Hundred', in *Kent Hundred Rolls Project*, ed. B. Jones (2006). Kent Archaeological Society, available online at http://www.kentarchaeology.ac/khrp/hrproject.pdf, accessed on 26 May 2011.

55   'Codsheath Hundred' and 'Hundred of Bircholt with the Barony', in *Kent Hundred Rolls Project*, available online at http://www.kentarchaeology.ac/khrp/hrproject.pdf, accessed on 26 May 2011.

56   Green, *Lives*, ii, appendix, pp. 456–7 no. ix.

57   *CClR, 1272–9*, p. 35; Labarge, *Simon de Montfort*, p. 270.

58   Significantly, a few days earlier, Edward instructed Bartholomew le Juvene to answer to Countess Eleanor for the issues and corn from her manors of Luton and Weston, once the debts that the countess owed to Edward for settling with her creditors overseas had been discharged: *CClR, 1272–9*, p. 35. The Dunstable annalist noted that Eleanor's lands were restored to her one year before her death: 'Annales prioratus de Dunstaplia', p. 259. See

also Figure 3. TNA, PRO: C 47/9/20, mm. 3–5 details the partition of Eleanor's Marshal properties between the Marshal co-heirs. For Eleanor's dower, see also *CClR, 1272–9*, p. 181; *CFR, 1272–1307*, pp. 44, 58; 'Annales prioratus de Dunstaplia', p. 265; TNA: PRO C 133/10/16 (1–3).

59   *CFR, 1272–1307*, p. 44; 'Annales prioratus de Dunstaplia', p. 265.

60   The Countess of Leicester's executors were Amaury de Montfort, Simon, vicar of Cleybroke (Leicestershire), Master Nicholas of Waltham and Master Nicholas de Heyham (alias Hecham), Archdeacon of Bedford, who had visited Eleanor at Dover in 1265: Green, *Lives*, ii, pp. 159, 457–8 no. xi; *CClR, 1272–9*, p. 181. See also p. 120.

61   *CClR, 1272–9*, p. 224. For Nicholas of Waltham, see also BnFr MS Clairambault 1188, ff. 31–31v, 31v–32.

62   *Chronica monasterii … Willelmi Rishanger*, p. 87; 'Annales prioratus de Dunstaplia', p. 259; 'Annales Londonienses', p. 86; *Chronica Johannis de Oxenedes*, p. 239. For the younger Eleanor's subsequent life and career, including her capture, and that of her brother, Amaury, and the siblings' imprisonment by the English king on her way to join her husband in 1275, see K. Norgate (2004, rev. M. Costambeys), 'Eleanor (c.1258–1282)', *ODNB*, available online at http://www.oxforddnb.com/view/article/19046, accessed on 27 August 2010; G. Richards (2009), *Welsh Noblewomen in the Thirteenth Century: An Historical Study of Medieval Welsh Law and Gender Roles*. Lampeter: Edwin Mellon Press, pp. 138–48. For Eleanor's acta as lady of Wales, and her concerns about the execution of her mother's will in England, see *The Acts of Welsh Rulers, 1120–1283*, ed. H. Pryce (2005). Cardiff: University of Wales Press, pp. 629–33 nos 432–6. See also ibid., pp. 579–80 nos 395–6, pp. 583–5 no. 398, pp. 620–5 no. 429.

63   See p. 1.

64   For this and another document, issued in 1284, whereby Amaury discharged his mother's debts to the French king, see BnFr MS Clairambault 1188, f. 32. See also Bémont, *Simon de Montfort*, pp. 369–70 no. li; Bémont, *Simon de Montfort* (2nd edn), p. 259 n. 1; Labarge, *Simon de Montfort*, p. 271. Edward, for his part, paid the nuns £63 1s. 8d. for the £220 16s. *par.* when he visited Paris in July 1286 from the moneys owed to Eleanor for her Marshal dower: *Issues of the Exchequer*, ed. F. Devon (1837). London: John Murray, p. 98; Bémont, *Simon de Montfort* (2nd edn), p. 259 n. 1.

Bibliography

1. MANUSCRIPT SOURCES

BIBLIOTHÈQUE NATIONALE DE FRANCE

Clairambault 1021 (Confraternity letters from St Albans Abbey).
Clairambault 1188 (Montfort family documents).

BRITISH LIBRARY

Add. 8877 (Eleanor de Montfort's household roll).
Cotton Otho D. III (St Albans Abbey cartulary).
Sloan 2435 (Aldobrandino of Siena, *Li Livres dou Santé*).

HAMPSHIRE RECORD OFFICE

11M59/B1 (Winchester pipe rolls).

SHAKESPEARE CENTRE ARCHIVE AND LIBRARY

DR10/1356 (Charter issued by Eleanor de Montfort).

THE NATIONAL ARCHIVES (FORMER PUBLIC RECORD OFFICE)

C 47 (Chancery: Miscellanea).
C 66 (Chancery: Patent Rolls).
C 133 (Chancery: Inquisitions Post Mortem).
E 101 (Exchequer: King's Remembrancer, Accounts Various).
E 159 (Exchequer: King's Remembrancer, Memoranda Rolls).
E 372 (Exchequer: Pipe Rolls).
KB 26 (Judicial Records: Curia Regis Rolls).
SC 1 (Special Collections: Ancient Correspondence).

2. PRINTED SOURCES

The Acts of Welsh Rulers, 1120–1283, ed. H. Pryce (2005). Cardiff: University of Wales Press.

Annales Cestrienses: Chronicle of the Abbey of S. Werburg, at Chester, ed. R. C. Christie (1887). Publications of the Record Society of Lancashire and Cheshire, vol. 14, available online at http://www.british-history.ac.uk/report.aspx?compid=67181.

Annales monastici, ed. H. R. Luard (1864–9). London: Longman, Rolls Series, 5 vols.

Aresta O. SS. ann. 1269 in 1 Reg. Parlam. Fo. 60, available online at http://ducange.enc.sorbonne.fr/APANARE.

The Beaulieu Cartulary, ed. S. F. Hockey (1974). Southampton: Southampton Record Series, vol. 17.

Bracton: de legibus et consuetudinibus Angliae, ed. G. Woodbine and trans. S. E. Thorne (1968–77). Cambridge, MA: Belknap Press of Harvard University, 3 vols.

Calendar of Documents relating to Ireland, 1171–1307, ed. H. S. Sweetman (1875–86). London: Longman, 5 vols.

Calendar of Inquisitions Miscellaneous, Volume I, 1219–1307 (1916). London: HMSO.

Calendar of Papal Registers relating to Great Britain and Ireland, Volume 1, 1198–1304, ed. W. H. Bliss (1893). London: HMSO, available online at http://www.british-history.ac.uk/source.aspx?pubid=980.

Calendar of the Charter Rolls (1916–). London: HMSO.

Calendar of the Close Rolls (1892–). London: HMSO.

Calendar of the Fine Rolls of the Reign of Henry III (2007–2011), available online at http://www.frh3.org.uk/home.html.

Calendar of the Liberate Rolls (1916–). London: HMSO.

Calendar of the Patent Rolls (1906–). London: HMSO.

The Cartulary of Bradenstoke Priory, ed. V. C. M. London (1979). Devizes: Wiltshire Record Society, vol. 35.

The Cartulary of Cirencester Abbey, Gloucestershire, Volume III, ed. C. D. Ross and M. Devine (1977). Oxford: Oxford University Press.

Catalogue des actes de Philippe-Auguste, ed. L. Delisle (1856). Paris: Auguste Durand.

Charters of the Redvers Family and the Earldom of Devon, 1090–1217, ed. R. Bearman (1994). Exeter: Devon and Cornwall Record Society, new series, vol. 37.

Chronica Albrici monachi trium fontium, ed. P. Scheffer-Boichorst (1874). Monumenta Germaniae Historica, SS 23.

Chronica Johannis de Oxenedes, ed. H. Ellis (1859). London: Longman, Rolls Series.

Chronica monasterii S. Albani, Willelmi Rishanger, ed. H. T. Riley (1865). London: Longman, Rolls Series.

The Chronicle of Bury St Edmunds, 1212–1301, ed. A. Gransden (1964). London: Thomas Nelson and Sons.

'The Chronicle of Melrose', in *The Church Historians of England, Vol. IV, Pt I*, ed. J. Stevenson (1856). London: Seeleys.

The Chronicle of Pierre de Langtoft, in French Verse, from the Earliest Period to the Death of King Edward I, ed. T. Wright (1868). London: Longman, Rolls Series.

Chronicles of the Reigns of Edward I, and Edward II, Volume I, ed. W. Stubbs (1882). London: Longman, Rolls Series.

Chronique des ducs de Brabant, Tome II, ed. E. de Dynter (1854). Bruxelles: L'Académie Royale de Belgique.

Close Rolls of the Reign of Henry III (1902–75). London: HMSO, 13 vols.

'Consuetudines sororum monasterii beati Dominici de Monte-Agri', in R. Creytens (ed., 1947), 'Les constitutions primitives des soeurs Dominicaines de Montargis', *Archivum Fratrum Praedicatorum*, 17, 41–84.

Curia Regis Rolls of the Reigns of Richard I, John and Henry III (1922–). London: HMSO.

De antiquis legibus liber. Cronica maiorum et vicecomitum Londoniarum, ed. T. Stapleton (1846). London: Camden Society.

The Dialogue concerning the Exchequer, book II, ch. XXVI, in E. F. Henderson (ed., 1896), *Select Historical Documents of the Middle Ages*. London: George Bell and Sons, available online at http://avalon.law.yale.edu/medieval/excheq.asp#b2p26.

Diplomatic Documents, Volume I, 1101–1272, ed. P. Chaplais (1964). London: HMSO.

Documents of the Baronial Movement of Reform and Rebellion, 1258–1267, ed. R. F. Treharne and I. J. Sanders (1973). Oxford: Clarendon Press.

Earldom of Gloucester Charters: The Charters and Scribes of the Earls and Countesses of Gloucester to A.D. 1217, ed. R. B. Patterson (1973). Oxford: Clarendon Press.

'Early Charters and Patrons of Leicester Abbey, Appendix: The Charters of Leicester Abbey, 1139–1265 ', ed. D. Crouch (2006), in J. Story, J. Bourne and R. Buckley (eds), *Leicester Abbey: Medieval History, Archaeology and Manuscript Studies*. Leicester: Leicestershire Archaeological Society, pp. 225–87.

Early Dominicans: Selected Writings, ed. S. Tugwell (1982). Mahwah, NJ: Paulist Press.

Flores historiarum, ed. H. R. Luard (1890). London: Longman, Rolls Series, 3 vols.

The Flowers of History by Roger of Wendover, ed. H. G. Hewlett (1886–9). London: Longman, Rolls Series, 3 vols.

Foedera, conventiones, litterae et cujuscunque generis acta publica, ed. T. Rymer (searchable text edition, 2006). Burlington, Ontario: TannerRitchie.

Genealogia ducum Brabantiae heredum Franciae, ed. I. Heller (1853). Monumenta Germaniae Historica, SS 25.

The Great Roll of the Pipe for the Sixteenth Year of the Reign of King John, ed. P. M. Barnes (1962). London: The Pipe Roll Society, new series, vol. 35.

The Great Roll of the Pipe for the Twenty-Sixth Year of the Reign of King Henry III, A.D. 1241–1242, ed. H. L. Cannon (1918). New Haven: Yale University Press.

Histoire des ducs de Normandie et des rois d'Angleterre, ed. F. Michel (1840). Paris: Jules Renouard.

L'histoire de Guillaume le Maréchal, ed. P. Meyer (1891–1901). Paris: La sociéte de l'histoire de France, 3 vols.

Historical Works of Gervase of Canterbury, ed. W. Stubbs (1879–80). London: Longman, Rolls Series, 2 vols.

History of William Marshal, ed. A. J. Holden (2002–6), trans. S. Gregory, with historical notes by D. Crouch. London: Anglo-Norman Text Society, 3 vols.

Issues of the Exchequer, ed. F. Devon (1837). London: John Murray.

Kent Hundred Rolls Project, ed. B. Jones (2006), Kent Archaeological Society, available online at http://www.kentarchaeology.ac/khrp/hrproject.pdf.

Lacock Abbey Charters, ed. K. H. Rogers (1979). Devizes: Wiltshire Record Society, vol. 34.

Layettes du trésor des chartres. Tome troisième, ed. J. de Laborde (1875), Paris: E. Plon.

The Letters of Adam Marsh, ed. C. H. Lawrence (2006, 2010). Oxford: Clarendon Press, 2 vols.

Letters of Medieval Women (2002), ed. A. Crawford. Stroud: Sutton.

The Life of St Edmund of Abingdon by Matthew Paris, ed. C. H. Lawrence (1999). London: Sandpiper.

Lettres des rois, reines, et autres personages des cours de France et d'Angleterre. Tome I, ed. M. Champollion-Figeac (1839). Paris: Imprimerie Royale.

'Liber constitutionum sororum ordinis praedicatorum' (1897), in *Analecta sacri ordinis fratrum predicatorum*, 3, 337–48.

Manners and Household Expenses of England in the Thirteenth and Fifteenth Centuries, ed. T. H. Turner (1841). London: Roxburghe Club.

Matthaei Parisiensis, monachi Sancti Albani, chronica majora, ed. H. R. Luard (1872–83). London: Longman, Rolls Series, 7 vols.

Matthae Parisiensis, monachi Sancti Albani, historia anglorum, ed. F. Madden (1872–83). London: Longman, Rolls Series, 3 vols.

The Metrical Chronicle of Robert of Gloucester, ed. W. A. Wright (1887). London: Longman, Rolls Series.

Oude Kronik van Brabant (1855). Codex Diplomaticus Neerlandicus, Utrecht, Second Series, deerde deel, part i.

Patent Rolls of the Reign of Henry III (1901–3). London: HMSO, 2 vols.

The Pipe Roll of the Bishopric of Winchester, 1210–11, ed. N. R. Holt (1964). Manchester: Manchester University Press.

Reading Abbey Cartularies, ed. B. R. Kemp (1986–7). London: Royal Historical Society, Camden Fourth Series, 2 vols.

Register of the Abbey of St Thomas, Dublin, ed. J. T. Gilbert (1899). London: Longman, Rolls Series.

Rotuli chartarum in turri Londinensi asservati, vol. I, pars 1, 1199–1216, ed. T. D. Hardy (1837). London: Record Commission.

Rotuli litterarum clausarum in Turri Londoniensi asservati, ed. T. D. Hardy (1833–4). London: Record Commission.

Rotuli litterarum patentium in Turri Londoniensi asservati, ed. T. D. Hardy (1835). London: Record Commission.

Royal and Other Historical Letters illustrative of the Reign of Henry III, ed. W. W. Shirley (1862–6). London: Longman, 2 vols.

The Royal Charter Witness Lists of Henry III (1226–1272), ed. M. Morris (2001). Kew: List and Index Society 291–2, 2 vols.

'The *Rules* of Robert Grosseteste' (1971), in D. Oschinsky ed. *Walter of Henley and Other Treatises on Estate Management and Accounting*. Oxford: Clarendon Press.

Statutes of Lincoln Cathedral: The Complete Text of "Liber niger" with Mr. Bradshaw's

Memorandums, eds H. Bradshaw and C. Wordsworth (1892). Cambridge: Cambridge University Press.

Statutes of the Realm, Volume I (1810). London: Record Commission.

Treaty Rolls, Volume I, 1234–1325 (1955). London: HMSO.

The Trotula, ed. M. H. Green (2001). Philadelphia, PA: University of Pennsylvania Press.

Vincent of Beauvais, De eruditione filiorum nobilium, ed. A. Steiner (1938). Menasha, WI: Medieval Academy of America.

'Visitationibus Odonis Rigaudi, archiepiscopi Rothomagensis', in Dom. M. Bouquet and L. Delisle (eds, 1840–1904), *Recueil des historiens des Gaules et de la France. Tome 21.* Paris: V. Palmé.

The Writings of Agnes of Harcourt: The Life of Isabelle of France and the Letter on Louis IX and Longchamp, ed. S. L. Field. (2003). Notre Dame, IN: University of Notre Dame Press.

3. SECONDARY SOURCES

Abulafia, D. S. H. (2004), 'Joanna, Countess of Toulouse (1165–1199)', *ODNB*, available online at http://www.oxforddnb.com/view/article/14818.

Alexandre-Bidon, D. and Lett, D. (1999), *Children in the Middle Ages, Fifth to Fifteenth Centuries*, trans. J. Gladding. Notre Dame, IN: University of Notre Dame Press.

Allen-Brown, R. (1955), 'Royal Castle-Building in England, 1154–1216', *EHR*, 276, 353–98.

Altschul, M. (1965), *A Baronial Family in Medieval England: The Clares, 1217–1314.* Baltimore: Johns Hopkins Press.

Arancón, M. R. G. (1980), 'Ricardo de Montfort al servicio de Teobaldo II de Navarra (1266)', *Principe de Viana*, 41, no. 160–1, 411–18.

Archer, R. E. (1992), '"How Ladies … Who Live on their Manors Ought to Manage their Households and Estates": Women as Landholders and Administrators in the Later Middle Ages', in P. J. P. Goldberg ed. *Woman is a Worthy Wight: Women in English Society, c. 1200–1500.* Stroud: Alan Sutton, pp. 149–81.

—(2003), 'Piety in Question: Noblewomen and Religion in the Later Middle Ages', in D. Wood ed. *Women and Religion in Medieval England.* Oxford: Oxbow, pp. 118–40.

Asaji, K. (2010), 'Household Accounts of the Countess of Leicester, 1265', in idem, *The Angevin Empire and the Community of the Realm in England.* Kansai: Kansai University Press, pp. 162–88.

Ashe, L. (2008) 'William Marshal, Lancelot and Arthur: Chivalry and Kingship', in C. P. Lewis ed. *Anglo-Norman Studies XXX: Proceedings of the Battle Conference 2007.* Woodbridge: Boydell.

Barrow, G. W. S. (1989 reprint), *Kingship and Unity: Scotland 1000–1306.* Edinburgh: Edinburgh University Press.

Bell, S. G. (1988), 'Medieval Women Book Owners: Arbiters of Lay Piety and Ambassadors of Culture', in M. Erler and M. Kowaleski (eds), *Women and Power in the Middle Ages.* Athens, GA: University of Georgia Press, pp. 149–87.

Bémont, C. (1884), *Simon de Montfort, Comte de Leicester.* Paris: Alphonse Picard, Libraire.

—(1930), *Simon de Montfort* (2nd edn), trans. E. F. Jacob. Oxford: Clarendon Press.

Bennett, J. M. (1996), *Ale, Beer and Brewsters in England: Women's Work in a Changing World, 1300–1600*. Oxford: Oxford University Press.

Biographie nationale, volume 1 (1866). Bruxelles: L'Academie Royale des Sciences, des Lettres et des Beaux-Arts de Belgique.

Birrell, J. (2006), 'Procuring, Preparing, and Serving Venison in Late Medieval England', in C. M. Woolgar, D. Serjeantson and T. Waldron (eds), *Food in Medieval England*. Oxford: Oxford University Press, pp. 176–88.

Blaauw, H. W. (1844), *The Barons' War Including the Battles of Lewes and Evesham*, London: Nichols and Son.

—and Pearson, C. H. (1871), *The Barons' War including the Battles of Lewes and Evesham* (2nd edn). London: Bell and Daldy.

Bouchard, C. B. (1987), *Sword, Miter and Cloister: Nobility and the Church in Burgundy, 980–1198*. Ithaca, NY: Cornell University Press.

Boulton, D'A. J. D. (1995), 'Classic Knighthood as Nobiliary Dignity: The Knighting of Counts and Kings' Sons in England, 1066–1272', in S. Church and R. Harvey (eds), *Medieval Knighthood, V*. Woodbridge: Boydell Press, pp. 41–100.

Boutaric, E. (1870), *Saint Louis et Alfonse de Poitiers*. Paris: Henri Plon.

Bradbury, J. (2004), *The Routledge Companion to Medieval Warfare*. London: Routledge.

Brooks, E. (1950), *Knights' Fees in Counties Wexford, Carlow and Kilkenny*. Ireland: Manuscripts Commission.

Brown, M. (2004), *The Wars of Scotland, 1214–1371*. Edinburgh: Edinburgh University Press.

Carpenter, D. A. (1980), 'The Fall of Hubert de Burgh', *Journal of British Studies*, 19, 1–17.

—(1990), *The Minority of Henry III*. London: Methuen.

—(1996), 'King, Magnates and Society: The Personal Rule of Henry III, 1234–58', in idem, *The Reign of Henry III*. London: Hambledon Press, pp. 75–106.

—(1996), 'The Lord Edward's Oath to Aid and Counsel Simon de Montfort, 15 October 1259', in idem, *The Reign of Henry III*. London: Hambledon Press, pp. 241–52.

—(1996), 'What Happened in 1258?', in idem, *The Reign of Henry III*, London: Hambledon Press, pp. 183–98.

—(2007), 'King Henry III and Saint Edward the Confessor: The Origins of the Cult', *EHR*, 122 (498), 865–91.

—(2008), 'Peter de Montfort', in *ODNB*, available online at http://www.oxforddnb.com/view/article/37845.

—(March 2008), 'Hubert de Burgh, Matilda de Mowbray, and Magna Carta's Protection of Widows', Fine of the Month, available online at http://www.finerollshenry3.org.uk/content/month/fm-03-2008.html.

Cavell, E. (2007), 'Aristocratic Widows and the Medieval Welsh Frontier: The Shropshire Evidence', *Transactions of the Royal Historical Society*, 17, 57–82.

Chaplais, P. (1952), 'The Making of the Treaty of Paris (1259) and the Royal Style', *EHR*, 67, 235–53.

Chibnall, M. (1991), *The Empress Matilda*. Oxford: Blackwell.

Clanchy, M. T. (1993), *From Memory to Written Record, England 1066–1307* (2nd edn). Oxford: Blackwell.

Coad, J. (2007), *Dover Castle*. London: English Heritage.

Cokayne, G. E. (1910–59), *The Complete Peerage*, ed. V. Gibbs et al. n.p.

Collectanea Topographica et Genealogica, Vol. VIII, (eds) F. Madden, B. Bandinel and J. G. Nichols (1843). London: Society of Antiquaries.

Crouch, D. (2002), *William Marshal: Knighthood, War and Chivalry, 1147–1219* (2nd edn). London: Pearson Education.

—(2006), 'Writing a Biography in the Thirteenth Century: The Construction and Composition of the "History of William Marshal"', in D. Bates, J. Crick and S. Hamilton (eds), *Writing Medieval Biography, 750–1250*. Woodbridge: Boydell, pp. 221–35.

de Hamel, C. (1986), *A History of Illuminated Manuscripts*. London: Guild.

de Laborderie, O., Maddicott, J. R., and Carpenter, D. A. (2000), 'The Last Hours of Simon de Montfort: A New Account', *EHR*, 115, 378–412.

Denholm-Young, N. (1937), *Seignorial Administration in England*. Oxford: Oxford University Press.

—(1947), *Richard of Cornwall*. Oxford: Basil Blackwell.

Dixon-Smith, S. (1999), 'The Image and Reality of Alms-Giving in the Great Halls of Henry III', *The Journal of the British Archaeological Association*, 152, pp. 76–96.

Douais, C. (1885), *Les Frères prêcheurs en Gascogne au XIIIme et au XIVme siècle*. Paris: Société historique de Gascogne, 2 vols.

Dugdale, W., *Monasticon anglicanum*, (eds) R. Dodsworth, J. Stevens, J. Caley, H. Ellis, B. Bandinel and R. C. Taylor (1817–30). London: Longman, Hurst, Rees, Orme and Brown, 6 vols in 8.

Evergates, T. (1999), 'Aristocratic Women in the County of Champagne', in idem (ed.), *Aristocratic Women in Medieval France*. Philadelphia, PA: University of Pennsylvania Press, pp. 74–110.

Farmer, S. (1986), 'Persuasive Voices: Clerical Images of Medieval Wives', *Speculum*, lxi, 517–43.

Flanagan, M. T. (2004), 'Clare, Isabel de, *suo jure* Countess of Pembroke (1171x6–1220)', *ODNB*, available online at http://www.oxforddnb.com/view/article/47208.

Gees, L. L. (2002), *Women, Art and Patronage from Henry III to Edward III: 1216–1377*. Woodbridge: Boydell Press.

Given-Wilson, C. (2003), *Chronicles: The Writing of History in Medieval England*. London: Hambledon.

Green, M. A. E. (1857), *Lives of the Princesses of England from the Norman Conquest, Volume II*. London: Longman, Brown, Green, Longman and Roberts.

Hallam, E. (2004), 'Eleanor, Countess of Pembroke and Leicester (1215?–1275)', *ODNB*, available online at http://www.oxforddnb.com/view/article/46703.

Harris, B. (2002), *English Aristocratic Women, 1450-1550: Marriage and Family, Property and Careers*. Oxford: Oxford University Press.

Hindsley O.P., L. P. (1997), 'Monastic Conversion: The Case of Margaret Ebner', in J. Muldoon (ed.), *Varieties of Religious Conversion in the Middle Ages*. Gainesville, FL: University Press of Florida, pp. 31–46.

Hogg, R. M. (2004), 'Basset, Philip (d. 1271)', *ODNB*, available online at http://www.oxforddnb.com/view/article/1643.

Holt, J. C. (1992), *Magna Carta* (2nd edn). Cambridge: Cambridge University Press.

—(1992), *The Northerners* (revised edn). Oxford: Clarendon Press.

—(1997), 'The "casus regis": The Law and Politics of Succession in the Plantagenet. Dominions, 1185–1247', in idem, *Colonial England, 1066–1215*. London: Hambledon Press, pp. 307–26.

Howell, M. (1998), *Eleanor of Provence: Queenship in Thirteenth-Century England*. Oxford: Blackwell.

—(2002), 'Royal Women of England and France in the Mid-Thirteenth Century: A Gendered Perspective', in B. K. U. Weiler and I. W. Rowlands (eds), *England and Europe in the Reign of Henry III (1216–1272)*. Aldershot: Ashgate, pp. 163–82.

Hoyle, V. (2008), 'The Bonds that Bind: Money Lending between Anglo-Jewish and Christian Women in the Plea Rolls of the Exchequer of the Jews, 1218–80', *Journal of Medieval History*, 34, 119–29.

Huneycutt, L. L. (1996), 'Public Lives, Private Ties: Royal Mothers in England and Scotland, 1070–1204', in J. C. Parsons and B. Wheeler (eds), *Medieval Mothering*. London: Garland, pp. 295–311.

—(2002), '"Alianora Regina Anglorum": Eleanor of Aquitaine and her Anglo-Norman Predecessors as Queens of England', in B. Wheeler and J. C. Parsons (eds), *Eleanor of Aquitaine: Lord and Lady*. Basingstoke: Palgrave Macmillan, pp. 115–32.

—(2003), *Matilda of Scotland: A Study in Medieval Queenship*. Woodbridge: Boydell Press.

Ireland, W. H. (1829), *England's Topographer, or a New and Complete History of the County of Kent, Volume II*. London: G. Virtue.

Johns, S. M. (2003), *Noblewomen, Aristocracy and Power in the Twelfth-Century Anglo-Norman Realm*. Manchester: Manchester University Press.

Jones, M. (2004), 'Geoffrey, Duke of Brittany (1158–1186)', *ODNB*, available online at http://www.oxforddnb.com/view/article/10533.

Kjær, L. (2011), 'Food, Drink and Ritualised Communication in the Household of Eleanor de Montfort, February to August 1265', *Journal of Medieval History*, 37, 75–89.

Labarge, M. W. (1962), *Simon de Montfort*. London: Eyre and Spottiswoode.

—(1965, repr. 2003), *Mistress, Maids and Men: Baronial Life in the Thirteenth Century*. Phoenix: London.

Lawrence, C. H. (1960), *Edmund of Abingdon: A Study in Hagiography and History*. Oxford: Clarendon Press.

—(1994), *The Friars: The Impact of the Early Mendicant Movement on Western Society*. Longman: Harlow.

—(2004), 'Edmund of Abingdon [St Edmund of Abingdon, Edmund Rich] (c.1174–1240)', *ODNB*, available online at http://www.oxforddnb.com/view/article/8503.

Lee, P. (2001), *Nunneries, Learning and Spirituality in Late Medieval English Society: The Dominican Priory of Dartford*. Woodbridge: York Medieval Press.

Little, A. G. (1892), *The Grey Friars in Oxford*. Oxford: The Oxford Historical Society.

Loengard, J. S. (1993), '"Rationabilis dos": Magna Carta and the Widow's "Fair Share" in the

Earlier Thirteenth Century', in S. S. Walker ed. *Wife and Widow in Medieval England.* Michigan: University of Michigan Press, pp. 59–80.

Loud, G. A. (1999), 'William the Bad or William the Unlucky? Kingship in Sicily, 1154–1166', *Haskins Society Journal*, 8, 99–113.

MacGregor, P. (1983), *Odiham Castle, 1200–1500.* Gloucester: Alan Sutton.

MacLehose, W. F. (1996), 'Nurturing Danger: High Medieval Medicine and the Problem(s) of the Child', in J. C. Parsons and B. Wheeler (eds), *Medieval Mothering.* London: Garland, pp. 3–24.

—(2010), 'Health and Science', in L. J. Wilkinson ed. *A Cultural History of Childhood and Family in the Middle Ages.* Oxford: Berg, pp. 161–78.

Maddicott, J. R. (1994), *Simon de Montfort.* Cambridge: Cambridge University Press.

—(2004), 'Montfort, Amaury de, Styled Eleventh Earl of Leicester (1242/3–c.1300)', *ODNB*, available online at http://www.oxforddnb.com/view/article/19045.

—(2004), 'Montfort, Guy de (c.1244–1291/2)', *ODNB*, available online at http://www.oxforddnb.com/view/article/19047.

Malay, J. L. (2009), 'Anne Clifford: Appropriating the Rhetoric of Queens to Become the Lady of the North', in E. Oakley-Brown and L. J. Wilkinson (eds), *The Rituals and Rhetoric of Queenship, Medieval to Early Modern.* Dublin: Four Courts Press, pp. 157–70.

Merlet, L. (1857), 'Procès pour la possession du comté de Bigorre, 1254–1503', *Bibliothèque de l'École des Chartres*, series 4, t. 3, 305–24.

Mertes, K. (1988), *The English Noble Household, 1250–1600.* Oxford: Basil Blackwell.

Monnas, L. (2008), *Merchants, Princes and Painters: Silk Fabrics in Italian and Northern Paintings, 1300–1500.* New Haven: Yale University Press.

Mullally, E. (1996), 'The Portrayal of Women in the *Histoire de Guillaume le Maréchal*', *Peritia*, 10, 351–62.

Murray, J. (1995), 'Thinking about Gender: The Diversity of Medieval Perspectives', in J. Carpenter and S. MacLean (eds), *Power of the Weak: Studies on Medieval Women.* Urbana, IL: University of Illinois Press, pp. 1–26.

Nelson, J. (2007), 'Scottish Queenship in the Thirteenth Century', in B. Weiler et al. (eds), *Thirteenth Century England XI: Proceedings of the Gregynog Conference 2005.* Woodbridge: Boydell Press, pp. 61–81.

Norgate, K. (2004, rev. M. Costambeys), 'Eleanor (c.1258–1282)', *ODNB*, available online at http://www.oxforddnb.com/view/article/19046.

—(2004, rev. T. Reuter), 'Matilda, Duchess of Saxony (1156–1189)', *ODNB*, available online at http://www.oxforddnb.com/view/article/18339.

O'Cléirigh, C. (1996), 'The Absentee Landlady and the Sturdy Robbers: Agnes de Valence', in C. E. Meek and M. K. Simms (eds), *The Fragility of her Sex? Medieval Irish Women in their European Context.* Dublin: Four Courts Press, pp. 101–18.

Ord, J. W. (1846), *The History and Antiquities of Cleveland.* London: Simpkin, Marshall and Co.

Orme, N. (1984), *From Childhood to Chivalry: The Education of the English Kings and Aristocracy, 1066–1530.* London: Methuen.

—(2001), *Medieval Children.* New Haven: Yale University Press.

Oxford Dictionary of National Biography. Oxford: Oxford University Press, 2004–11, available online at http://www.oxforddnb.com.

Painter, S. (1982 reprint), *William Marshal: Knight-Errant, Baron and Regent of England*. Toronto: University of Toronto Press.

Parsons, J. C. (1993), 'Mothers, Daughters, Marriage, Power: Some Plantagenet Evidence, 1150–1500', in idem ed. *Medieval Queenship*. Stroud: Sutton, pp. 63–78.

—(1995), *Eleanor of Castile: Queen and Society in Thirteenth-Century England*. New York: St Martin's Press.

—(1996), 'The Pregnant Queen as Counsellor and the Medieval Construction of Motherhood', in J. C. Parsons and B. Wheeler (eds), *Medieval Mothering*. London: Garland, pp. 39–61.

—(1998), '"Que nos in infancia lactauit": The Impact of Childhood Care-Givers on Plantagenet Family Relationships in the Thirteenth and Early Fourteenth Centuries', in C. M. Rousseau and J. T. Rosenthal (eds), *Women, Marriage and Family in Medieval Christendom: Essays in Memory of Michael M. Sheehan. C. S. B.*, Kalamazoo, MI: Western Michigan University, pp. 289–324.

Patterson, R. B. (2004/5), 'Isabella, *suo jure* Countess of Gloucester (c.1160–1217)', *ODNB*, available online at http://www.oxforddnb.com/view/article/46705.

Petit-Dutaillis, C. (repr. 1966), *The Feudal Monarchy in France and England from the Tenth to the Thirteenth Century*. New York: Harper and Row.

Pettifer, A. (1995), *English Castles: A Guide by Counties*. Woodbridge: Boydell Press.

Phillips, K. M. (2003), *Medieval Maidens: Young Women and Gender in England, 1270–1540*. Manchester: Manchester University Press.

Pollard, A. F. (2004), 'Monmouth, John of (c.1182–1248)', rev. R. R. Davies, *ODNB*, available online at http://www.oxforddnb.com/view/article/18959.

Poulson, G. (1840), *The History and Antiquities of the Seigniory of Holderness, Volume I*. Hull: Robert Brown.

Pounds, N. J. G. (1990), *The Medieval Castle in England and Wales*. Cambridge: Cambridge University Press.

Power, D. (2004), *The Norman Frontier in the Twelfth and Early Thirteenth Centuries*. Cambridge: Cambridge University Press.

Powicke, F. M. (1947), *King Henry III and the Lord Edward*. Oxford: Clarendon Press, 2 vols.

—(1949), 'Guy de Montfort (1265–71)', in idem, *Ways of Medieval Life and Thought*. London: Odhams Press, pp. 69–88.

Prestwich, M. (1988), *Edward I*. New Haven: Yale University Press.

Prinet, M. (1917), 'Deux monuments funéraires de l'abbaye de Saint-Antoine des Champs', *Bulletin de la Société de l'histoire de Paris et de l'Ile-de-France*, 80–3.

Ranft, P. (2002), *Women in Western Intellectual Culture, 600–1500*. Basingstoke: Palgrave Macmillan.

Rezak, B. B. (1988), 'Women, Seals, and Power in Medieval France, 1150–1350', in M. Erler and M. Kowaleski (eds), *Women and Power in the Middle Ages*. Athens, GA: University of Georgia Press.

Richards, G. (2009), *Welsh Noblewomen in the Thirteenth Century: An Historical Study of Medieval Welsh Law and Gender Roles*. Lampeter: Edwin Mellon Press.

Ricketts, P. (2003), 'Widows, Religious Patronage and Family Identity: Some Cases from Twelfth-Century Yorkshire', *Haskins Society Journal*, 14, 117–36.

Ridgeway, H. W. (1989), 'Foreign Favourites and Henry III's Problems of Patronage, 1247–1258', *EHR*, 104, 590–610.

Rogers, N. (ed.), *The Friars in Medieval Britain: Proceedings of the 2007 Harlaxton Symposium*. Donington: Shaun Tyas.

Röhrkasten, J. (2004), *The Mendicant Houses of Medieval London, 1221–1539*. Münster: Lit Verlag Münster.

Rosemann, P. W. (2004), *Peter Lombard*. Oxford: Oxford University Press.

Sanders, I. J. (1951), 'The Texts of the Treaty of Paris', *EHR*, 66, 81–97.

Scott, W. W. (2004), 'Margaret, Countess of Kent (1187x95–1259)', *ODNB*, available online at http://www.oxforddnb.com/view/article/49377.

Seabourne, G. (2007), 'Eleanor of Brittany and her Treatment by King John and Henry III', *Nottingham Medieval Studies*, 51, 73–110.

Shadis, M. (2009), *Berenguela of Castile (1180–1246) and Political Women in the High Middle Ages*. New York: Palgrave MacMillan.

Smets, G. (1908), *Henri I, duc de Brabant, 1190–1235*. Bruxelles: Lamertin.

Smith, J. A. (2010), '"Clausura districta": Conceiving Space and Community for Dominican Nuns in the Thirteenth Century', *Parergon*, 27(2), 13–36.

Stacey, R. (1987), *Politics, Policy and Finance under Henry III, 1216–1245*. Oxford: Clarendon Press.

Stafford, P. (1997), *Queen Emma and Queen Edith: Queenship and Women's Power in Eleventh-Century England*. Oxford: Blackwell.

Strickland, M. (2005), 'Enforcers of Magna Carta (*act.* 1215–16)', *ODNB*, available online at http://www.oxforddnb.com/view/theme/93691.

Stringer, K. J. (1985), *Earl David of Huntingdon: A Study in Anglo-Scottish History*. Edinburgh: Edinburgh University Press.

Taylor, C. S. (1889), *An Analysis of the Domesday Survey of Gloucestershire*. Bristol and Gloucestershire Archaeology Society.

Thompson, S. (1991), *Women Religious: The Founding of English Nunneries after the Norman Conquest*. Oxford: Clarendon Press.

Vale, M. (2001), *The Princely Court: Medieval Courts and Culture in North-West Europe*. Oxford: Oxford University Press.

Vaughan, R. (1958), *Matthew Paris*. Cambridge: Cambridge University Press.

Vincent, N. (1996), *Peter des Roches: An Alien in English Politics, 1205–1238*. Cambridge: Cambridge University Press.

—(1999), 'Isabella of Angoulême: John's Jezebel', in S. D. Church (ed.), *King John: New Interpretations*. Woodbridge: Boydell Press, pp. 165–219.

—(2004), 'Aubigny, Philip d' (d. 1236)', *ODNB*, available online at http://www.oxforddnb.com/view/article/47227.

—(2004), 'Henry of Almain (1235–1271)', *ODNB*, available online at http://www.oxforddnb.com/view/article/12958.

—(2004), 'Richard, First Earl of Cornwall and King of Germany (1209–1272)', *ODNB*, available online at http://www.oxforddnb.com/view/article/23501.

Walker, R. F. (1972), 'Hubert de Burgh and Wales', *EHR*, 87, 465–94.

—(2004), 'William Marshal (II), Fifth Earl of Pembroke (c. 1190–1231), magnate', *ODNB*, available online at http://www.oxforddnb.com/view/article/18127.

Ward, J. C. (1992), *English Noblewomen in the Later Middle Ages*. Harlow: Longman.

—(2002), *Women in Medieval Europe, 1200–1500*. Harlow: Pearson Education.

Warren, W. L. (1961), *King John*. London: Eyre Methuen.

Waugh, S. L. (1988), *The Lordship of England: Royal Wardships and Marriages in English Society and Politics, 1217–1327*. Princeton, NJ: Princeton University Press.

Weiler, B. (2007), *Kingship, Rebellion and Political Culture: England and Germany, c. 1215–c.1250*. Basingstoke: Palgrave Macmillan.

West, F. J. (2004), 'Burgh, Hubert de, Earl of Kent (c.1170–1243)', *ODNB*, available online at http://www.oxforddnb.com/view/article/3991.

Westerhoff, D. (2008), *Death and the Noble Body in Medieval England*. Woodbridge: Boydell Press.

Wilkinson, L. J. (2003), 'The *Rules* of Robert Grosseteste Reconsidered: The Lady as Estate and Household Manager', in C. Beattie, A. Maslakovic and S. Rees Jones (eds), *The Medieval Household in Christian Europe, c. 850-c. 1550: Managing Power, Wealth and the Body*. Turnhout, Belgium: Brepols, pp. 293–306.

—(2007), *Women in Thirteenth-Century Lincolnshire*. Woodbridge: Boydell Press.

—(2009), 'The Imperial Marriage of Isabella of England, Henry III's Sister', in E. Oakley-Brown and L. J. Wilkinson (eds), *The Rituals and Rhetoric of Queenship, Medieval to Early Modern*. Dublin: Four Courts Press, pp. 20–36.

—(2010), 'Education', in idem ed. *A Cultural History of Childhood and Family*. Oxford: Berg.

Woolgar, C. M. (1999), *The Great Household in Late Medieval England*. New Haven: Yale University Press.

Youngs, D. (2006), *The Life Cycle in Western Europe, c. 1300–c. 1500*. Manchester: Manchester University Press.

Index